Standby Studio

Anne Hailes

Takes You Behind the Scenes
as Ulster Television
'Goes on Air'

Published in Belfast by Shanway Press, 2009.

t: 028 90 222 070
e:info@shanway.com

ISBN: 978-0-9560101-4-8

For my
family and friends
past, present and future

Standby Studio

This book holds untold memories of special years.
When Anne Hailes, then Anne Shaw, joined Ulster Television three weeks before the company went 'on air' in 1959, she was part of an exciting and unique time in the history of Northern Ireland.
From a clerk typist she became a production assistant working with the most famous names of the day.
'Standby Studio' was her call before the live programmes were transmitted into the homes of the country.
Her memories come from all angles, the characters, the stories, the disasters, the delights and above all, the humour.
They are all here in this first hand account of those special years when Ulster Television came to town.

1. A Decade Remembered 7
2. Something Unique 11
3. The Stage is Set 15
4. The Twists and Turns of Life 25
5. Local Heroes 31
6. Exciting Imports 45
7. Girl Power 60s Style 57
8. The Lighter Side of Life 65
9. Naughtiness and The Big Freeze 71
10. The Long Walk Home 77
11. A Comic Genius 83
12. Picture Perfect 89
13. All Part of Growing Up 95
14. Midnight Oil 101
15. Setting Goal Posts 109
16. Imposing Figures 115
17. So Many Characters 121
18. Music of Folk and Friends 129
19. Hallowe'en 2008. One Year To Go 135
20. The Pace of Change 139
21. Show Biz Come to Town 147
22. McPeake Phenomenon 151
23. First Hand Reporting of History 155
24. Hands and Hearts Across the Border 163
25. Special Men in my Life 167
26. Some of the Greats 175
27. The Split Personality of a Gentleman 183
28. Changing Values 187
29. Looking Back 191
30. A Toast to Absent Friends 197
31. The Wee Woman from Outram Street 199

Acknowledgements 201

Index 203

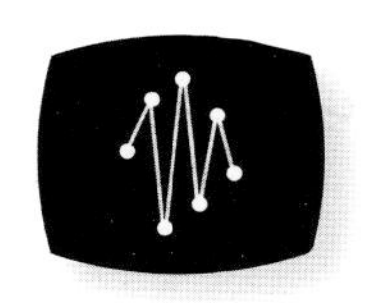

1959 - 2009

1
A Decade Remembered

With flags and window boxes, Ulster Television takes up residence in Havelock House 1959.

Are you old enough to remember the 1960s? If you are, you'll have plenty of memories to conjure with. If not, I hope you'll enjoy reading of those times. They say if you remember the 60s you didn't live them, flower power, peace and love, tension in Cuba with the Bay of Pigs invasion, the build up to the Troubles in Northern Ireland and the birth of Ulster Television. Two events brought this book about, an autobiography by Dr. R. Brumwell Henderson published in 2003, and a meeting in October 1999.

Brum Henderson's book, *A Life in Television* was mainly a view of Ulster Television from the boardroom and his experiences over 30 years, as founder, the first managing director and subsequently chairman.

It challenged me to write a view from the studio floor.

In today's jargon, there is no 'time line' to this story. Basically it charts my course from 1959 until 1966 when I left Ulster Television for the first time. It weaves a story of kinetic energy swirling around a small number of people, the colourful characters who came and went and the fun we had. Studio One was the initial playground. Studio Two opened in 1962 in time for the third anniversary. It was live broadcasting in black and white. Colour was still ten years away.

I began life in television as a clerk typist but soon became a production assistant working with programme directors on a variety of programmes. Hence the name of the book - as we approached transmission time, the PA would call – *Standby Studio* – hearts would turn over in delicious apprehension and we were off.

The second spur to putting pen to paper was a meeting of many of the original members of Ulster Television at a restaurant in Belfast, a party held to celebrate our 40th birthday.

We came from all over Europe to raise a glass to the good old days. It was the first get-together of its kind and technicians, programme directors, production assistants, front of camera, secretaries and accountants and more, talked about the fun and excitement of the formative years. And what stories we had to tell. Time can play tricks with recollections and we may remember the good times rather than the bad. This is a miscellany of memories told by friends and colleagues who have, like me, drawn as accurately as possible on our memories during those years. A little poetic licence here and there, a minimum of exaggeration but the truth as we saw it in those golden days.

*

What was happening in Northern Ireland during that decade? There was the introduction of direct flights to the Continent with ten-day holidays in Italy for £25.6s.6d, a bank rate of 4% and the launching of the £15 million P & O liner 'Canberra'. Ireland's first crematorium was opened on the outskirts of Belfast, whilst in Bradbury Place, not far from Ulster Television, the unique little Toll House, home of a local chimney sweep was demolished and, at the cost of £90,000 Malone Golf Club made their new home at a 271 acre site at Drumbeg, Co. Antrim.

In the early 60s there were alarming reports – unfounded - that the Grand Opera House was to be turned into an American bowling alley and the Empire, a theatre which played host to entertainers like Florrie Ford, Lillie Langtry, Marie Lloyd and Jessie Matthews, closed its doors for the last time.

About the same time Northern Ireland was swept by winds of 103 miles per hour causing five deaths and over £1 million worth of damage. In February 1963 many will remember with a shiver the blizzards which left one third of the Province without power or communications. In Belfast the death took place of Gipsy Castella who claimed to be the most tattooed woman in the world and 1963 also saw newspaper reports that a young local man, Jim Galway, had been appointed principal flautist with the Covent Garden Orchestra. Imagine, when he reached the age of 69 in December 2008 he'd sold over 30 million records.

And, to celebrate his visit to Northern Ireland, a 35 lb piece of Giant's Causeway rock ignored formalities at the border to speed on to Dublin to be presented to President John F. Kennedy.

Belfast's reputation as a conference centre was reported as being on the 'up grade' when a Northern Ireland Tourist Board spokesman announced, "the opening of more hotels in and around the city and the consequent availability of several hundred extra beds has naturally helped with the accommodation problem."

It was the decade when *Lady Chatterley* appeared on the national scene and John Profumo, British Secretary of State, for War and his friends provided more spicy reading. With unemployment rising to the highest since 1947, gangsters saw fit to relieve the Glasgow to London mail train of £2.5 million. B.P. struck oil in the North Sea and a 70 mile-per-hour speed limit was introduced on our roads.

On an October day in 1966 came the tragic news that 116 children and 28 adults had died when a coal tip slipped down into the village school in Aberfan in Wales.

International headlines announced that the Soviets had shot down an American U2 spy plane piloted by Gary Powers and another Soviet caused flash bulbs to pop at the conclusion of the 1960 United Nations General Assembly when an angry Nikita Khrushchev faced British Prime Minister Harold Macmillan and pounded out his point on the table with his shoe. Another Russian, Major Yuri Gargarin, began the space race which ended later in the decade with the amazing televised picture of two Americans walking on the surface of the moon.

As the Beatles hit America, Cassius Clay hit opponents with his newly adopted Muslim name, Muhammad Ali and John Lennon announced that he was more popular than Jesus. In an interview with the *Evening Standard* in 1966 Lennon claimed that Christianity will go and that 'we are more popular than Jesus now.' And Marilyn Monroe died.

Who can forget that it was the decade which stunned the world with the news that President John F. Kennedy had been assassinated and saw the beginnings of unimagined civil unrest in Northern Ireland.

There was good news too.
On Saturday 31st October 1959, something happened which made the 60s special,
Ulster Television went 'On Air'
and nothing was the same again.

Looking at Life

with Rowel Friers

"Normal service will be resumed in a few minutes"

Belfast Telegraph

Maurice O'Callaghan whose voice heralded the arrival of Ulster's new television station.

2
Something Unique

Imagine the scene. Late autumn sunshine on a narrow street in Belfast, long rows of red brick, two up two down terrace houses, they said it was the longest street of its kind in Northern Ireland.

In the shadow of the gasworks, Havelock Street ran into Vernon Street and the residents were out in force. Alex's corner shop was the headquarters for information, that's where the 'television people' bought their sweets and cigarettes and dropped hints.

And today was the day, Saturday 31st October 1959. Men rushed home from work, women gathered on the pavement in front of the pale blue building at the top of the street. Children ran round them playing tig and hop scotch, little knowing that in an hour or so they would be on television enjoying the opening party in Studio One, hosted by comedienne and actress, Beatrice Lillie. The smell of fireworks was in the air and there was a running commentary. The craic was great. "Mrs. are you famous?" "Hey, there's him, thingamajig, what do you call yer man?"   "Mister, can you get me on TV?"

After weeks of preparation, right on their doorstep, a new television station was born with style and fanfare. At teatime around 97,000 screens would jump into action as the Ulster Television symbol and the first few notes of *The Mountains of Mourne* were heard in front rooms all over Northern Ireland.

From early morning newspapermen were trying to catch a local 'front of camera' personality to get a quote and, weighed down with cameras, photographers hung around the buzzing foyer waiting for a front page scoop, florists vans were pulling in to unload bouquets. A veritable anthill hiving with activity. The smell of fresh paint and perfume filled the air. Frantic last minute spit and polish and in reception, in administrative and sales offices, technical area, studio, makeup rooms and canteen, there was excited apprehension.

In homes up and down the country families were getting ready too. We were told that our typical audience was the wee woman in nearby Outram Street. She was the salt of the earth, the working wife who looked after her man, brought up the children and enjoyed watching television when she got the chance. She would really appreciate home grown talent on the screen, local entertainers, ads for the items she shopped for, Kennedy's bread, Cookstown sausages, the Ulster Bank and honest to God Belfast voices telling her all about everything.

Audrey Corry was waiting for her husband Norman to come home early from work. She had finished feeding baby Alan who was only five months old. As he lay on the settee she saw to Laura, who at three years of age, had little interest in Sir Laurence Olivier. Peter Corry was yet to be born but like the rest of the family his passion was to be music and he appeared on Ulster Television many times as he built his career as one of Ireland's leading singers. "It was a rush getting everything ready so we wouldn't miss the start of this new station, there was great anticipation and I remember the opening and the symbol coming onto the screen as the fireworks were going off outside".

Andrew Dougal, later chief executive of Chest, Heart & Stroke NI, was in a panic when the family discovered their set had 'gone on the blink'. They couldn't get the new station. In apparent innocence he went along to a neighbour's house, knocked the door and announced: "We can't get Ulster Television," then asked if the elderly man would be watching *Robin Hood*, no doubt tears in his eyes! At nine years of age it was one of his first successful negotiations.

Deane Houston was only eight yet he remembers sitting on the floor, short trousers and socks, the fire lit and the new television set in the left hand corner of the room. "I remember looking up at the screen and seeing the logo appear then the theme tune for *Robin Hood* and Friar Tuck falling off a log in a fight. It was a big occasion and I was all on my own to enjoy it. The Sheriff of Nottingham made quite an impression. Suddenly I was seeing good and evil appearing on the screen right in front of me." Throughout his adult life Deane has worked to improve the lives of others and maybe the tussle between right and wrong, even in a programme like *Robin Hood,* had a lasting impact on the small child.

On the Falls Road, in her granny's house, Liz Gough was waiting. *Teatime with Tommy* was to become their special programme and as her father Tony was a great singer, they were required to sit quietly and appreciate the artists, sometimes joining in. "Looking back I remember everything in black and white that opening night, even the room. We'd saved to get the set and it really was a very special time." She remembers the advertisements. "The *Smash* potato spacemen, the *Daz* ads, and we always wondered how they got the sparkle into the ring of confidence for *Colgate* toothpaste."

In the Curzon cinema further up the Ormeau Road from Havelock House, Billy Blaney was worried. He was projectionist and his film that week was *Carry on Sergeant.* "The worry was that no one would come to the picture house that night, but they did although the numbers were down." Little did he know then that some years later he would be leaving his secure job and good wage to join the film library staff at the new television station.

In Ballymurphy, Da Taylor had the first television set in an area where there was great poverty but tremendous community spirit. Joe Graham tells me that Da had a tricycle with a box on front and he went around selling ice creams for a ha'penny each so he was known and loved amongst the children. "When he bought his television he placed it strategically in the centre of the front room and lined up apple boxes in rows and then invited the kids in to watch programmes like *Romper Room,* charging them a penny a time. During the commercials Da would emerge from the scullery with the ice creams but it was a great afternoon's entertainment for the price!" At night the mothers would pile in to watch programmes and anyone who hung around the windows hoping to get a free show was soon chased. "Ulster Television brought a local dimension to be enjoyed, especially the ads with the top of the commercial pops being *Barney's Bread* and the famous Hughes bap." Barney Hughes, the master baker and philanthropist inspired one of Belfast's most famous street songs: *My Aunt Jane, she called me in, she gave me tea out of her wee tin, half a bap with sugar on the top and three black lumps out of her wee shop.* These 'economy' loaves baked by Hughes were nutritious and beneficial for the digestive system and so gave rise to another saying, *Barney Hughes's bread, sticks to your belly like lead.*

According to Joe, UTV emerged at a significant time in Belfast. Teenagers began to catch up with their counterparts in England and the Dancette record player became the must-have accessory. Joe divided his loyalty, sporting an Elvis Presley quiff and wearing Beatle boots. He tells me that he actually saw the Beatles when they were taking time out at the Alverno Hotel on the upper Springfield Road, then called Hannahstown Road on the outskirts of Belfast!

*

All over the country people were tuning in, holding aerials up in the air, looking for wire coat hangers to bend in an effort to get a better picture. At the transmitter on Black Mountain the boys were setting up ready to beam the pictures far and wide.

What happened next is the essence of this book because what happened next was a major success story in the family of independent television companies throughout the United Kingdom even though it was the smallest area on their network map. Memories can be clear as day or slightly distorted but they belong to the people who were in at the beginning and our memories are honest, just as they and I remember them.

This is a story of those early days, the first half dozen years: the humour, the drama, the 'visiting firemen' as we called our guests. People like Tom Jones, Bing Crosby and Brendan Behan and the local men and women, including Gloria Hunniford, Romper Room's Miss Adrienne and comedian Frank Carson, who all became professionals and set the scene for years to come. For broadcasters and writers it was an introduction to a vibrant medium in which to express themselves, the belligerent and the gentle but always the entertaining. For me, a young woman known in those days as Anne Shaw, it was the beginning of the best adventure of my life, first as a filing clerk, then within a few months, a production assistant in the studio and in years to come, in front of camera.

Of course, things change especially in the world of television but those early days reflected in these pages were surely the best of times, with talk of the stars and the modest personalities who graced the screen as well as those of us who worked behind the camera in this small powerhouse of a building. We've all had a hand in a unique experience.

This is our story.

The State opening of Parliament 9th February 1960. Belfast Telegraph

Brian Waddell, Fred Corbett and Paddy Scott, the men behind planning programme content and soon after the opening, a news and current affairs service.

3
The stage is set

Opening day began in earnest at 11.00 that morning as we gathered to hear the plans, aware that we stood in the eye of the storm. Tension built as the minutes ticked away. We were in our best dresses, shirt and tie, nothing was overlooked.

As a girl of 17 I signed on as a clerk in the film library at Ulster Television, those two magic words. Jeans and tee shirts had yet to be invented so I arrived dressed demurely in a coffee coloured wool suit and cream blouse, seamed stocking, Cuban heeled shoes, white gloves and a hint of makeup.

Monday 5th October 1959, three weeks before the opening.

My father, John Shaw, drove me to the rather dilapidated building on the corner of Havelock Street and Ormeau Road. The front door was yet to be put in place, so it was a matter of climbing up the steep rusty fire escape leading to the general office where I was confronted by a row of desks, girls with their heads down typing, their manual Adlers clacking away. In one corner sat a Telex printer purring, just waiting to spring into life as programme details arrived from network companies in England. There was a buzz, a smell of Gestetner ink and a friendly greeting from everyone. It was mesmerising and slightly daunting. There were only half a dozen people in the long room with Howard Martin in charge, Ronnie McCoy the accountant and Tom Dawson who was to become familiar in the coming weeks because, in this office, he scrutinised expenses sheets, calculated wages and signed the cheques.

That morning I saw all this through a blur of excitement.

I'd just finished a year at Miss Isabel Elliott's Belfast Shorthand Institute and Secretarial College. This famous institution was next door to the Regency Cinema in Royal Avenue, Belfast, a big temptation which, with my friend Marilyn Mackie Todd, was often given into. If it wasn't the pictures we'd be roaming nearby Smithfield, the glorious market where you could get anything from a needle to an anchor.

At Miss Elliott's we'd covered spelling so I was a bit embarrassed when, during my typing test, the gentleman who was interviewing me leaned over my shoulder saying: "We'll be using English spelling here, not American. Programme is spelt 'programme' not 'program'." He was Colin Lecky Thompson and I think I swung it when he asked me if I'd any special ambition as I was growing up. "I always wanted to be a boy," I told him. I knew exactly what I meant; in 1959 boys could travel the world but it was difficult for girls. Months later he told me he was puzzled to know what I was getting at, so he offered me the job!

In those days things were instant. Interview on Thursday, phone call on Saturday and I began the following Monday, 5th October 1959. My annual wage was the princely sum of £320, although Cliff Richard had just made No. 1 with *Living Doll* and was reputedly earning £30,000. Twenty-two year old Buddy Holly died in a plane crash that year. Pearl Carr and Teddy Johnston sang the Eurovision entry *Sing Little Birdie* and *Six-Five Special, Oh Boy, Cool for Cats* and *Boy Meets Girl* were to become required viewing for teenagers.

Somewhere in Belfast an up and coming comic was planning an audition piece for the new television station. He saw himself with the interviewer introducing him.

'Tonight we welcome Frank Carson RC.'

'Good evening.'

'RC - does that mean you are Roman Catholic?'

'Ah no no, no no. I'm a rat catcher.'

'A rat catcher?'

'Yes, I am a professional rat catcher.'

'Tell me about it.'

'Well, I'll fill you in first. Rats don't get on with mice, they are different religions. I caught one the other day in a fruit shop. It was 18 years old.'

'How do you know it was 18 years old?'

'It had a date in its mouth.'

Or maybe the one about being a road sweeper who'd worked in the shipyard for 23 years.

'I brought my brush with me.'

Interviewer: 'Surely not the same brush for 23 years?'

'Yes, the same brush just seven new heads and eleven new shafts.'

Or perhaps he'd do his travelogue.

In Canada a young woman called Gloria Hunniford was planning to come home to Portadown for a few weeks before returning to get engaged to the handsomest man she had ever met.

Derek Bailey was working his way up the career ladder at the Pye factory in Larne and Tom Jones was working nights in a paper mill and about to become lead singer with The Senators.

When I arrived that glorious Monday morning, the build-up had begun. The old shirt factory, some say bought for £6000, was being transformed into a television studio, offices were taking shape, state of the art equipment was arriving every day and a work force of about 40 thrusting young people was gathering.

The word had gone out for weeks beforehand, a voice over a test card with two announcements, one made by actor Maurice O'Callaghan and the other by one of the founders of the company, Brum Henderson, at one time earmarked to be an onscreen presenter.

"Ulster Television comes on the air on October 31st " they intoned, "bringing some of the most exciting independent television programmes to Northern Ireland. You cannot afford to miss shows like *Sunday Night at the London Palladium*. You can have some of the most famous international stars by your fireside this winter brought to you by Ulster Television, your own local station." Both announcements ended with the advice that, if the Independent Broadcasting Authority test card was of a poor quality, you should see your dealer at once, and the strap line - "Prepare in time for Channel 9". This set the scene. Now the stage was ready.

*

Three weeks after my arrival at the top of the fire escape, there was a grand doorway leading into the finished foyer, glamorous receptionist and potted palms strategically placed. The talking point was a landscape painting by Angela, Countess of Antrim, wife of the chairman and a well respected painter who also sculpted in stone and bronze. Her art work graced one complete wall and it depicted life in Belfast, with the addition of a shiny new TV mast sitting high on the Black Mountain.

The momentum had begun and it was reflected in the local newspapers.

On Tuesday 27th October 1959, alongside an advertisement for a weekend return airfare Belfast–London by Viscount aircraft for £8, were reports of 98 miles per hour winds, a 'near all time record' according to the meteorological men.

The next day headlines were still about the storm and the damage caused; workers trying to get the railway tracks back in place and the telephone poles upright. There was concern about conditions for the weekend's celebrations at Havelock House.

On the 29th October front page news was that Marty Wilde, the idol of teenage girls, was to marry Joyce Baker one of the Vernon Girls, dancers on the programme *Boy Meets Girl*. On this day the advertising of television sets began in earnest with the cleverly named Ulster Telefusion offering £3 initial payment and 6/- per week rental.

More ads on 30th October.

'No TV? Why?' asked Telectro Agencies in Fountain Street. 'Look in tomorrow and you can look in tomorrow night'. RGD were offering connoisseur sets to the '1.100.000 people in Ulster who can now enjoy commercial television in addition to BBC/TV. Model 610 needs no special adjustment for ITV reception'. EKCO distributor V. Leonard in Berry Street took a whole page in the Belfast Telegraph to feature their 'slim line 17" table model with new 110 degree full-vision tube giving 19 sq. ins. More picture area, only 65 guineas.' A toss-up between this and the Belfast Co-op 17" table model at only 62 guineas.

In the middle of all this excitement, C&A featured their Outsize Week – up to 50 inch Hip. Coats with beaver lamb collar 6 guineas, dramatic design black lace dress 39/11d.'

The 4th Edition of the *Telegraph* on Friday, 15 pages for tuppence ha'penny, carried a huge ad from Ulster Television itself. 'All set for Channel 9 Tomorrow at 4.45 p.m.' Inside was Rowel Friers' first cartoon about the new station. He showed a BBC studio with an announcer, suspiciously like Michael Baguley, addressing the camera as the technicians huddled round a monitor in the corner watching the UTV symbol and waiting for the new station to go on air. The legend read: *'Normal service will be resumed in a few minutes'*. Normal service was never resumed once the cheeky young challenger appeared the following day at 4.45 p.m.

Sir Laurence Olivier

There has always been competition, the tabloid commercial channel against the broadsheet dignity of the British Broadcasting Corporation, incidentally a wonderful training ground for many broadcasters over the years including yours truly. Competition that night also came from three theatres in Belfast, The Ulster Operatic Company was putting on the *Merry Widow* in the Opera House, comedian James Young was performing in the Group Theatre and of the seven city cinemas, Vincent Price was drawing the crowds in the *Return of the Fly* at the Royal Hippodrome. There were also 19 busy suburban 'picture houses' as we called them plus dancing in the Orpheus and Capronis. Plenty of alternatives but they all felt the draught as people decided to stay at home and gaze in wonder at Sir Laurence Olivier, Adrienne McGuill and Robin Hood.

Opening day began in earnest at 11.00 that morning as we gathered to hear the plans, aware that we stood in the eye of the storm. Tension built as the minutes ticked away. We were in our best dresses, shirt and tie, nothing was overlooked. In the street, the locals gathered, enjoying every moment calling out to every one arriving and departing, most in big posh cars. It was controlled mayhem which somehow came to a calm climax at 4.45 p.m. when the red light went on that Hallowe'en afternoon.

The opening ceremony was performed by actor and top drawer celebrity Sir Laurence Olivier with a glittering list of guests amongst them Lady Peel, better known as character actress Beatrice Lillie, who was quite beside herself with celebration.

Our front of camera personnel were polished to a shine and the equipment well tested when the time came for the first notes of *The Mountains of Mourne* calling viewers to attention. The Ulster Television logo also made its debut late afternoon on Saturday, 31st October 1959, preceding the station opening.

First came the ITA tuning caption for 30" - make sure your picture was the best it could be. Then the signature tune *Seamus* for two and a half minutes - get the dishes finished up and settle down. Then the UTV announcer would confirm you were indeed watching Ulster Television. After all this came the 'station ident'. This was affectionately known as the coat rack, a series of seven dots appearing one at a time in an uneven pattern across the screen, each with its accompanying bong. A line then joined the dots reminiscent of a silhouette of the Mourne Mountains, a stylised technical wave form, more to do with setting up the picture than a romantic image of a local landmark. The sequence finished by proudly revealing the legend Ulster Television.

Many believed the ingenious logo held another message. Placed over a map of Northern Ireland, the seven dots represented some of the large towns and cities, roughly positioned from west to east they linked – Strabane, Londonderry, Enniskillen, Coleraine, Armagh, Ballymena and Belfast.

Then came the formal proceedings with a welcome by the Governor of Northern Ireland, Lord Wakehurst. He told the opening night audience, "In Northern Ireland we have been so long without independent television, it has made me intensely curious about it." He then introduced the star of the evening, Sir Laurence Olivier.

Looking back to newspaper reports of that day, there seemed to be a feeling that first night nerves were shared by distinguished veterans and homegrown personalities alike, trembling scripts held in shaking hands; boxer Freddie Gilroy dashing into the studio, 'a too hasty entrance' according to one reviewer. There was local input during the network programme, *Greetings to Ulster* compered by Macdonald Hobley, when J.G. Devlin and Elizabeth Begley sent messages from *A Shilling for the Evil Day* rehearsals, a play in which Maurice O'Callaghan and James Ellis also appeared. Technical advisor was Hubert (Hibby) Wilmot, director of Belfast's Arts Theatre.

Then it was on with the business of the day and the announcer gave a run down of programmes for the evening. On opening night that honour fell to a 21 year old local girl, Adrienne McGuill and it was a first step to lasting fame as will be revealed. During the evening she charmed the audience telling them of Sunday night's offering which included *Ulster Rich and Rare*, a film made and narrated by Lord Wakehurst, Joe Tomelty's play on *Armchair Theatre* and *The Palladium*. So the excitement continued and the audience grew.

At the time there were 1.5 million people living in Northern Ireland. It was the smallest television region in the United Kingdom but it had its own dedicated studio and 45,000 homes owned television sets and that number was increasing every day. Ulster Television was unique because transmission penetrated into Scotland, the Isle of Man and over the border into the Republic of Ireland, and this new opportunity for local businesses to advertise was immediately taken up. The additional coverage was attractive to advertising agencies when buying time for their clients. Advertising revenue was, and is, the lifeblood of independent television. Locally there were just four agencies but the station had its own effective sales office, led by the flamboyant Basil Lapworth, and between them commercial breaks were well filled. The important challenge, however, was to increase the set count and soon it was 60,000 and then 90,000 and growing.

There's a story which demonstrates the power of television. On the afternoon Scotland first saw commercial television, one of the ads was for Murray Mints '*the too good to hurry mints*', a tube which became famous. There was outrage next morning, however, when sweet shops from the highlands to the lowlands were inundated with customers wanting to buy Murray Mints but there was no stock in any shop. More accurately, there were no stocks left because every shop carrying a small experimental supply was sold out.

Working from Ulster Television sales office, Basil Singleton also sold 'air time'. He reports that cigarette and beer advertisements were allowed only during the day with no spirits being advertised at all, thanks to a mutual agreement within the Distillers Association to ensure there would be no competition between the drinks firms.

Advertisements were sold in multiples of five seconds. A ten second 'flash', a single visual on a slide and a voice over, cost £10.00. 50 years on, 10 seconds during the commercial break in *Coronation Street* will cost in the region of £1500. It's interesting that *Robin Hood* was scheduled early in the day to hold the audience into the early evening, all because of advertising. Where BBC once stood for 'best in British culture', it soon became 'beat the bloody commercials'!

Basil remembers Frank Carson messing around during rehearsals joking with the crew. "You won't bloody well sell them." he announced to camera holding the product, this was amended during transmission to: "It's the way I tell them" and so his catchword was born. On another occasion during a live commercial for Namosa Tea, the presenter 'dried', forgot his words and just looked into the camera like a frightened rabbit. Naturally the client demanded compensation. Ulster Television offered a free 30 seconds slot featuring a public donation to charity not realising that advertising a charity was forbidden. It was literally learning on the job.

Early on the opening day many of the ads were

Opposite left:
The Right Honourable The Lord Wakehurst KG GCMG OstJ. 3rd Governor of Northern Ireland.

Right:
The first newspaper picture of the New Faces. Ivor Mills, Brian Durkin, Jimmy Greene. Front Row: Anne Gregg, Ernest Strathdee and Adrienne McGuill.

local. The first was a 60 second film for Gallaghers. Others included, Kenneth Vard Furs, Joseph Kavanagh, Johnstons Umbrellas, Kennedy's Bread and Denny's Sausages. There was one 'live' ad for Brands department store, 60 seconds from Studio One. As the evening progressed and the price of advertising increased, the slots were filled by big names, Max Factor, Ajax, Caramac Sweets, Palmolive and Pal Dog Meat. The last ad of the evening was for Mars Bars.

Although transmission was limited outside our own borders, the on-screen personalities became pinups from Donegal to Douglas, Stranraer to Strabane and one of the most popular regulars making a name for himself was Frank Carson.

*

When I interviewed him for this book, we met in a small restaurant on Belfast's Lisburn Road and Frank told me of his audition and how he decided on the travel piece. As usual, he was generous with his time and memories and loved being surrounded by an adoring audience of diners hanging onto his every word.

"Anne Gregg and Ivor Mills were there for the auditions and they asked me what I could do. I told them 'I do a travelogue, it's very funny'.

'Let's have it,' said Ivor.

'Ireland is divided into two parts called Northern Ireland and Eire, it gets its name from a former prime minister Mr. Deevil Eire. Ireland is composed of four parts, Ulster Munster Linfield and Celtic. The capital of Ireland is called Dublin, the main street being O'Connell Street named in memory of the late Red Hugh O'Connell, a Dublin butcher who committed suicide and didn't leave a sausage.
Not far from Dublin is Cork which is famous as a touring centre because of Tipperary to which it is a long way from.
In Tipperary arises the famous River Shannon, famous in verse and song. One of the best known songs being O Shannon Doughah I love Your Daughter and Shannon Harvest Moon.'

He passed the audition!

Back to Hallowe'en night when the late afternoon air was thick with mist, fireworks and excitement. We were all spruced up to the nines, girls in fashionable bouffant hairstyles, fresh colourful dresses with nipped in waists.

The little office I worked in was above the front door. I had typed a list of all the commercials and films for the evening schedule and filed it for the film library boys to lay hands on as they were needed. My friend Mary Hunter and I opened the window above the front door and leaned out as far as we could to catch a glimpse of the VIPs as they arrived. As Sir Laurence Olivier's car pulled in, I leaned out that extra little inch and my back suspenders parted from their belt. I can still feel the painful ping. With my drindle skirt over my head, Mary had to kneel down to staple them back in place before I could go and join the celebrations! A case of make do and mend. And thank goodness no one barged in.

My job in the film library was to type the name, duration and catalogue number for every film coming into the big room on the top floor. Rows and rows of shelves quickly filled with reels all standing like silver soldiers at attention. They were waiting to be loaded onto a trolley and taken downstairs to master control for that day's transmission. One of the young librarians remembers how important it was to correctly assemble three or four commercials onto one reel, with a starburst inserted between each, ready for showing during the break in programmes.

Ivan Foster with his friend Albert Wallace were the two likely lads of Ulster Television. They were close friends, like brothers, full of fun and delighted to be working in the vital world of television. The two had something of a reputation. Although their adventures were harmless, there was always something to report next day in the canteen.

Ivan, who was destined to become well known to the public, had joined the company on 21st September 1959. In blazer and flannels he was that most important person, a messenger at the front desk, then a newsroom runner before promotion to the film library. His 'boss' in reception was Joan Henderson and his job was to run errands, including going to the chemist to buy stockings for a lady announcer. On the one occasion this request was made, he stoutly refused believing it was not part of his duties and contrary to the manly image of a 60s teenager! On the opening day he personally received the great and the good ushering them into the studio, ahead of the managing director who was the actual host

A young Ivan Foster working in the film library, one of the dedicated number, many ex-cinema projectionists. Amongst them, Joe Lyttle, John Meehan, Michael McCashin, Pat Devine and Eric Lennox. Eric even turned his garage into a working cinema, using tip-up seats and red plush curtains from the Troxy on the Shore Road in Belfast.

but Ivan, always having the courage of his convictions, led the way.

"I remember us being a tight knit group at a unique time with directors and studio cameramen coming from the network companies in England and Scotland as our programme schedule expanded. Working in UTV was a passport to anywhere, we used to walk into concerts on the strength of it. It was considered glamorous."

Promotion soon followed. In the film library it was hard work rather than glamour. 107 commercials were transmitted every day with some repeats. News film was shot on 16mm and the commercials and major films on 35 mm and they kept coming. Apart from daily feature movies or news material, a full days reel of commercials carried over an hour's worth of film.

In 1963 Ivan lost his driving licence and appeared before Bangor Magistrates court in fear and trepidation of losing his job. He didn't but it's funny how things work out. Because he had no licence, one memorable weekend he and Albert travelled to Portrush by train. They arrived on the Belfast platform with seconds to spare, jumping into the first carriage they came to. The carriage was already occupied by five girls on their way to a Christian convention in the north coast town. "We smoked our fags, talked the big talk, we were really impressive!" Ivan remembers with a smile. "Getting out of the carriage at Portrush, one of the girls, Hazel, smiled at me and said: 'You've laughed at us all the way here. God says in Genesis 'My Spirit shall not always strive with Man'."

Although at the time he didn't understand what this meant, the meeting made a lasting impression on the young man. It was a time of confusion.

Ivan was an only son and so was Albert. They had a lot in common but, on the evening following his father's funeral Albert told Ivan that he was saved and would follow the path of Christianity. "I was mad at him, I went up in smoke, I'd have no one to go to dances with, to the pubs and the general round of events frequented by teenagers back then. I'd lost a friend." A few days later, pondering this news, Hazel's words came to him. "Suddenly it made sense, I instantly knew what she meant." He realised that God was giving him the choice of repenting of sin and wrong doing. To follow Him or go his own way, treading forever the empty road he was on. The choice for the young man was easy to make. It was in Albert's home on 5th April 1964 that Ivan was converted and eventually became the Reverend Ivan Foster of the Free Presbyterian Church.

Even though I'd known him since 1959, we'd lost touch until one day in the troubled 70s when we met in the swing doors of the News Letter offices in Donegall Street. He remembers my perfect double take!

"I think you were seriously taken aback to see me wearing a dog collar," he joked when we talked again for this book. I assured him I was. He'd left UTV at the end of 1964 to become a student in the Free Church and when we met in the swing doors he was a well known public figure, a minister in Ian Paisley's Free Presbyterian Church of Ulster, (formed to maintain biblical Protestantism and expose what it sees as the errors of Catholicism), and later to become for a time a Democratic Unionist Party politician who was much in evidence at protest rallies. Although a friend and associate of the Rev. Dr. Ian Paisley, in November 2006 Ivan became the most prominent Free Presbyterian to openly challenge Paisley's decision to enter into a power-sharing government with Sinn Féin and he went on to denounce Paisley's decision from the pulpit of his church in January 2007. Speaking on BBC Newsline just 36 hours before the DUP and Sinn Fein were due to nominate their choices for first and deputy first minister he said: "The thought of one so highly esteemed and loved as Ian Paisley in political coalition with Martin McGuinness I would say is heartbreaking to most, if not every, Free Presbyterian."

Before he left Havelock House to join his church he had worked his way up to assistant news film editor and like the rest of us his memories are of people. George Shields, a quiet man with a mischievous sense of humour who ran the film library meticulously,

The Reverend Ivan Foster. *Irish News.*

Film librarian Olive Courtney with Anne Shaw.

hundreds of reels of film in those days, all documented and immediately accessible. George's right hand was Olive Courtney who suffered Dyane's muscular dystrophy. Initially she climbed laboriously up three flights of stairs until the lift was installed but soon had to give in to a wheelchair. Ivan remembers the day she fell in the rain but refused any help and struggled up herself. Only afterwards did he understand that the physical pressure of helping would have hurt her too much. He and I talked of how we all clubbed together to collect Green Shield stamps to get her a motorised wheelchair and our dismay when it wouldn't work on the carpets in the building. She must have been disappointed but she chose to dwell on the gesture made by her friends rather than the failure of our mission. Olive was a wonderful example to us all, her Christianity touched believer and non-believer alike and we benefited from knowing her.

In 1965 Ivan Foster met Ann, whom he married in March 1968. She had been a member of Dr. Paisley's father's church in Ballymena. The couple have six children and 16 grandchildren. Ann was principal of the independent Christian school they founded in 1979 until her retirement from that position in June 2006. Ivan has ministered in congregations in the west of the province which he pioneered since his ordination in 1968. He retired as minister of Kilskeery Free Presbyterian Church at the beginning of November 2008. When we talked, he was ministering to a Free Presbyterian congregation in Tavistock, Devon, on a part-time basis during a vacancy.

Did he ever meet Hazel again? "Yes. Outside C&A store in Donegall Place," he said. "She ran for her life when she saw me! She ran into the store and I chased her round the counters. When I caught up with her and told what had happened, she couldn't believe it, she a Baptist and me a Free Presbyterian. I was able to tell her I'd a lot to thank her for."

*

As I've said, things moved very fast in the days after the opening and it wasn't long before I was given the job of schedules clerk listing the day's transmission details on paper, everything seen on the screen from a five second ident to a two hour feature film, the announcers links, the commercials and the studio programmes. Then I applied for and, at my second attempt, got the post of production assistant in the studio, timing programmes and working closely with the director. It was then that I met some of the most famous people on the scene at that time. There were only a few of us in this much sought after job and we were the best-paid girls in Northern Ireland. It was a time of Biba, Mary Quant, freedom and flower power. Over the next four years my salary rose from £320 per year to £1,100. I was rich and I was happy.

Brenda Adams with Anne Hailes nee Shaw!

Double your Money host Hughie Green and the famous TV Post featuring the Thompson Twins.

4
The Twists and Turns of Life

One evening it was the turn of a very young good looking priest to give his homily. During the commercial break he was rushed into the small and only studio, and sat down at a desk facing the camera. It was explained that the shadow of the cross was on the canvas wall behind him, his script would be in front of him should he need to glance down and, when the little red light appeared below the camera lens, he should smile, say good evening and give his address.

I expect everyone comes to a crossroads at least once in their lives, turn one way and the result is one thing, turn the other way and it's something else. I'll never forget mine; it came one Wednesday night in the early 60s at 7.00 p.m. I'd just been appointed production assistant to the programme director working in the studio control room. We'd finished the evening programme and were leaving Studio One when one of the guests, a moody gentleman who had been eyeing me up and down all afternoon, cornered me in the corridor between make-up and the front door.

"I want you to come and have dinner with me, I think you're wonderful." Demurely and being only 21, I explained that I was going to visit my Auntie Joan in hospital that evening so couldn't possibly have dinner with him. He wasn't pleased and persisted. "I want you to have dinner with me." "Sorry I've told you I'm going to see my Auntie Joan." Somewhat exasperated he barked, "You can see your Auntie Joan any time, you can't have dinner with Harold Robbins any time." I still declined. He went on to become a multi-millionaire writer with five wives under his belt! He must have had *The Carpetbaggers* in his head at that time as it was written in 1964, one of so many sexually explicit novels. By the way, apparently he left each of his wives $1m in his will. Can't help wondering!

And what about Tom Jones who came to promote his first hit record *It's Not Unusual*? At first the BBC refused it airtime but thanks to the pirate station Radio Caroline, teenagers heard it and took a shine to the voice and the man in his black leather trousers and big Edwardian shirts. He was known as 'sex on legs' and when I walked into the dressing room that afternoon to ask him to sign a contract, he was standing, bare chest but for medallion round his neck and a rabbit's foot hanging from his belt, his good luck charm he explained.

I wished him well with the single. "Thanks love," he said in that melting, lilting, dark brown voice, "it's a one off and I'm going to enjoy it while it lasts." He needn't have worried, like Ulster Television itself, Tom Jones when on to great things.
Years later he is reported to have said, "I'm not looking forward to retiring. The biggest fear for any performer is that it will all be taken away, it's so much part of you, a physical thing. If I'm not able to sing, I won't know what to do." He has aged well, even his grey hair has a certain appeal and his voice is as good as ever.

I remember a beautiful Burmese woman schooling me in how to curtsey and address her King who was being interviewed on the teatime programme *Roundabout* and I'll never forget Gladys Aylward, the tiny missionary who brought her children over the mountains to the *Inn of the Six Happiness.*

In the film of her story, Ingrid Bergman portrayed the young English parlour maid who, at the age of 26, became a probationer at the China Inland Mission Centre in London and left for China in 1930. There, in Yangchen she set up an inn for the mule caravan drivers to rest, have food and some good old fashioned religion. She became the government foot inspector when foot binding of women was banned. She quelled a riot in the men's prison when soldiers were afraid to intervene. She was instrumental in prison reform and became respected as Ai-weh-deh – *Virtuous One*. Gladys began to 'buy' children who were being misused and eventually built a family of over 100 boys and girls. She became a Chinese citizen, lived frugally and dressed like those around her. When the Japanese invaded, this feisty woman gathered up her children and took them to the mountains. They walked for twelve days and nights and escaped across the Yellow River to safety. In failing health she returned to England in 1947 and died in 1970.

A few years before she died I talked to her when she visited the studios. A tiny woman who came up to my shoulder, dressed in the traditional working clothes of the Chinese, navy pyjama-like suit. She had wispy grey hair and a devastating smile. In those days we had the rich and famous, celebrity and royalty passing through but she is my warmest memory. Just proves you don't have to be big and dominating. Steely little ladies of a modest disposition can pack a powerful punch.

*

Before recording machines, every programme was 'live', including *End the Day*. A minister or priest came in late in the evening, and after rehearsing his four minute talk in the makeup room, he was ushered into the studio, sat down at an antique desk in front of a fixed camera and told to begin when the red light showed.

The epilogue was given each night at close down, about 10.30 p.m. It was known as the G-Spot – G standing for God in this case. It was strictly shared between the churches and allocated according to the number of followers in each. One evening it was the turn of a young good looking priest to give his homily. During the commercial break he was rushed into the small and only studio, and positioned facing the camera. It was explained that the shadow of the cross was cast on the canvas wall behind him - a technique achieved by using a 'gobo' - his script would be in front of him should he need to glance down and, when the little red light appeared below the camera lens, he should smile, say good evening and give his address. The camera was 'locked off', no need for a cameraman as this was a straight to camera piece, nothing could go wrong.

He was alone, waiting.

We were in the control room. I was watching the second hand as it ticked to the top of the hour. "Standby studio, cue studio". The red light went on. The young cleric smiled into the camera – and stood up. For three minutes and 33 seconds we heard his message and saw only the fly front of his trousers.

*

In those days, for technical reasons, men had to change into blue shirts. Clergy wore special blue dog collars and writer Denis Ireland, a regular contributor with snowy white hair, had to be powdered down from head to neck to avoid flare. We talked in technical and non-technical jargon, flare, motor boating, reverse polarity, barn doors and cycs, this was short for cyclorama the huge canvas curtain which surrounded the studio to block out unsightly walls and technical paraphernalia. The boys were warned not to stand against the bank of monitors in Studio One control room as they might become impotent because of the Rontgen rays, the early name for x-rays. Sadly, over the years, a notable number of women were diagnosed with breast cancer and I often wonder if there was any connection. The drug of choice for the sophisticated was the purple heart which apparently made the user pee purple but did little else and the slimming pill of choice was *Pondrex,* it didn't do much either.

The memories are legion and come at me from all angles. The hot sunny day we filmed Louis Armstrong arriving at the old Nutts Corner Airport and the local jazz band marching out on to the tarmac to give him a musical escort.

A perfect spring morning, everything was fresh and there was an excitement in the air. Louis Armstrong was on his way. By lunchtime the sun was shining and it was warm and the chosen few were on the tarmac of Nutt's Corner airport.

Wednesday, 25th April 1962 and Louis Armstrong was coming to town to play the King's Hall.

He was a legend. Jazz trumpeter and singer, raised in poverty in uptown New Orleans, learned the cornet at the age of 12 in the band of the 'New Orleans Home for Colored Waifs' where he served his time for general delinquency. At 18 years of age he was playing with Kid Ory's Creole Band and on the Mississippi riverboats before joining his mentor King Oliver in 1922. Anyone with a love of jazz knew he was someone very special and we were about to meet him.

The British European Airways Vanguard taxied to a standstill scattering hundreds of hares living beside the runways and enjoying the heat from the engines. The red carpet was in place. Jimmy Compton and his Jazz Men were at the ready. They tuned up, a cacophony of brass and wind. As the door opened, the band came together in a glorious jazz version of *When Irish Eyes are Smiling* to greet a small rotund gentleman who hesitantly put his head round the corner, his black face creased into the most amazing and genuine smile, the famous teeth shining and the eyes nearly popping out of their sockets. He was 62 and at the end of a gruelling tour, he'd just flown in from Paris and although tired, he was every inch the showman. Journalist Billy Simpson recalled he wore a grey pinstripe suit and pink and white checked shirt with a jazzy bow tie. I remember his wife, the fourth, coming down the steps, elegant and poised. Lucille was born in Queens and she also had a musical background being the first dark skin dancer at the Cotton Club. She was not only his wife, she was his musical and tour companion.

As 'Satchmo', short for satchel mouth, stepped onto the red carpet, he appeared surprised. 'I didn't expect anything like this,' he said and there was a cheer as the band played *The Saints* and marched him in true New Orleans style to the arrivals hall where crowds of fans were waiting. As the celebrations continued, we returned to Havelock House with the film which had to be processed in time for *Roundabout* that teatime. Director Derek Bailey's green Triumph Herald was floating on air as we drove back to Belfast - and so were we.

A bird's eye view of Louis Armstrong arriving at the Grand Central Hotel

As we were racing round the Horse Shoe Bend into the city on a cloud of happiness, Louis was preparing to be driven through 2000 cheering fans, his pale coloured Jaguar and his band's coach having to make umpteen stops until it reached the Royal Avenue Hotel. Newspaper reports described how they were preceded by an open topped lorry filled with local musicians. Rodney Foster's Jazz band and the White Eagles played their tribute all the way to the front door. The public were out in their finery and the noise was deafening! The famous All-Stars were equally taken aback with the welcome, Trummy Young trombonist, pianist Billy Kyle, drummer Danny Barcelona, Joe Darensbourg clarinetist, bassist Billy Cronk and vocalist Jewell Brown, names still on collector's record sleeves dating from that day in 1962.

Many of those who knew their jazz reckoned Armstrong to be the most creative of all jazz musicians but he was at the end of a series of one night stands all over Europe and he was drained. Reporters noticed his exhaustion during the press conference. The smile was switched on for photographers as the big handkerchief came out to mop the famous brow. On the night however, with the King's Hall boxing ring his stage, Louis Daniel Armstrong belted out the old favourites, *Blueberry Hill, Saint Louis Blues* and *The Saints* and the audience rose to their feet and danced in the aisles. Although reviews of the concert were ecstatic, according to the press, the numbers were disappointing and the promoters lost money.

The same boxing ring hosted a very different set of musicians two years later. Although they'd played in Dublin and then in the Ritz Cinema in Belfast 12 months before, a year made a difference to their status as idols, so it was much heralded that on Monday

2nd November the Fab Four were coming to town. This time, in the King's Hall at Balmoral, the Beatles performed to thousands rather than hundreds. Being members of the media and especially of a television company, tickets were forthcoming! I went along with Alan, my husband to be, my brother Johnny Shaw and his friend Elizabeth Wilton. They were about 12 and it was a struggle to hold them up so they could see over the heads of the jumping crowds. But even from the fringes, we saw the Beatles, we heard the Beatles and it was indeed fabulous. Like so many things, it's the taking part which is every bit as exciting as the performance and that night we were all part of the spectacle and the hysteria.

*

It's interesting that at 63 Louis Armstrong was one of the oldest artists to have a number one song in the Billboard Top 100 and it happened at the same time the Beatles were appearing in Belfast. On top of that, this elderly jazz icon had knocked their hit *Can't Buy Me Love* off that top spot with his recording of *Hello Dolly*. Armstrong died six years later still topping the bill and his coffin was carried by, amongst others, Bing Crosby, Ella Fitzgerald, Duke Ellington, Dizzy Gillespie, Pearl Bailey, Count Basie and Frank Sinatra. What a support group. On the eve of the year 2000, President Bill Clinton announced that one of Louis trumpets was to be included in a millennial time capsule to be opened in 100 years time, and in 2001 the airport in New Orleans was renamed Louis Armstrong International Airport in his honour.

And I shook his hand.

*

I shook another famous hand belonging to one of Louis Armstrong's pall bearers. On a wet windy day I drove with the film crew to Baltray Golf Club, just south of the border between the North and South of Ireland, to interview an entertainment legend, Bing Crosby.

In 1948 apparently Crosby was voted the most admired man alive, even more admired than Pope Pius X11. But he was an interesting man for another reason. It was said that he resented time being taken up with live daytime broadcasting as it kept him from his beloved golf so he developed the art of pre-recording and became a pioneer in this field. Golf was a consideration but in fact, his main aim was to achieve better quality through recording, to eliminate mistakes and control the timing of programmes. He was involved in the technical side of recording using the best equipment, especially microphones which had to be placed in the most effective positions for the ultimate in sound quality. He bought in German built magnetic tape recorders and in the late 40s invested $50.000 in the Ampex company to produce more machines. This enabled Crosby to pick and choose the jokes that went down best with the live audience, cut out any material that didn't get a reaction and so have control over the finished show. On one occasion some of the best jokes were cut out to give time for another song; the show turned out to be so dull that, during the edit, the jokes were put in again but the audience reaction was lost so a 'laugh track' was inserted. This was the beginning of a trend which is prevalent today, especially on radio.

He also recorded hit songs in the privacy of the studio. This he preferred as he didn't need to don the hated toupee the network demanded he wear in front of an audience.

The Ampex recording machine was later developed to record pictures on videotape and it was this machine which arrived in Ulster Television some months after the opening and revolutionised the output from the station.

*

The Beatles came and went, the Rolling Stones followed and Adam Faith was my all time favourite. It was a heady time. Tom Jones had to rush back into makeup when a little boy, waiting in the crowd of autograph hunters at the front door, left sticky hand marks all over his shiny suit. Sponging-down fell to makeup artist Jill McCord and her colleague Connie Larmour. Lucky girls. They also had the dubious task of keeping Oliver Reed sober until he appeared on camera. I don't think it worked because when I met him on his way to studio he was in very good form. Hooded eyes and a slightly leering smile didn't make him the breathtaking ladies man he was reputed to be - at least not to me on the back staircase of Havelock House!

Through the years there have been stories of celebrities being incapable of appearing on the screen and the fault is often levelled at the presenter of the show which is unfair. George Best fell foul of the effects of alcohol in 1991 with Terry Wogan, before that Oliver Reed caused embarrassment on Michael Aspel's show when he performed an exuberant song and dance. On one occasion socialite Tara Palmer-Tompkinson was almost incoherent on Frank Skinner's television show. One day in October 2008, singer Kerry Katona caused concern on the ITV's *This Morning*, hosted by Philip Schofield and Fern Britton when she explained that medication the night before was causing her to act in an erratic manner and to slur her words during the interview. It seems to me that there should always be someone on hand to alert the director or producer if there is any doubt. Rather like the day an actor was booked for a live South African sherry commercial. He rehearsed with the actual sherry, then had a few 'refreshments' in the board room before transmission; fell down stairs on the way to the studio, was helped into place, propped up and yet, so professional was he, he was word perfect for the thirty second commercial before collapsing in a heap as we got the sign 'clear studio'.

It's been said that theatre is an illusion, well, so is television. It's not always as it seems.

I went in front of camera years later to present and produce programmes including *Ask Anne* and those days again brought fun and challenge. But it was cold tea in the wine glasses the day we cooked a Christmas dinner in the studio and the turkey came out of the oven looking underdone and anaemic. Quick as a flash and before we went to the finished table, the bird was whipped out to makeup where it was basted with a good thick coating of Revlon's Toasted Beige foundation. Funny how you make things work. When we featured a couple of fierce Rottweilers on one programme, I admit I was scared. They snarled and wouldn't lie still but my method of self-calming worked like a dream. When I held a hanky saturated with lavender essence under each wet nose, they fell relaxed at my feet like pampered poodles.

Of course, time moves on and television like most creative businesses has changed beyond imagining.

In those far off days of the '60s, people wished each other good luck when they went into a studio. Today many television studios are factories where programmes are manufactured and in general, creativity has been left behind. There's no time to develop subjects, the sound bite rules. With the 'credit crunch' of late 2008 onwards, many reporters were criticised for becoming pundits and bloggers, giving an opinion rather than a balanced account. People began to feel the media was leading the way, causing panic with their dire predictions. But these commentators had access to top bankers and politicians and were only reporting what they had found out, possibly getting carried away with immediate information before thinking of the over-all effect it might have on savers and borrowers. Many would say the result added to the depression and the fear. In the 'old' days that wouldn't have happened. Then every story was balanced, analysis by the pundits was important, opinion less so. Sometimes objective journalism was forgotten in the frenzy of the more recent economic story.

Undoubtedly cut backs have devastated the television industry, especially in Northern Ireland, where in 2008 and into 2009 familiar faces on the screen, intimate friends to the viewer, simply disappeared and for the first time unions had little clout.

The most important room in the house – makeup. Jill McCord prepares Adrienne McGuill for appearing on Romper Room.

In the 60s trades union activists were powerful. Pay and conditions were based on film industry practices and this meant rigid breaks for studio staff during the day, set start and finish times and if there was a requirement to work over midnight, as happened most often for technicians in Master Control, they were into Golden Time. This was expensive overtime.

50 years later with the downturn in television advertising, with Ofcom (the independent regulator and competition authority for the communication industries in the United Kingdom) proposing a reduction in regional hours, plus the 'credit crunch', all combined to leave little room for negotiation between unions and management and management had their way. It was a bitter time, so unlike the glory days when both the administrative and creative sides of the business joined in the raw enthusiasm of setting up a television studio and shaping programmes, adhering to budgets, battling to understand new technology and taking pride in being part of pioneering work.

Without doubt, the early 60s were a most exciting and stimulating time when friendships were well made and long treasured.

Ivor Mills

5
Local Heroes

The farmer brought in half a dozen young lambs bedded down on straw which caused one director of the night to have a serious attack of hay fever. And the ballet dancers had four false starts as the 'foldback' system which carried the music from the turntable in the control room on to the studio floor, failed!

When all the technical plans were laid and underway during the year of 1959, the 'faces' were auditioned. Television was a unique medium and although BBC was broadcasting a limited news service in Northern Ireland, this upstart independent television was new, exciting, vital and visual and ready to tackle anything.

That meant recruiting beautiful and talented people, one for everyone. Ernest Strathdee was a man's man, an international rugby player, a man of the cloth, a good pair of hands to cover sport and religion. Brian Durkin was a Newry man, a teacher, steady, reliable and knowledgeable, with a deep voice and a great smile. Jimmy Greene, an actor and a fine man who spoke with authority and had a sense of humour. Then came Ivor Mills, handsome, dry wit and a slightly superior air. They each had their strengths and they each had their following and all were much loved by their audiences. It was, however, two young women who captured the public's imagination.

Adrienne McGuill was only 21 when she was selected to be the first person to appear on screen and Anne Gregg, a 19 year old civil servant, became the face of *Roundabout* co-hosting the first evening magazine programme on regional television alongside Ivor Mills.

Anne was beautiful and she was competent. She and Ivor had the sort of on-screen chemistry which is commonplace, indeed essential, today but it led to rumours which were a great weight for the people involved to bear and for the rest of us to counter.

In those far off days, the front of camera personalities were the personal property of the public, or so the public thought. We were protective of each other and one incident sums it up for me. At seventeen my father opened an account with the Belfast Savings Bank in King Street mainly because they didn't issue cheque books and he felt with my huge salary of £320 a year, it was wiser to put such temptation beyond my pen. One lunch hour I went into the branch to withdraw 10/- and the teller went off to record the transaction. Immediately a sly sort of a character stood in his place. "You work in Ulster Television," he whined. "Yes," I was always proud to admit to that. "You could tell me," he was like Uriah Heep. "is there any truth in the rumour about Anne Gregg and Ivor Mills?" How dare he. I drew myself up to my full height and demanded the manager. I withdrew all my money, 17/6d, and took it to the Ulster Bank where it has resided ever since!

It was a decade when careers moved fast.

Anne was much sought after on the network and in 1962 she left Ulster Television to join Anglia TV's *About Anglia* before moving to the BBC in London. Always a writer, she joined *Good Housekeeping* magazine as features editor rising to become the deputy editor before she took over the editorship of *Woman's Journal* in 1978. Although she continued to write, Anne returned to television two years later as reporter on the *Holiday* programme. When she resigned in 1991 the public were up in arms with over one thousand protests to the BBC when a much younger woman, Anneka Rice, replaced her. It was seen as the first case of an apparent ageist attitude within the media, which later affected the careers of Anna Ford, Selina Scott, Moira Stuart and Miriam O'Reilly and *Strictly Come Dancing* choreographer Arlene Phillips.

Management: the men who moulded Ulster Television.
Basil Lapworth sales, Gordon Duffield publicity, S.E Reynolds programme controller, Brum Henderson managing director, Barry Johnston company secretary and Colin Lecky Thompson presentation.

Anne wasn't off screen for long, however, as ITV invited her to host a series about 'Christianity in the United States' which led to a full diary including many travel programmes and books. In 2003, France awarded her the Médaille d'Or du Tourisme. Sadly, on 6th September 2006, at the age of 66, Anne lost her life to cancer.

Anne and Adrienne were two girls in a thousand, the number of young women who applied for the positions. Both had interesting backgrounds, Adrienne's mother claimed James James, composer of the Welsh national anthem *Land of my Fathers,* was a distant great uncle, whilst Anne's uncle was R.H. McCandless doyen of stage actors and directors in Northern Ireland.

It was as a pupil at Strathearn School in Belfast that she was first introduced to amateur drama. The stage became a great love and gained her much attention. She took leading roles with the Drama Circle winning awards at Ulster Drama Festival competitions at the Grand Opera House but, despite an ambition to turn professional, instead she entered the Civil Service joining the Ministry of Finance at Stormont.

When she arrived at Havelock House, we all knew she was special and although this was a new world, Anne took to it like a duck to water. The youngest resident presenter on British independent television, Anne attributed her audition success not only to her experience on the stage but to her deep voice. Hers was a voice and a face which were to win the hearts of the public.

In those days interviewers had one special weapon in their armoury, the programme controller, S.E. Reynolds. A senior figure on the network he had come to Ulster from ABC Television to help set up the station along professional lines and to coach the studio staff. He knew about show business, after all at one time he had run a circus! He was one of the first ever television producers, working at Alexandra Palace before the war. Every night after the show, Anne and Ivor would sit with him and dissect the programme, examine the weaknesses and build on the strengths and together they honed a near perfect product. The strength of *Roundabout* was a willingness to take on anything. The 'in town tonight' theory covered everything from a farmer with something to say, to ballet dancers appearing at the Grand Opera House to Ivy Benson and her All Girls dance band, a dozen good looking young women musicians who played in the Villa Marina, Isle of Man during the summers of the late 50s and 60s.

The farmer brought in half a dozen young lambs bedded down on straw which caused one director of the night to have a serious attack of hay fever and the ballet dancers had four false starts as the 'foldback' system which carried the music from the turntable in the control room on to the studio floor, failed! It was unintentionally hysterically funny as, in full tutu and pointes, the ballerina was poised, arm gracefully in the air, head turned coquettishly towards her partner – and nothing happened. Remember this was live television. On the fifth introduction the music from *Swan Lake* filled the studio and saved the day.

*

Screens could have gone dark the day Adrienne was hijacked by students as she arrived at Havelock House. They intended holding her for ransom during their annual charity 'raise and give day' known locally as RAG day. She was driven round town in the back of an open topped car. Despite bravely trying to make a bolt for it at red traffic lights in Royal Avenue, the boys were too quick. Their placards read, 'Adrienne won't be Appearing Today' thinking this would encourage the company to cough up the ransom. Members of management were not amused. They did not enter in to the spirit so Adrienne was taken to a flat in the student quarter of Belfast and held prisoner overnight.

"They were very nice, allowed me to ring my parents and tell them it was all a joke and I was warm and well-fed. Next day I was released and went back to work."

There was always a suspicion that the excellent publicity department within Ulster Television looked a little too smug with the resulting newspaper coverage. It was headed up by S. Gordon Duffield, a *Telegraph* journalist with additional responsibility for entertainment and editor of *Kine Weekly*. This meant he was in touch with showbiz so television was a natural progression.

"There were two principal groups bidding for the franchise. One headed by Lord Antrim and the other, chaired by the Duke of Abercorn which included my great friend, George Lodge, of the Grand Opera House and the adjoining Hippodrome." George Lodge invited Gordon to join the consortium in their bid for the new television station. "Assuming that the contract would come from Stormont they had omitted to appoint any Catholics to their group. Lord Antrim must have had some insider knowledge that the questions would be coming from the ITA and his group was balanced to include Catholics and Protestants. On the day, when the question came to George Lodge, 'How many shareholders are Catholic and how many are Protestant?' The answer didn't please. When the same question was put to Lord Antrim's team the answer helped swing the contract in their direction."

Far from being the end of the road for Gordon, a member of the winning consortium, theatre manager Hibby Wilmot, offered him a job setting up a publicity and promotion department at double his *Telegraph* salary. He had no hesitation in accepting. Jack Kinney, who was clerk of works and Mr. Fix-it in Ulster Television, was running out of letters as he approached Gordon's new office. As a result, for some weeks, the door bore the legend 'Pub Man'. On another occasion it was Jack, under directions from on high, who pinned the notice on the downstairs gentleman's loo during a drought. *If going to the toilet only No 1. Don't flush.*

In an early example of multi-skilling, one of Gordon's jobs was organising towels for the gentleman's toilets in the new building. "It was so fraught that I mixed up the paperwork and gave the contract to two companies. Early one morning a young lad came running to say there was trouble in the gents. I didn't know what to expect! When I got there two men were having a stand-off! They were facing each other like two cowboys one with a mallet in his hand the other with a hammer in his and each with a roll of towelling under his arm. I ended up making a deal promising there would be plenty of development in other areas in the building and the world of installing towels would be divided between them."

Preview was one of the top programmes, Robert McLarnon presented, Derek Bailey directed and Gordon Duffield was the producer.

Apart from publicity, Gordon was the obvious man to set up the entertainment programme, *Preview* with a budget of £20 each week. But such was the appeal of this new area of exposure, there was no difficulty persuading men like Richard Harris to travel to Belfast to talk about the latest film. At school we collected sweetie cigarette cards, little cards with international film stars smiling out. Without doubt the one I remember best, and collected most, was Richard Todd star of *The Hasty Heart* and *The Dam Busters* playing Wing Commander Guy Gibson. He was born in Dublin and his father, an international rugby player, was capped three times for Ireland. Richard Todd was heart stoppingly handsome to an impressionable teenager and I think my heart actually did stop for a few seconds when Gordon brought him to Havelock House to appear on *Preview*. He was charming and every bit as handsome as I remembered him on my card collection. He was the Brad Pitt of the day I suppose and, as I write, still handsome and charming.

When Jim Creagh joined the staff in 1961 it was as assistant to Gordon Duffield. He arrived into a completely new environment, quite different from the Irish News where he was receiving news releases from Ulster Television day and daily as the company looked for coverage in the local press. When he considered a job with the new station, however, he was hesitant, there might be nothing there after a while and he had a good job with the paper. "I asked my colleague Alex Toner who said, go for it, you're talking about tomorrow's world." So it was. Soon Jim was press officer selling the concept of television, now writing and sending out the news stories to local press and embarking on a campaign to increase the number of sets throughout the country.

Gloria Hunniford gets to meet my hero. After that I was determined to become a production assistant. Derek Bailey, Gloria and Gordon Duffield with Richard Todd.

Initially the coverage was limited, with Londonderry not well served, something to which they took great exception. "At public meetings we were lambasted, had we forgotten about this area? Was it cost? It didn't help that I arrived in a big company BMW so the point was well made that Derry is only an hour and a half up the road!" Before long, the West was on the map and the transmission signal was excellent thanks to the Strabane booster transmitter which went on air at the beginning of 63, and later the little studio established in the Diamond, manned by Cyril Troy.

In 1966, as Head of Press, Publicity and Presentation and eventually assistant MD, Jim was looking after transmission content and presentation but he was also instrumental in compiling an important document - the first marketing guide to Northern Ireland, a ready-reckoner of trades and professions.

He loved the cut and thrust of those early days, the fact that regional broadcasting reflected 'parish pump' issues, indeed this was the essence of Ulster Television because its raison d'être was to carry news of local problems, the chit chat and the talent as well as investigative journalism which often strayed into contentious areas of politics and religion.

But there was always the shadow of the IBA, the lords and masters, they who had to be obeyed.

"I remember their first visit to Northern Ireland. I talked to Harper Brown, manager at the Midland Hotel, and explained that the dinner we were holding for them was big time. We talked about it, I didn't want it to be too formal so I suggested instead of the traditional long tables with the formal top table we should break with convention and have individual tables. We'd place a businessman, a personality, staff members and an IBA representative at each table. Harper agreed with this idea and we sat down, made up cards with all the names, shuffled them about and devised the place settings. It worked, everyone enjoyed the dinner and the IBA were impressed."

Years later, when the images were dark and frightening, telling the positive side of Northern Ireland to the rest of the UK also fell into Jim's in-tray. There was a poster campaign, Frank Carson dominated tube stations and television commercials. There was Frank strolling through a beautiful and sunny Belfast, relaxed and chatting to people doing their shopping. 'Where is this?' he asks the viewer and proudly answers, 'Northern Ireland'. Another busy scene and he pops the question: 'Who has the highest unemployment in the UK? Not us.' There was one short film with a farmer walking down the main street of Ballymena followed by a pig on a string with passers-by pointing and laughing but when an E-type jaguar glides past them, well, that was common place, no one gave it a second glance. So gradually the myths were dispelled, an optimistic message struck home and people became curious. The result was that, over the years, many thousands have come to see for themselves and liked what they saw.

A lot of stars came through the doors into the studio but politicians also were given the floor, even as a programme was on the air. Gerry Fitt burst through the studio control room into the excitement of the '62 election programme which was in full swing in Studio One.

He had just won the Dock Division seat from the Unionists. He'd be representing the area in which he had been born and reared at the Northern Ireland Parliament and this enthusiastic man wanted to celebrate. He was on a roll. Four years later he won West Belfast for Republican Labour and went on to become a founder member of the SDLP.

Even Monte Carlo rally drivers roared in through the scene dock doors and once a pipistrelle bat bit the presenter and took off at a high rate of knots – the bat that is!

It was heady stuff, everyday was an adventure and I don't recall being any happier than I was during those first years of Ulster Television. There were romances by the dozen. Some ended in marriage. Some in tears. We were a family, sometimes to the exclusion of our own families and on occasions that brought heartbreak. We also lost friends through accident, illness, and suicide. It was intense. There was no small talk. It was getting right in to the heart of the matter and exploring it from every angle. The friendships forged in the first six years of Ulster Television are as strong today as they were then and writing this book has been a great opportunity for us all to get together again. It's also been an opportunity to include other aspects of life during the early 60s. Tangents are great things and I'll probably go off on quite a few!

In those days, as with the setting up of the original consortium, balance was still important. Any argument had to voice a counter argument. Balance meant equality and accuracy, staff left politics and religion at the front door, these subjects were only aired on programmes. This meant a unionist and a nationalist, a worker and a boss, a Catholic and a Protestant, each putting their point of view; it made for good television especially in the 70s when Rev. Dr. Ian Paisley and Gerry Fitt came head to head. The sparks flew, microphones were ripped off and flung aside and there was a lot of stomping out of the studio in a temperamental huff. Or so it seemed. On one such occasion Paisley announced he'd had enough. He left the set and headed for makeup to remove his Crème Puff powder. The programme concluded with a calm goodnight and as the end captions ran, Fitt too headed to the washhand basin. I was behind him with my clipboard and contracts. Although politicians didn't get paid for their appearances, they still had to sign a contract even in retrospect.

I was apprehensive when the two met in the brightly lit room, mirrors surrounded by light bulbs and glamorous makeup artists in attendance. Instead of a frosty silence, the reverend gentleman turned to the founding member of the SDLP and asked him what plane he was getting over to London the next morning. "I'm going for the early one," Fitt replied. "Keep me a seat Gerry if you're there first. See you tomorrow." And he was off with a wave. I felt that was wrong. Whipping up the public via the television set, each preaching what I saw as intolerance and then, out of sight, being colleagues prepared to share opinions on a flight to London en route to take up their seats in the House of Commons. It was the first time I was aware of the manipulation of the masses through the media, especially the medium of television. It has always happened and always will. At least in those days both sides of the argument were aired, today such scrupulous fairness seems no longer a prerequisite.

The new television act of 1963 issued by the Independent Television Authority laid down a code for programme makers. It gave guidance on general standards including bad language which wasn't tolerated; the portrayal of violence and any scenes of a sexual nature – bed hopping was out. The Authority became stronger as the years progressed with powers over programme schedules, advertising content and timing. If there was any doubt, the programme makers would call in the authority representative to view the content and give a ruling. If a company fell foul of the guidelines it could mean punishment. After three warnings the axe would fall and the company could loose the contract.

Within Ulster Television, at management level, there were apparent tensions but on the studio floor and in the production offices we were happy to work away enjoying great relationships and regular challenges, especially for those who were in front of camera.

Whilst Anne Gregg was exposed to the cut and thrust of a nightly magazine and news programme, Adrienne began her television career in 'the announcers box'. It was about six foot square. A desk, a swivel chair, a locked-off camera pointing at the announcer and a joy stick to move the camera a little to the left or right, up or down plus a switch to turn the microphone on or off.

Adrienne McGuill.

Like Anne Gregg, Adrienne wanted to be an actress and she followed her star to London to attend the Guildhall School of Music and Drama where her courses included child psychology, something that was to play a big part in her future job prospects. After only 12 months she had to return home due to her parents illness but acting was still in the blood so she joined Hibby Wilmot's Belfast Arts Theatre Company as a member of the stage management team. It wasn't long before she was on the stage and in a period of three years took part in 48 productions, acting in 38 of them. That all changed one day in 1959, however, when she spotted an advertisement looking for staff for the new commercial television station, and that included announcers.

She ticked all the boxes and opened the station on the night of Hallowe'en 1959.

"It was like a dream come true but I was terribly nervous. I sat there completely terrified with my finger on the switch that turned on the mike to bring my voice into thousands of homes. I knew what I had to say, I'd rehearsed it over and over but when I threw the switch there was this awful banging noise, bang, bang, bang. I immediately turned the mike off. Then I realised it was my heart beating but I thought everyone else would hear it too."

Thankfully she got herself under control, turned the mike on, smiled into the camera lens and uttered the immortal words. "Good evening everyone. My name is Adrienne McGuill and I am your announcer. I shall be telling you about all the programmes you will see on Ulster Television. Tomorrow night at 9 o'clock we present *Armchair Theatre*. The play is called *A Shilling for the Evil Day* starring local actors Elizabeth Begley and James Devlin. Earlier at 8 o'clock we visit *Sunday Night at the London Palladium.*"

What a day it was for the young woman working alongside Sir Laurence Olivier, hovering, avuncular and slightly the worse for celebratory drinks but the consummate professional. He had opened the new station and in her photograph album, Adrienne cherishes a little scrap of paper on which Olivier had written the four items he would include in his Epilogue at the end of the evening. He'd chosen quotes from Hamlet, Joseph Addison's hymn *The Spacious Firmament on High*, St. Patrick and the Bible.

After a party in the Grand Central Hotel, infiltrated I'm reliably informed, by some thrusting young reporters including Eddie McIlwaine destined to be one of Northern Ireland's foremost

Hibby Wilmott, governing director of the Belfast Arts Theatre conducting Sam Cree's new play Married Bliss. September 1965. The cast included Maurice O'Callaghan, Lilia Webster, J. J. Murphy and Catherine Gibson.
Belfast Telegraph

journalists, the guests came back to Havelock House. Olivier requested a Bible for his Epilogue. No Bible. Thankfully there was time for someone to rush home, grab the good book and get back to the studio before the noble knight appeared on screen, serene and soberly holding the Bible.

Jimmy Greene remembers somewhere along the line Olivier came to 'Let there be light and there was ....' He paused apparently and someone somewhere took it as a cue and pulled a switch and additional lights blazed.

Jimmy was a local actor from the Ormeau Road whose father worked in the shipyard in the 30s. There was no theatrical influence in the family at all. When we talked through the memories in 2008 he was 76 which meant he was 27 when he joined the company. In the theatre his contempories were Harold Goldblatt, Bob McCandless, J.G (Jimmy) Devlin and Billy Miller, later to become famous as the Holywood star Stephen Boyd. Boyd was the early day Liam Neeson. After attending Ballyclare High School he worked between an insurance office and travel agency by day and acted in the evening and at weekends. He gained his professional Equity card in Belfast and found employment in London theatres where he augmented his wages by working in restaurants, as a doorman at the Odeon Theatre and busking. But talent will out and soon he was appearing in major BBC television productions and then Holywood and films.

Ivor Mills was invited to the Ritz Cinema Belfast to attend the morning preview screening of the epic *Ben Hur* starring Boyd. There was great excitement. The press were out in force and personalities were in attendance. As Mrs. Millar, mother of the star, was coming down the steps onto Fisherwick Place, Ivor asked her had she enjoyed the film. "Well," she confided, "it was a long sit." At three and a half hours it certainly was.

It's interesting that, if Elizabeth Taylor hadn't taken seriously ill, Stephen Boyd would have played Mark Antony in *Cleopatra* but the film was delayed and he moved on to other roles. The young man from Glengormley, Co. Antrim carved out a busy career in films before fading from the headlines in the late sixties. He did, however, make a comeback with his roles in the American series *Hawaii Five-O.*

Billy Millar, as most fellow actors knew him, died suddenly in 1977, a massive heart attack claiming his life whilst playing golf in California where he is buried.

*

Ivor Mills had film star looks too, a tall handsome matinee idol of a man, talented, teacher, musician and an impeccably dressed interviewer without fear.

As things came to a head and with Hallowe'en fast approaching, new people arrived daily and the canteen was the hub of the universe. Ivor queued like the rest of us and one day he asked for a cup of tea but didn't have the 4d. required, paper money but no coins. On the other side of the counter, Margaret stood her ground. No way would she accept big notes, that would rob her cash till of change. Stand off.

'Take it or leave it' was her attitude and she meant it. These girls were from the local area, they were here first and Margaret wasn't going to be put out by anyone who thought he was God's gift. On the other hand, Ivor wasn't used to such an ultimatum. A schoolmaster, what he said was law – usually. The stalemate was resolved when, with a flourish, Ivor produced his cheque book and with great aplomb made out a cheque to the Gardner Merchant catering company for four pence.

With equal dignity, Margaret accepted it and put it into the till. Everyone was satisfied and there was a ripple of applause. The pair were firm friends thereafter although Ivor always had the correct change for future transactions.

He fared somewhat better the day he was interviewing a top businessman about this new-fangled piece of office equipment called a Dictaphone. A young typist, Sheila Hewitt, was invited to put the case for the secretary. Her boss had bought her a new dress for the occasion and she had her hair done and her nails polished. Appearing on television was a event and you had to look your best. As the interview progressed, the men were lauding this inventive time saving device, Ivor turned to Sheila and asked for her opinion. She didn't hesitate. "It's wonderful if you like that sort of thing," she said. "But, you've got to consider it can't sit on the bosses knee and give him a cuddle." With that she got up from her seat, walked to Ivor, sat down on his knee and gave him a big kiss. She was a hit! Before joining British European Airways as their hostess to the VIPs, Sheila became a regular contributor for a few months but she wasn't forgotten and eventually joined the staff as the much loved makeup artist, Sheila Dundee.

We were a strange mix of people and personalities and remarkably, we gelled. We were colourful in every way, the worldly television people from the network and the local men who were still boys with bright sweaters and corduroy trousers. The girls in floral drindle skirts and high heels. The big fashion statement was the expensive Jaeger elasticated belt worn with tight ski pants, although only the older more glamorous girls wore these!

We even had our own in-house folk group who became well known throughout Northern Ireland. Miles Scott, Leslie Bingham, Allen McMurtry and Gerry O'Kane - The Irish Rovers.

Life was so exciting, fast and every day brought a new high and inside the building we began to work as a unit.

As the staff built over the days, a few of us were sitting at one of the dozen tables or so which made up the small canteen. A smiling gentleman approached balancing a cup and saucer and a large fruit scone. "May I join you?" Certainly he could, we introduced ourselves and so did he. "I'm Stanley Wyllie, transmission control." We welcomed him, all except one of the secretaries who launched into a diatribe about how much she hoped he wasn't the Stanley Wyllie who played the organ at the Ritz Cinema in town. She hated organ music, she said, so when the organ rose up out of the pit during the break between the B movie and the big film, all rainbow lights flashing and the organist waving to the audience and launching into the top 20 of the day, she was under her seat with her ears covered! The Compton organ was all lights and gizmos and Stanley, in his white dress coat with a flower in his buttonhole was famous and a firm favourite with Belfast audience, except this one girl he proposed sitting opposite.

As he sat, in his gentle way, he replied to her that he was indeed that Stanley Wyllie. Quick as a flash she smiled up at him. "Well," she said, "I'm glad you're not as bad as I thought you were. Can I pass you the sugar?"

In fact Stanley was one of the top organists in the UK giving recitals until his sudden death in 2003. When, in 1959, he swopped the organ console at the Ritz for the buttons on the desk in Master Control in Havelock House, the Compton was bought by a Mr. Carrington who installed it in his country pub, The Plough, Great Munden in Hertfordshire. Twenty-six years later, on one of his visits to London to give a guest recital on the giant Wurlitzer in the South Bank Polytec, Stanley visited Great Munden to say hello to his old friend Compton. At the end of the evening, Stanley was delighted when he was presented with a trombone stop from the organ. It was a valued keepsake.

So Stanley and the secretary Bernadette became friends and we began to learn of each other's background, had we worked elsewhere or, like me, arrived straight from shorthand and typing school?

*

That was the way of it in the early days. We were a family, 30, then 35 then 40 and so it grew. There were spats of course, but we got over them. It was, however, the impact of sudden death that had the most dreadful impact of all.

A floor manager is the conduit between the 'box' where director, PA and sound engineer sit, and the studio floor. Through headphones he hears instructions and organises the guests, gives the interviewer time cues and in general, manages the business of the studio. He can communicate through a tiny microphone, being heard only in the box. Even now, as I write, I can still hear David Marshall's familiar voice in my head.

There will be many people reading this who will remember the day in August 1968 when news came through of a fatal crash at Ballynure on the Larne Road. A trailer broke away from the cab of an articulated truck, veered on to the wrong side of the road and fell on top of a Renault 4 returning to Belfast after a family day out. Inside was a family of five, only the baby survived. Our colleague floor manager David Marshall 32, his wife Annette, an actress and interviewer on BBC's *Scene Around Six,* and their little daughters Jessica and Louise were killed. Annette's sister, Diana

There was music everywhere. On the roof Robert McLarnon with Acker Bilk's Paramount Jazz Band.

David Marshal (right) with director John Scholz Conway, studio crew and dancers during a break in With a Fiddle and a Flute rehearsals.

Payne and her brother-in-law Jimmy Greene raised the baby, Maggie who in 2008, 40 years later had two children of her own.

*

In the early 60s the average age of the staff in the Ulster Television studio complex was 23. They were innocent days although those who fell into the 23+ range did exciting things like going out for dinner and to the theatre. The sub-23 year olds, my group, preferred to go to Barry's amusements on a Saturday or drive along the coast to Helen's Bay for a picnic round a campfire. If someone could get their dad's car we were up for anything. Eventually I shared a black Ford Popular with my brother Mike Shaw and it opened up new vistas and gave me a feeling of great freedom.

Movement within the staff was rapid, one day a floor manager the next a director, one day a filing clerk the next a production assistant and for Adrienne McGuill, announcing led to much excitement and a high profile.

Soon she was sitting in a big comfy armchair with a cuddly teddy bear on her knee as she introduced stories *For the Very Young,* tales of Sean the Leprechaun and Danny the Dormouse written by Sheila St. Clair with illustrations by Rowel Friers. This glamorous presenter immediately engaged the little ones as she greeted them. "Hello boys and girls, I'm going to tell you a story." She was invited to their parties, she visited hospitals, she was the darling of football teams, she once had makeup advice from the advisor to the royal household and she had the honour of travelling on the maiden voyage of the Belfast built P&O liner, the *SS Canberra*. Women's programmes followed, *A Matter of Taste* and *Women Only,* live fashion shows with beautiful models Grace Emanual and Patricia Mancerelli. Live cookery included making an omelette one afternoon and there was panic when the cooker went on fire and the extinguishers came out in a hurry and the viewers saw a real drama. Always cool and always dressed impeccably, Adrienne took it in her stride.

We exchanged experiences sitting in her lovely home overlooking Belfast Lough. I told her of an *Ask Anne* programme in the 80s about breast cancer when, during the half hour, we included a fashion show featuring swimwear especially designed for women who had undergone a mastectomy. During the show one of my guests explained that before there were prostheses to wear inside a bra, she used a little bag filled with birdseed. This took on the shape of the breast and looked very natural under her clothing. One day, however, when she was doing the housework and cleaning round the toilet it fell out and splashed into the loo. "I fished it out," she said with a big smile, "ran the tap over it and put it in the hot press to dry. A couple of days later when I went to get it I discovered all the seeds had germinated and I had a flourishing garden of green shoots!"

I like to think that programme broke down many of the barriers and fears surrounding the word cancer. Little did I know how I'd draw on that lovely lady's honesty and humour when I too had to face breast cancer in 2000.

Certainly Adrienne was breaking new ground for women and giving them a voice through her programmes in the early 60s. But there was one programme which made her a household name for men, women and especially children.

"1964 will always be my most exciting year, that's when I was selected to become Miss Adrienne in *Romper Room*."

This Talbot Television programme was franchised internationally to many television companies with millions of young viewers; locally it went on air on December 28th of that year, the latest of 166 centres throughout the world and an immediate hit. The set was like a colourful classroom, props included a tall red pillar-box for the children to post their letters and, as often happened, when a curious child would disappear they were usually found hiding in the box. Eventually it was given a fitted base and no one went missing after that. There was the magic mirror too and even adults got a little thrill when Miss Adrienne saw them sitting at home as she watched them watching her. She would hold up her Magic Mirror to camera, an ordinary but large hand mirror. She held it in front of her face saying, "Magic Mirror tell me today, will I see my friends at play?" As she said this, a swirling pattern was superimposed in the centre of the mirror and the camera pushed into until it filled frame, at which point Adrienne did a quick change for a hoop with a handle. When the effect faded, children at home could see her face looking out at them through the 'mirror'. At this point she would say, "and I can see Rosemary, Sheila, Bill and Michael," about ten names of children who had written in. Sometimes, just sometimes, she'd run out of names so she would feature the technical and studio staff, once it was senior management. We were as thrilled as any child, although one grown man of my acquaintance still feels aggrieved that she never saw a Houston in her mirror.

Earlier that month Adrienne flew to Baltimore to train to become the glamorous 'Miss Adrienne', the champion of children of four and five years of age. When she was in the States that December, she decided to take a sightseeing tour and paid five dollars for the coach journey. "Lady," said the driver, "I'm sorry but there just ain't no one else who wants this tour. Would you mind if we leave the coach and use the limousine." She travelled in luxury and it was the beginning of a magical time in her life which saw her become the most recognised face in Northern Ireland and having the honour to represent Talbot Television with her Romper Room series at the Cannes film festival.

During the ten-day course in Baltimore, Adrienne studied the techniques of running a television kindergarten, she learned about being a Do-Bee not a Don't-Bee, met Willie the Weatherman and Mr. Music. 'Do-bee a door closer, don't-bee a door slammer.' she would say not only to the children in the studio but also to her colleagues in the production office. Soon we were all singing her theme tune, "I always do what's right, I never do anything wrong, I'm a Romper Room Do-be, I Do-be all day long."

It began as a live programme, five days a week at 4.40 in the afternoon, entertaining and educational, it was designed to draw out self-expression and physical fitness. It was 20 minutes of unpredictable live television, full of tension and there were plenty of stories to tell, like a five year old Leonardo DiCaprio who apparently distinguished himself on one American show by relieving himself in the corner of the set.

One lovely spring day in 2009, 14 old timers sat round our table at home and we talked over lunch. The memories of *Romper Room* came thick and fast. About the red haired guy from Lisburn. He was being noisy and Adrienne asked him to be quiet. "Do you remember Adrienne?" asked Paul Irwin who was a sound engineer. "He turned round to you and told you to f*** away off!" "And do you remember Charlie McKeown," came from Bill Armstrong. "When everyone else was trying to be a Good Do Be, he always said he wanted to be a Bad Do Be." Charlie was a technical man and had no badness in him. Allen McMurtry a racks engineer, recalled how the son of one member of staff settled into the brightly lit studio and, once on air, looked up at the ceiling and asked very loudly "What are all those bloody lights for?" You can't beat live television. "And do you remember the day one of the children wanted to go to the toilet." This from Adrienne. "I called for Auntie Connie to come and take her out to the loo. Then another hand went up, and another. They all trooped out after Auntie Connie and I was left to fill the programme with no children!"

Miss Adrienne obviously had a great influence on young Simon Crook who loved appearing on Romper Room so much that he and joined Ulster Television as a cameraman years later.

We talked about the characters who came to teach us how television was done 'on the mainland'. That didn't go down well. One superior director from London arrived on the first flight and left on the last flight. He was so objectionable the boys took him to Studio Three – the pub – and suggested a few drinks before rehearsals. He was well up for it but what he didn't realise that the spirit measure in Northern Ireland was different to his local. We enjoyed a quarter of a gill measure whereas in England the measure was a sixth of a gill. He was so paralytic by 6 o'clock he had to be poured onto the plane. So much for someone who thought he could teach the paddies how to lower their drink!

Eric Caves talked about the *Cheyenne* feature film which came in three reels but somehow part three was transmitted first and part one last. "No one even noticed." Alan Hailes told the story of the Religious Advisory Panel going into the control room to watch a religious programme and give their advice. By some mischance, instead of a religious programme appearing on the screen, up came an X-rated movie. Someone added that rumour has it they watched it right through! It was Billy Blaney who remembered a war film being shown on a Sunday afternoon. "When the title caption came upon camera, the props man held a lit cigar under the caption card so the smoke would add atmosphere." This was the mindset, be adventurous!

In later years, because each *Romper Room* videotape was erased after transmission ready for the following day's recording, it appears there are no records of the early programmes anywhere in the world. But badges and mugs are still treasured in Northern Ireland homes and those of us who worked on the programme, or watched it, remember something which was unique. As for Adrienne, she never lost her love of children. She and her husband the late Harry Catherwood, a respected businessman and a member of the board of directors at Ulster Television, were blessed with four children; in fact their daughter Andrea followed her mother into the media as an international television journalist.

For her work, a lot of it with young people through Action Medical Research, Adrienne was awarded the MBE in 2004 and five years later was appointed a deputy Lord Lieutenant for the County Borough of Belfast.

*

People came and went in the first few years of Ulster Television. Roy Alcorn, who died in 2008, joined the staff to become the third floor manager following in the footsteps of Derek Bailey and Andy Crockart. But Roy never settled. Teaching children was more

Roy Alcorn, floor manager, who quit television to return to teaching and cameraman, later director/producer, Bob Brien.

important and he returned to his profession within 18 months and was a much valued teacher and the first to produce a school musical. *Annie Get Your Gun* staged by the staff and pupils at Regent House School in Newtownards. He first left teaching in the late 50s to join the James Ellis theatre company, Bridge. The company came about when the Group Theatre in Belfast was hesitant to put on Sam Thompson's *Over the Bridge*, a contentious piece exposing sectarianism between Catholics and Protestant workers in the Belfast shipyard. So Ellis formed a touring company and Roy was a mainstay of the group and was elated when they made it to the West End and the Shaftesbury Theatre. The fact that the notice to close went up on the first night was a drawback but not surprising as it was the week of Princess Margaret's wedding and at a time when no one knew or cared about the yard workers who came over the Queen's Bridge in Belfast. When the new television company was looking for staff, Roy took up the challenge of a new area of creative life. But the love of teaching and of knowledge was too much and was well demonstrated when he and his wife Lucy represented Northern Ireland three times on the BBC radio programme *Round Britain Quiz* in the days when it was hosted by Franklin Englemann. They were the first husband and wife team to take part. They appeared with Angela Rippon on *Master Team* and Roy faced Magnus Magnusson on *Mastermind* with his superb general knowledge and his specialist subject, films.

Even in those days we had an *X-Factor* competition when Shelagh McKay from Dervock in Co. Antrim, was chosen from thousands of entries to become a presenter. She was a social worker based in West Belfast when her friend Daphne Harkness noticed in the newspaper that Ulster Television were looking for a new 'face'. 23-year-old Shelagh wrote in, passed the audition and suddenly was on screen interviewing on *Roundabout*. She enjoyed the studio work but being thrown in at the deep-end isn't easy and after a year, when she married, she decided to go back to her welfare work. She was offered and accepted a job as head of personnel in the Training Executive. "I loved it and it lead on to another period of time at Queen's University studying special needs then teaching children with learning difficulties. I enjoyed Ulster Television but unlike Queen's where you were told directly if your essay was awful and how to put it right, there was no such direction." A lot of people found that. Some succeeded, some were wise enough to move on to find fulfilment in their chosen subject. Some stayed but never really cut the mustard. It's a wise person who knows which route to take.

When we talked in 2009 Shelagh told me of her work with L'Arche, an international federation of 131 communities all over the world where people with and without learning disabilities live together in a spirit of friendship, sharing their talents and their gifts and where everyone's presence is valued. With plans for more, at that time there was just one centre in Northern Ireland with Shelagh on the Board of Directors.

⁂

But back to the story, October 1959 and the opening day beckoned. Little did I know that I would turn down dinner with a millionaire, be electrified by Ronnie Drew's eyes and that my suspenders would snap at just the wrong time.

Anne Gregg and Paddy Scott.

Tommy James

6
Exciting Imports

Inventiveness was well illustrated when one of the boys got an SOS from his wife on Christmas Eve to buy Christmas wrapping paper to parcel the gifts for delivery that evening. He rushed out but in his hurry didn't notice he'd bought birthday paper by mistake. Necessity is the mother of invention so he spent the next hour scribbling until every sheet read 'Happy Birthday Jesus'.

Teatime with Tommy is still legend in Northern Ireland. The host, Tommy James, was a cockney from the Mile End Road in London who came to work in a Belfast music shop, demonstrating and selling pianos. He took the ear of the managing director of the time, Brum Henderson, who liked his style and offered him a job as musical director, records librarian and accompanist for singers on programmes. A man destined to become the famous Mr. Music on *Romper Room* and host of a number of shows in coming years. Actress Leila Webster MBE, appeared on Tommy's live shows, one where the set was built round a campfire! "I was scared stiff. Very young and inexperienced. I sang *The Gypsy Love Song*. On the bill was trombone player George Chisholm from *The Black and White Minstrel* show. I was over the moon to meet him in person. And we did sketches as well. I think it was a special Christmas show when I sang *The Black Velvet Band* with comedian Tom Raymond and Brian Durkin and Ernie Strathdee was there too. I was dressed as a school girl with pigtails and a straw hat doing all the wrong things and singing in a broad Belfast accent!"

From the beginning Tommy impressed with his easy style and ready smile. Within a couple of years he was given a regular programme of his own every teatime, Monday to Friday. The natural title was *Teatime with Tommy*. Tommy introduced both local and international artists accompanying them on piano, giving many their first chance on television, including Gloria Hunniford, Denise McKenna and her cousin Eleanor Nodwell. Eleanor was one of the finalists in the Irish heats for the Eurovision Song Contest in 1969, Dana came second and Muriel Day from Newtownards was the winner. Muriel went on to perform in the Madrid finals, looking stunning in a green mini-dress made by local designer Alice Campbell. She and her backing group, The Lindsays, sang *The Wages of Love* on the first Eurovision to be broadcast in colour. Lulu was joint winner that year with *Boom Bang A Bang* and Muriel came seventh. She was well known throughout Ireland when she sang with her husband Dave Glover and his Showband and she was a regular on *Teatime*.

Actor Derek Thompson, probably better known as Charlie Fairhead in the BBC medical series *Casualty,* was only 15 when he appeared on *Teatime with Tommy* with his twin sister Elaine. They sang hits like *Yellow Bird*. The set was a desert island and

Regular visitors to Studio 1, Elaine and Derek, the Thompson Twins. Derek became nationally famous as Charlie Fairhead in the BBC programme Casualty.

prominent was a bunch of bananas with some big drooping leaves which trembled in time to the chorus. The cameraman was up a ladder and the camera on a raised platform so the two winsome children could look up, through the leaves and sing to their audience, *"yellow bird, up high in banana tree"*.

That day the climate in the studio was in sympathy! No bigger than a large bedroom, it housed three Marconi Vidicon cameras, small and inexpensive but requiring a great deal of light on the subject. This was achieved using powerful television 'bulbs', each in a metal box with adjustable side panels, known as barn doors. Dozens of these lights were slung from rigs fixed into the ceiling. On a hot day, when the ventilation system was under pressure, temperatures reached 115 degrees Fahrenheit, over 46 degrees Celsius and conditions for staff and artists were grim.

Another 'find' was Roger Whittaker, a platinum, gold and silver record award winner later in his career. He arrived in the UK from Kenya to study zoology and marine biology at the University of Bangor in Wales, but he had another talent. Roger sang and whistled not just well, but very well. He had the dilemma of showbiz verses university and showbiz won.

Roger was singing in a Belfast pub when director John Scholz Conway happened to call in for a drink, and, as they say, the rest is history. As a result Roger became one of the Ulster Television family and ended up with a 13 week series of his own, *This and That*, the first local programme sold to the all powerful network. And then there was Val Doonican. It's firmly believed that Tommy rejected Val at the first audition but relented and gave him a spot, five guineas for five minutes. This led to a booking on *Sunday Night at the London Palladium* in 1963 resulting in national and then international fame for the Waterford man who wore big cardigans and sang sitting in a rocking chair.

Mike Kent, who came to Ulster Television from 'the network', directed amongst other things, the Tommy shows and he remembers the constant round of auditions, rehearsals and recordings. Being used to the discipline of network studios, Mike stuck rigidly to the red light rule. If this warning light was on outside the studio doors, it meant we were 'on air', either live or recording and it was a restricted area. No one was allowed to enter. On one occasion, when the managing director accompanied by three VIPs dared open the door into the control room during the news, Mr. Kent risked all by telling him in no uncertain terms and at the top of his voice, to get out and shut the something-or-other door after him!

Strict discipline was important and adhered to, especially in the days of live broadcasting. Distraction could spell disaster. Any member of the team leaving the control room to go onto the studio floor had to ask permission of the floor manager. There were 'pleases' and 'thank yous' and respect between colleagues was shown.

In those days, three or four programmes were being transmitted every day from Studio One. Often there was only the duration of an announcement previewing future programmes or the national news bulletin from ITN in London to get organised. Five or ten minutes to turn the studio round from a news desk to a magazine set, or a jazz programme like *Room at the Top* or *Teatime with Tommy* featuring Tony Martin on drums and George Newman, a chiropodist by trade, on double bass.

An example of the ingenuity of the studio crew came one day cameraman Bill Armstrong, who took many of the pictures in this book, suggested putting tiny lights on the end of Tony's drum sticks, dimming the studio lights during transmission and the result was light years ahead of its time with the sticks seeming to spin a web of coloured arcs in time with the music.

Tony was a natural comedian and I'll never forget the day we were all invited to a wedding, one of the many internal romances which came to fruition. When the minister stood up at the reception with his glass of orange juice and said, 'Ladies and gentlemen, be upstanding for the Queen', Tony jumped up and exclaimed in a excited shout, 'The Queen! The Queen? No one told me the Queen was going to be here.' To say we younger and less reverent guests fell about laughing is something of an understatement.

We laughed a lot in those days as we bounced along on a wave of happiness being inventive and creative. Inventiveness was well illustrated when one of the boys got an SOS from his wife on Christmas Eve to buy Christmas wrapping paper to parcel last minute gifts for delivery that evening. He rushed out but in his hurry didn't notice he'd bought birthday paper by mistake. Necessity is the mother of invention so he spent the next hour scribbling until every sheet read 'Happy Birthday Jesus'.

*

Along side *Romper Room, Teatime with Tommy,* was probably the most popular and memorable programme to come out of Havelock House. Saturday morning was dedicated to auditions. Reminiscent of hundreds of X-Factor contestants in the mid 2000s hopefuls squeezed into the big production office on the top floor or the studio on the ground floor. Mike would meet the auditionees, full of encouragement, full of enthusiasm but often that was the last they would see of him. The standard was pretty awful and he admits that he would resort to letting them down gently over the studio speaker rather than face to face. Zandra Smyth was the regular production assistant on *Tommy* and her total dislike was the song *40 Shades of Green* which she heard over and over again. Sometimes I sat in for Zandra and I discovered that for some reason sopranos thought they would score with a number from *The Merry Widow* and to this day my least favourite song in the world is *Vilja Oh Viljas the Nymph of the Wood.* That high note still makes me cringe.

About that time, we moved into a larger, airier studio. As the

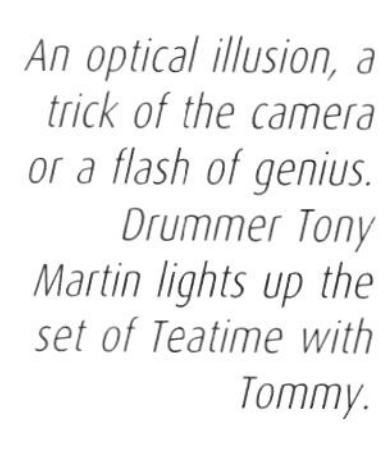

An optical illusion, a trick of the camera or a flash of genius. Drummer Tony Martin lights up the set of Teatime with Tommy.

An early visitor to the studios was Patricia Phoenix (Elsie Tanner in Coronation Street) with Adrienne McGuill and the Lord Mayor of Belfast Sir William Jenkins.

foundations for Studio Two were being laid, management and their guests, the Lord Mayor and local dignitaries, placed a time capsule for future generations to discover. It contained a *Belfast Telegraph* and a *TV Post.* The job was performed by Anne and Adrienne each wearing their mothers fur coats. Also inside was a *Daily Express* of that day, a programme schedule, a UTV key ring, a book of matches bearing the message *Strike the Right Choice with Ulster Television* and some pounds, shillings and pence.

The new studio was important for many reasons not least because a daily news service was introduced and news became one of the strengths of the station from that day forward.

Ronnie McCoy remembers that at one time there was a plan to develop ground along the Lagan Embankment for a new custom-built complex and one of the wives was sent undercover to suss out the costs of this beautiful site overlooking the river. It didn't work out. UTV stayed where it was on Ormeau Road opposite the gas works and the ground went to Dunnes Stores for a shopping complex.

Back to Tommy. Once an act was selected it was a matter of recording five three-minute numbers, one for each weekday transmission - 25 guineas for five slots, all done in half a day.

It was during studio rehearsals on Friday 22nd November 1963 that someone ignored the protocol, flung open the control room door shouting 'Kennedy's been assassinated'. This time Mike Kent didn't throw them out.

A man of many parts, director Mike Kent with Adrienne McGuill and Danny the Doormouse.

The President had been shot at 6.30 pm our time, pronounced dead at seven and the official announcement came from the White House to us at 7.33 pm. It was 1.33 pm in Washington, DC.

I was at home, having tea, the television was broken and we were listening to the radio. I have rarely experienced such frustration. Wanting to be at the heart of the news, I jumped into our black Ford Popular and sped to Havelock House.

In Studio Two there had been a moment's silence as the enormity of the situation sank in. Then the work of a news organisation began. Mike stood the crew down, thanked the artists who were rehearsing for the following week's *Teatime* shows and set about getting a programme ready for transmission that evening. The 35th President of the United States was a charismatic world figure and there was no shortage of local material so, on that Friday evening, as events were still unfolding in Dallas and Washington, our programme went live on the air.

Everyone pitched in, unions didn't count, no matter what had to be done the person who was free and able would take it on.

John Scholz Conway was senior director at the time and he'd been responsible for persuading Mike Kent to come to Ulster, first as a floor manager but soon appointed the youngest director on the ITV network. He was only 24 and had already spent four years in the RAF. "John made it sound so positive that I just packed up and came across." Mike was talking to me from his home in La Var Province in France. I remember him as an all-rounder ready to take on anything. Tall, dark and handsome, he was well suited to the television life and relished it.

"I tried to do a little of everything. At one time I read the links between programmes, I modelled, interviewed the Minister of Transport about the new MI, even sang *Fly me to the Moon* with Dusty Springfield on one programme. You wouldn't get away with it today! One minute it was directing a farming programme out in the fields with the film crew, the next in the studio with writer Sheila St. Clair recording *Sean the Leprechaun* and then covering the local reaction of a world event like the assassination of Kennedy. We were a small team in Ulster Television, all working together and never knowing what each day would bring."

*

That was the attraction of the compact little station, it was the centre of the universe for local news and was to remain so throughout the difficult and sad years of The Troubles. Mainly during the 70s into the 80s, television crews from around the world came to land on the doorstep of Havelock House, sweeping in and out as the events unfolded. They were news hounds. They were offered facilities, information, contacts and countless cups of tea. With the speed of their news gathering they sometimes had to leave the scene in indecent haste which made it difficult for local journalists to go back for a follow-up interview. Whereas visiting crews were 'sent' on a story, for the local reporter it was telling a story in which they were intimately involved. Newsreader Kate Smith admitted to me how she would look away from the studio monitor once she had introduced a film clip showing some atrocity. It was the only way she could cope with reading the terrible news and control her emotions throughout a difficult half hour programme.

In 1976, journalists covered the story which became known as the Kingsmill Massacre. On January 5th, in a revenge attack for the killing of six Catholics the previous day, reports spoke of sixteen workmates, five Catholics and eleven Protestants going home towards Bessbrook. Four of the Catholics got out at Whitecross, the others continued their journey. Further along the road, the coach was stopped by a group of men, armed and waiting. It was assumed it was a British Army or RUC checkpoint so, when they were ordered out and lined up against the coach, the men obeyed. At this point the only Catholic was told to step forward. His colleagues tried to stop him identifying himself as they soon realised these men could be loyalists come to kill a Catholic. They wanted to protect him. He was told, however, to get on down the road and not to look back. His friends and the bus driver were shot. Ten men were shot dead. The eleventh, although very badly wounded, survived the attack which in all, took less than a minute.

The boys from the network. John Scholz Conway, Don Keating, Eddie Crook, Mike Kent, Tony Finigan and John Floyd. Front row: Frank Holmes, Colin Lecky Thompson, Alan Smith, Frank Brady and Pat Dowd with ubiquitous. Bushmills prominent.

Paul Clark told me that he thought he had coped with the trauma of covering the story and interviewing the people most closely involved. But, like so many of my colleagues the shock was delayed. Not until the tenth anniversary did it hit home and he wept for the things he had seen and heard. These men and women who report or film or record in any way the atrocities of our country are usually forgotten, and left to live with their vivid memories. I remember reporter Ivan Little, a hardened newsman, sitting by himself in the UTV canteen, his back to the room his face to the wall as he tried to come to terms with the dreadful events he had reported on that day. I hope someday the public will realise how brave and compassionate these people have been and continue to be. In a small place like Northern Ireland, it's important to understand what's going on and never to leave a situation without a goodbye or with bad grace. It's a tribute to local reporters from all branches of the media, camera crews and newsrooms that they handled what they had to do with sensitivity and courage.

*

In those early days of the 60s, a local television crew was always welcome, the teapot was on the table, scones especially baked for the entourage and cream cakes the pièce de résistance. What a crowd! Unions dictated there should be a cameraman, a sound man, lighting man, sometimes make-up, sometimes a producer, but always a director and his production assistant.

Gloria Hunniford worked with director John Scholz Conway as his PA. He was more than a director to us, he was a mentor to many in the studio. After all, he worked cameras on the legendary, live and difficult *Armchair Theatre* Sunday evening drama series.

Johanna Helmut Scholz was born in Vienna and after the war was an interpreter and also a cameraman for the American Army based in Austria. He then wondered what to do when that came to an end. Why not a try the new kid on the block - television He rang ABC, offered his services, got a job and worked on the first programme ever televised.

Associated British Corporation was one of a number of commercial television companies set up by cinema chains in the 1950s. These cinema moguls were worried that television was taking away their audiences so, in an attempt to safeguard their business and with the encouragement of the Independent Television Authority, they became involved in the new medium. It was from this company that many technicians and studio directors came to help set up Ulster Television.

When John came to Belfast and the attraction of a brand new television station, he thought it would be easier to have a more straightforward name. He was pondering this change just as he was passing the road sign to Conway Street and John Conway was born. Not long after this, he reverted to his family name again, apparently at the request of his grandfather who was bequeathing an inheritance. As a result, all the programme paper work and the credit captions had to be amended to accommodate the change and John Scholz Conway became a well-known name on the screens of Ulster.

Tony Finigan came to local television, again from ABC London, as studio director and later took on the position of Head of Programmes. This Englishman was "mad about electricity" and became a scientist at the General Electric Company, and ended up, as he put it, stopping unexploded German bombs going off. We talked in his home in Groomsport in Co. Down, just before he died in November 2008. Looking out over the sea, relaxed in his eighties and comfortable in his red socks, he described how the sergeant would locate the bomb and then he would move in to burn it out or blow it up. After the war GEC produced heating and cooking appliances and were associated with television companies, including Ulster, "a perfect circle." In the middle of this circle, Tony attended Guildhall School and worked for some years in repertory before becoming a theatre director. He appeared in a couple of films and now and again he pops up in old black and white movies shown on a Sunday afternoon television or a specialist channel for these vintage works of art.

Frank Carson checks the script with director John Scholz Conway

Again, as for so many young enthusiastic theatre people, television caught Tony's attention in the mid 50s and he too worked on the ultimate television production of the time, ABC's *Armchair Theatre*, a 50 minute live play plus two commercial breaks of 2 min. 35 sec. each. As floor manager he described the frantic rush getting the studio re-arranged and the actors a glass of water during those breaks.

"The dread was a camera going down and out of action but on one occasion the worst nightmare of all happened - an actor died from a massive heart attack during the live transmission and the rest improvised and filled in the gaps. The show must go on you know."

It was in November 1958 when just over halfway through transmission of *Underground* directed by William Kotcheff, the Welsh actor Gareth Jones began to feel unwell and in the makeup room, between two of his scenes, he collapsed and died.

Tony Finigan taken in Groomsport shortly before he died.

Colin Lecky Thompson, later Head of Presentation in UTV, saw the drama unfold. He was duty transmission controller overseeing the ABC'S station output from Master Control.

"We were sitting at the control desk watching the play when the director called through to us from the studio saying 'someone has died on set'. I asked, 'Shall we run a standby film?' We always had three different standbys, a 20 minute, half hour and 47 minutes. 'We're going to go ahead with the play,' he replied. Between a quick rewrite during a commercial break of 2 minutes and 35 seconds and a lot of ad libbing from the actors, the show carried on and came out on time."

Director Sydney Newman had improvised a way of coping with the missing actor, 'shoot it like a football match' he said and instantly restructured the script as the production assistant, Verity Lambert, took over directing cameras. She had graduated from a secretarial job in Granada's press office to eventually become a legendary producer, awarded an OBE in 2002, with such titles as *Minder* and *Doctor Who* on her credits. She left more than £2.5 million in her will when she died in 2007.

*

In those days the money for writers was in London's West End theatre land rather than in television and as Tony remembers, the pool of good writers dried up and for various reasons *Armchair Theatre* came to an end. He began to look around and spotted an opportunity with the new station about to open in this far off place called Northern Ireland. "I loved it immediately, the enthusiasm, the incredible social life, one studio, three cameras and offices incomplete."

He directed many of the commercials and recalled makeup artist Connie Larmour being selected for her beautiful hands and nails to show off Lunn's jewellery from the elbow down, and me wielding a Ewbank carpet sweeper, in shot from the knees down. One day the local chemist met me on the Ormeau Road with the delighted comment that he'd seen me on television the night before. "Not me." "Oh yes – you, I'd recognise your legs anywhere." Secretary Mary Hunter found fame when she was chosen to provide the Praying Hands to introduce the Epilogue. She also had the distinction of being auditioned by film director and then UTV managing director, William MacQuitty. "He asked some of us to the studio to see how we would come across as continuity announcers and after my piece I was mortified when he announced, 'typical Northern Ireland accent'. I didn't get the job."

We got the princely sum of three guineas for any part of our body - purposely - in shot. Money from America.

The man who started me on my career in the media was Colin Lecky-Thompson, born in Rangoon where his English father was a member of the police force. Colin was always quite exotic to us, his secretary Mary Hunter and to me, a junior member of his team, especially the day he asked Mary to go into Belfast to the only delicatessen in the country to buy popadoms and the makings for an Indian meal. He even looked slightly Burmese and put it to good use one day in the Grand Central Hotel when a group of HODs – otherwise known as Heads of Department – were meeting to discuss programming and especially religious input.

"I learned to tread very carefully on the religious front especially as I was sitting on the Religious Advisory Committee."

The first panel, formed at the outset of the company in 1959, consisted of the Rt. Rev. R. C. H. Elliott, former Dean of Belfast and Bishop of Connor representing the Church of Ireland; the Most Rev. Dr. Cahal Daly, in 1990 appointed Cardinal Archbishop of Armagh; the Very Rev. Dr. Jack Withers, later Moderator of the Presbyterian Church and the Rev. George E. Good, President of the Methodist Church.

Many noted churchmen who served on the religious advisory panel in those early days include the Venerable Archdeacon Eric Barber, Holywood, Co. Down; Rev. David Burke, Rev Horace Uprichard, Rev. E. R. Lindsay, former President of the Methodist Church, the Rev. George Loane and Father Hugh P. Murphy Ahoghill and later St. Mary's Star of the Sea Whitehouse, Co. Antrim.

When he was stationed at St. Mary's, I called with Father Hugh one Sunday. I'd been to morning worship in the Methodist church in Whiteabbey village and on the way home my car mysteriously turned into the grounds and pulled up at his front door. It wasn't planned. It just happened. I rang the bell and he opened the door, no greeting just a smile and a nod and a call to the kitchen behind him, "Mary, the third piece of chicken has arrived." His housekeeper had cooked three chicken breasts for the two of them, there was one extra waiting – as it happened, for me. It turned out to be a divine appointment and we talked about many things and sorted a lot of problems. He died not long afterward. I recall now how, in 1978, we'd received the shock news that Father Hugh had been kidnapped from his home in Ahoghill. The former Royal Navy chaplain was taken in response to the IRA abduction and murder of RUC Constable William Turbitt.

The kidnappers said that they would return the priest in the same condition. Many people were on their knees, some for the first time in years, praying for the release of this compassionate man of the people. Thankfully our prayers were answered.

*

As Head of Presentation in 1960, Colin Lecky Thompson soon discovered that the religious balance in Ulster Television programming schedules was very important and that it was vital to stick to the rotation laid down, based on the numbers representing the various faiths.

"Being new to Northern Ireland I just couldn't follow the intricacies of the local scene and at one of the religious meetings held in the Grand Central Hotel, it all got a bit heavy so, for some reason, I proceeded to sit cross legged on the floor with my arms folded Buddha style! As you can imagine, there was absolute confusion! What was I doing sitting in the middle of the dining room of an important downtown hotel? 'I'm a Buddhist,' I announced although it wasn't true. No one knew what to say but it broke the tension."

The Religious Advisory Panel was all important from the beginning but it was to become even more so as the Troubles took hold.

Those were the days that we had to stick strips of Sellotape from one corner of the window to the other and then up and down as well as across. This was to prevent the glass flying should a bomb go off outside. There were many scares and indeed, in the late 70s, the building was firebombed but thankfully, no one was hurt.

General Election November 1965. Fred Corbett Head of News (right) checks progress with John Cole and studio guests Austin Currie, William Craig and Sam Napier.

In the beginning, there were regular religious programmes and evening epilogues but later in the 60s and 70s something more was required. Lord Robin Eames, Archbishop of Armagh and Primate of All Ireland before his retirement in 2006, gives credit to Brum Henderson for being conscious of the need for spontaneous words of comfort following serious civil upheaval and terrorist atrocities. Brum Henderson and the panel prepared a list of clergy willing to undertake a live homily at short notice. "We would be phoned around 7 o'clock and asked to come to Havelock House for a spot at about 10.30, so it was literally listening to the news and making notes on the back of an envelope. That suited me," he added, "I'm not a person for scripts. It was a matter of speaking to the camera and speaking your mind and I appreciated the trust which was put in us."

Robin Eames was one of the senior churchmen who attended strategy meetings with Henderson as they reflected on the immorality of what was happening in Northern Ireland and planned how best they could serve the people through the medium of television. He had, and still has, a career dedicated to the service of others, a vocation recognised by the Queen when she awarded him the Order of Merit on his retirement. This is her personal appointment and she decided to invite him to join an elite group of 24 people who have been recognised for outstanding contribution and great achievement to the arts, learning, and science and literature.

*

Colin Lecky Thompson was part of this early scene. As luck would have it, I'd phoned him just after New Year 2009 as he was celebrating his birthday, happily retired and living in Crawley, West Sussex. We reminisced. He talked of 'his girls', Mary, me, then Jill McKinley who came to work for him when I became a PA, Claire Kennedy who followed me into studio work and, of course his journey to Ulster Television.

In 1959 he was working in ABC one of the first television stations, located originally in London and relocated to Didsbury Manchester were he was the transmission controller who was responsible for guiding the first transmission through from the technical control area to the home transmitter. It was on such a weekend as he sat calling for announcers to standby, ensuring films were laced into the telecine machines and ready to roll with the feature film and the all important commercials were in the correct sequence, that a tall stranger stepped on to the hallowed ground of Master Control and stood behind Colin watching what was going on.

"During a commercial break I was introduced to him. Brum Henderson. He was very polite and thanked me for allowing him to stand in and watch. He was just leaving when all hell let loose; a machine broke down and I had to think quickly. I asked the actor in the continuity studio to talk for two minutes about the evening programmes as we got organised." Henderson was impressed with the operation and invited Colin to Belfast to meet the top men who offered him the job of Head of Presentation. "It was a big step up for me and took me away from the hands-on of transmission control and into administration, setting up a new system of daily broadcasting, schedules, training programmes, interviewing for a number of jobs." I remind him, with great gratitude, that I was one of that number.

Mr. Lecky-T stayed in the province for over ten years and saw the beginnings of the Troubles from his position as Programme Controller at Downtown Radio before returning to England to take up a job with Border Television in Carlisle.

I'd lost contact for years until, at a conference in London, I met Tom Lecky-Thompson. Could there be a connection? There was and Tom put me in touch with my first boss. When we talked for this book I asked about Tom. Colin relates a fascinating story about his brother, a test pilot who was involved in one of the final and most important test runs of the vertical take-off jet, a concept which was developed at Short Brothers in Belfast.

His journey began at the top of the Post Office tower in London. Down in the lift, a fast taxi to Euston Station where a Harrier jump

Still having fun 50 years later! Shirley Andrews, Anne Shaw and Mary Hunter.

jet was sitting on a piece of land prepared for the exercise. He took off vertically in a cloud of dust and muck, guiding it carefully until he was clear of the buildings and then shot off across the Atlantic, apparently refuelling in mid-air three times on the way to New York. Once there he followed the path of the Hudson River, past Ellis Island, the Statue of Liberty, the Brooklyn Bridge to the area cleared for set down. Once on land, he jumped into a yellow cab which raced him to the Empire State Building where be was taken to the top in a high-speed lift. The test run was hailed as a success.

I'm sure Tom was thinking of that adventure when he heard the remarkable story of Chesley B. Sullenberger the Second who guided his disabled US Airways Airbus 320 to land safely in the Hudson River in February 2009. A mid-air collision with a flock of geese did the damage and his calm control of the situation saved the lives of all 155 passengers.

Colin looked back almost 50 years as we talked.

"We were all there on the opening day of UTV, of course. All the work had been done for that evening although we were planning ahead as well in the hope that there would be a tomorrow. It all went like clockwork and the transmission controllers were very relieved, we were on such a high so I was able to enjoy the party in the boardroom even though I was in tears."

The TC's were like gods, they literally controlled everything that left Havelock House on the airwaves, up to the transmitter on Black Mountain and then radiated into the towns and cities and villages. There was Pat Dowd, Gus Dixon, Nick McCafferty, Glen Clugston a very fine jazz trumpeter and another musician, organist Stanley Wyllie.

There were many tricks played on the local boys. The final sequence before closedown included the Queen sitting side-saddle on her magnificent horse. A drum roll and then the National Anthem. The night came when Stanley called 'Roll Telecine' and up came the Queen as usual but the boys had contrived that, although the public heard the National Anthem as usual, in the control room it was the drum roll of *Robin Hood and his Merry Men*. Panic!

As in all television stations, the hub of the building was Master Control, the nerve centre where the engineers sat surrounded by machinery, microphones, faders, and cigarettes. Those were the days when we ate cigarettes, our own and other peoples. I graduated from Olivier to menthol and finally Balkan Sobrani cocktail, dark tobacco wrapped in a variety of brightly coloured papers, shocking pink, turquoise, black. Adrienne McGuill traded various colours for the lime green variety as they complimented her lovely new lime green dress. We girls thought we were something else, so wealthy, so sophisticated! In retrospect, most of us were far from sophisticated.

In all we numbered about 35 in the pre-transmission days, many were the big boys, the men who had come to Belfast from Manchester and London, from the established television companies - the 'network'. They had worked on live programmes like *Armchair Theatre, Sunday Night at the London Palladium,* and to us impressionable girls, they were glamorous.

We were probably more at home with our own local boys, however, young men who gathered to fill the job vacancies and were as excited as we were.

In 1959, Eric Caves, destined to become Chief Engineer and great source of information for this book, applied for a job as assistant engineer and was taken on a tour of the building by Frank Brady, Supervisory Engineer. "An empty cement shell," Eric remembers. "This is where we'll have telecine' said Frank pointing to a blank wall. 'Here will be Master Control. Over there will be the announcer's box.' We were surrounded by bricklayers, joiners and electricians hammering and sawing." On12th September, Eric got a letter of acceptance and reported for duty.

"I was elated. Craig Fleming, Jack Williamson, Frank Holmes, Jim Bilney, Davie Jones and Norman Laking and I walked into town and celebrated over coffee in Campbell's. We were the bees knees

The originals: the men who put Ulster Television in the picture. Tom Reid lighting department, and cameras Brian Furness, Alan Hailes, Bob Brien, Ernie Barrett and Don Keating. The sixth cameraman, missing from this picture, was Pat Terrins.

on £440 a year."

Campbell's was a famous coffee shop opposite the City Hall where the writers, playwrights and actors met, so the boys were in good company.

A fascinating place. Every Saturday morning the little café overlooking the flower sellers outside the City Hall played host to literary men - Jack Loudan, W.R. Rodgers, Denis Ireland, William Conor and Joe Tomelty. I liked to go there and gaze upon Ralph Bud Bossance, Sam Hanna Bell and Rowel Friers. Campbell's was somewhere happy people wanted to be!

Norman left his mode of transport behind that day, an old hearse with pink gingham curtains! We used to pile into it and go to Carrickfergus where the Sports and Social Club had a GP 14 yacht and we sailed in Belfast Lough before fish and chips on the way home. That was all to come.

For Eric and the others, an intense six weeks followed. "The Pye telecine machines were installed and training began. Faults were purposely introduced to the machinery so the young enthusiastic engineers were themselves tested."

Putting a television station on the air was a big responsibility. Battling with warm weather when atmospherics disturbed the electronic signal and the familiar caption would appear *Normal Service will be Resumed as soon as Possible*. You don't see that now in this digitally sophisticated age. "When we got the recording machine in 1963 we had to get used to that too. Charlie White and Craig Fleming were in charge. One night something happened to the 'heads' on the machine, they weren't lining up and we saw the strange picture of two girls playing harps with strings bent in the middle!"

When we went on air, however, apart from film, everything

transmitted by Ulster Television was live because there was no recording equipment to suit our station. Even some local commercials were live, most 30 seconds but the most fearful of all was the four minute 'ad mag', a horrendously difficult mini magazine programme where the two actors had to memorise a script and the product order as they wandered round the set. It just had to go well as there was no alternative. It usually took the shape of a husband and wife chatting through their day and mentioning everything from food to holidays. Apart from the actors, the studio had to be on its toes getting props in place in between shots and the timing was crucial 'in' on time and 'out' on time, to the split second. For the PA it was a nightmare counting down to the 'out', the floor manager relaying with hand signalled instructions to speed up or slow down. If it ran over time, too bad. The transmission controller was only looking at the clock and he cut away from the studio to the network programme absolutely on time and UTV had to live with the consequences of a lost commercial and the wrath of the advertiser.

*

Many fascinating colleagues arrived on or about the opening day, all with television history and tales to tell. There were some names to get your tongue round and in Havelock House; lecturer and teacher Brian Baird sailed through his audition as announcer as he was the only one of dozens who could get his tongue round the name of ITN newscaster Reginald Bosanquet. Some said Bo-sankee, others Bosan-ket but he scored with the correct 'Bos-ankay'. Bosanquet became a legend who lived hard and worked hard and whose father, cricketer Bernard, was the inventor of the 'googly', a style of bowling that has a habit of sneaking round the bat and scattering the bails. Diction is all important as I discovered on one occasion. An *Ask Anne* programme on disabled access featured me being pushed round Belfast in a wheelchair. The following year I planned to revisit the most inaccessible places and asked the film library to hunt out the original piece on Ask Anne in a wheelchair. Days later they came back to me, "Can't find it anywhere," said the librarian, "searched the place, there's nothing here about an afghan in a wheelchair."

The majority of 'imports' were men, some tall and good-looking, some not so tall but still interesting. The local girls were warned about this influx from the network. "Just be careful," a senior manager said, "these men use coarse language and think

Eric Caves and Frank Holmes at the original Master Control with Adrienne McGuill in the announcers 'box'.

you girls are very gullible."

Some did, but we weren't.

Sports presenter, Ernie Strathdee, was my father's great friend, they had sport and 'a jar' in common. He was my hero. He won nine caps playing rugby for Ireland, a member of the Grand Slam side of 1948 and the Triple Crown in 1949. He captained the team against Australia and against France. Ernie died in a tragic fire in Belfast's Regency Hotel in July 1971, he was only 50 years of age. The managing director, Brum Henderson, paid tribute to him. "He was one of the most able broadcasters ever to emerge in Northern Ireland. We are all the poorer for his loss." That was certainly true. In my early days in television, it was Ernie who kept me right. His sage advice to a young girl faced with sophisticated imports was: "Don't listen to them when they 'f and blind'. If you get really cross," he told me, "just say ee-llaass-ttiicc.

Ernie Strathdee, a favourite especially with followers of Irish rugby!

Gloria Hunniford

7
Girl Power 60s Style

In those days I don't think we knew what sexual harassment was. If you got chased round the filing cabinet it usually ended up in a giggle and was the main conversation over scones and coffee in the canteen.
We blushed with outrage when someone described the colour of his new car as being 'nipple pink'! The most sophisticated chat up line from one English gentleman colleague was, "would you expect me to buy a chair without sitting in it first?" You had to laugh!

What a mixture we were and how interesting to chart the course of the women who crossed the threshold of that Palace of Variety known and loved as Havelock House and how many stayed in the 'business'.

We believed ourselves glamorous. We worked in television and we had the enthusiasm of youth. If the world is peopled by only two types of individual, drains and radiators, then we certainly were full-on radiators. Mostly we were innocent of the ways of life, indeed, when I first applied for the job as studio production assistant, the programme controller gently told me I had "the delightful disadvantage of being too young. There are very worldly men working here," he continued, "who might take advantage of a young lady like you." Well, I was a bit affronted but in retrospect I know what he was getting at although I still think he was wrong. We weren't taken advantage of but some things were a mystery. I simply didn't understand when a network director stopped outside the gentlemen's toilet as we dashed downstairs to the studio, "You go on dear, I'm just going to shake hands with the wife's best friend."

In those days I don't think we knew what sexual harassment was. If you got chased round the filing cabinet it usually ended up in a giggle and was the main conversation over scones and coffee in the canteen. We blushed with outrage when someone described the colour of his new car as being 'nipple pink'! The most sophisticated chat up line from one English gentleman colleague was, "would you expect me to buy a chair without sitting in it first?" You had to laugh! And we certainly did when one of the makeup artists, a beautiful and sophisticated girl, reported that she had been approached in Linenhall Street the night before. This was one of the 'red light' areas. There was no one around. It was misty and dark. The poor woman was minding her own business when suddenly a man stepped out of a shadowy doorway exposing all he possessed. Quick as a flash, she tapped it with her umbrella and said haughtily. "Put that thing away young man, I've seen better on a goat."

If someone got serious about someone else, everyone knew and I think that stopped any unwanted situations arising or bullying tactics taking hold. So naïve were we, we didn't even know how to take a compliment. I was going out on a date with a very nice freelance cameraman and he admired the dress I was wearing. To cover my embarrassment I replied the unforgivable – 'oh, this old thing' – routine. "You girls in Northern Ireland don't know how to take a compliment and that's very hurtful," was all he said and it taught me a lesson. It's ridiculous to think of in this day and age but one day I made a phone call to a programme director and he said, "you've a very sexy voice on the phone." I was somewhat gobsmacked, taken aback, it put a completely different aspect on our friendship after that, for me anyway, and I could hardly look him in the eye for weeks.

Today some of the things that happened would be reported. For instance, when walking up stairs in my flouncy skirt with rows and rows of butterflies in horizontal hands, as usual tight waist and tucked in white blouse, one of the senior technical managers came up behind me, smacked me on the bottom and said, "Nancy girl, you've a quare pair of child bearing hips". He always maintained Anne was short for Nancy. It didn't occur to me to challenge his rudeness. I only felt slightly aggrieved that I had big hips but comforted myself that if ever I had children I'd be quids in. On another occasion we were preparing a cookery demonstration and during a break, someone in the props department got all the potatoes, put them in pairs and draped a sausage suggestively over them. This was for my benefit as I was the production assistant on the programme and bound to be the first one to see the display. Harassment or a bit of male humour? Easier to ignore than make an issue of it and we soon became mature enough to handle these little asides.

As women workers in Northern Ireland we were well paid and the male talent was attractive both inside the building and out, the visiting 'firemen' as they were called, the singers, the show bands, the sportsmen. The big smoke for men in those days was the extra long Peter Stuyvesant cigarette and the commercial reps. who worked for the company were hugely attractive. Like the ITN newsmen, all over six feet and handsome. We seemed to party all the time. Gloria Hunniford's 21st and the glorious white dress

The serious expressions belie the fun behind the cameras.
Alan Hailes, Billy Vennard, Colin McCallum, Tom Reid, Fred Faulkner, Derek Bailey, Maurice Harper and Ian Hill.
Seated: Hugh Greer, John Floyd, John Scholz Conway, Gloria Hunniford, Don Keating and Connie Larmour.

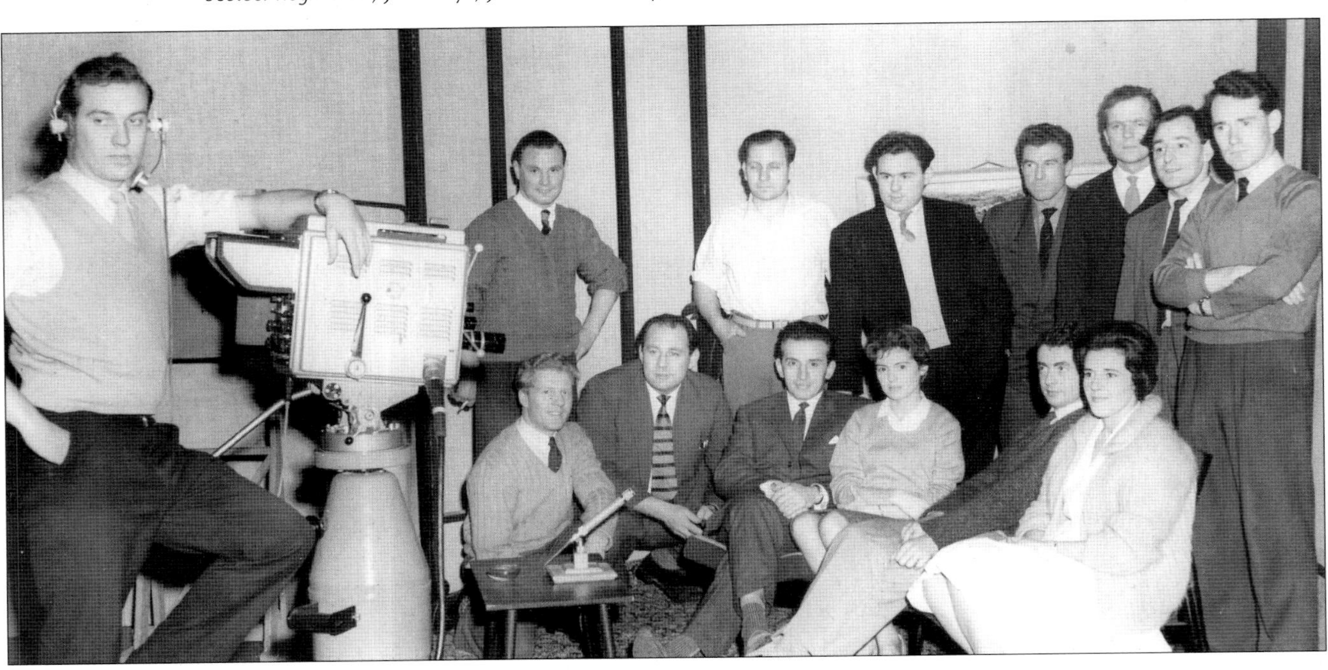

with black spots she wore. My own coming of age in the Pig and Chicken for which I wore scarlet and danced the night away. One of the happiest nights of my life.

Belfast was beginning to buzz after the grey post-war days and the girls and the boys took advantage of it.

John Hewitt, author of two outstanding books recording the history of local RAF pilots, remembers those days. He was just a lad yet he knew every ballroom there was. He rhymes them off, "Orpheus, great sprung floor, Betty Staff in Queens Street, Gala at the Albert Clock, the Plaza, Milanos, singer P. J. Proby in the Boom Boom Room wearing tight white silk pants and an emerald cloak. The girls pulled him off the stage despite the wire cage round him for protection! Then there was the Jazz Club near the Great Northern Railway. We went to the Royal Bar in Ann Street wearing suits which were too tight and I remember the Rolling Stones in the Ritz and in the Flamingo Ballroom in Ballymena." The Flamingo was famous. Ireland's first commercial ballroom opened in December 1959 boasting the popular acts of the time, Joe Dolan, Acker Bilk and Roy Orbison, as well as the mighty Rolling Stones.

John played snooker with Alex 'Hurricane' Higgins in the Jam Pot off Donegall Road when Alex had to carry an old wooden Guinness box to stand on. "I would mitch school and he'd challenge us for a shilling then he'd let you beat him. It would be double or quits and that would go on till about 10/- was in the pot and of course he won. But he was a lovely fella. He used a brush shaft tapered and chalked at the end. Imagine, prize money was £350 for big tournaments in those days and then it went up to half a million and beyond.

"I was fascinated by television and the whole new experience of advertisements. We lived in Silvio Street off the Crumlin Road and we'd no television but the woman two doors down had, the only TV in the street, so we all crowded in. They were great days."

It seemed they were great days for everyone. But for many of the girls in Ulster Television it was a man's world and this presented a dilemma. Obviously there were marriages within those first years but the unfortunate side effect was that one or other had to leave the company. It applied to at least six couples at that time as there was no protection against sex discrimination in employment until 1976 when legislation was put in place against this happening. Too late for us and in those days it was always the girl who left. A pity but we all moved on to other jobs or motherhood or both. After her marriage to cameraman Don Keating, Gloria Hunniford moved to the BBC and begin a new career in broadcasting, her first step on a path which took her to the top. For me, I fell in love with a handsome cameraman who smoked a pipe, wore a big hairy sweater and drove a sports car with his initials on the hubcap. I boasted about him and his custom-made hubcaps. It was some time later that he burst my bubble by telling me that AH didn't stand for Alan Hailes but for Austin Healey. We went on to marry, have Michael and Susie, and remain in the media, he in Ulster Television and me to public relations then journalism.

*

Then one day Gloria phoned me from her production office in Broadcasting House, Ormeau Avenue, Belfast. It was a Tuesday morning and I was sitting on the edge of the bed.

"I'm doing a new BBC radio programme called *Taste of Hunni.* Will you go to six supermarkets and take six or eight items and compare the prices, we're calling it the consumer spot. Need it 10 o'clock Thursday morning. OK?" No bother I'd certainly do that. "Will I leave it at reception?" "No - bring it to the studio." It dawned on me. "You mean you want me to speak this." "Yes." "Oh Gloria, do you think I can do this all right?" "If I didn't think you could do it I wouldn't be asking you, so get your butt up here on Thursday morning."

Her faith in me, and her direct approach, changed my life.

We'd been friends for years, since she came through the doors of Ulster Television in 1960. In those days, not only did a representative of the GPO come in on a regular basis to wash and disinfect all the telephones but new members of staff were brought round and introduced to everyone. She was special, a singer who'd just come home to Portadown from Canada, an international traveller! Gloria had her first taste of radio and television in Kingston, Ontario and it came about in an unusual way.

She was working at the tourist attraction Old Fort Henry when a colleague in the accounts department mentioned that she sang every day on a local programme called *Lunch Box.* Quite literally this girl would leave work during her lunch hour, dash down to the television station, sing her songs and be back before the hour was out. "One day I asked her if I could go along and within minutes they were asking if I could sing any Irish songs. Well, of course I

Peter Tomelty with the Tommy James Trio, Tommy, Tony Martin and George Newman.

could. If you could sing *When Irish Eyes* or *40 Shades of Green* you were on and soon I had a spot of my own during my lunch break and eventually my own 25 minute radio programme, I think it was called *Gloria's Requests.* For an eager beaver like me it was terrific. I was still a teenager so it was a great chance to learn about radio – and learn every Irish song in the book."

We nearly lost Gloria to Canada. It was very close.

"I came home for Christmas in 1959 to see my parents and let them know I was fine and pacify my father with the promise that I would stay, fully intending to go back to Canada. I'd fallen in love with the most handsome man I'd ever seen in my life and was one step away from being engaged! But I'm a firm believer in fate and when my clever father cut out the ad for a production assistant in this new television station, I applied and decided if I got the job I was meant to stay. If not, I was on the first boat back to Canada."

She didn't get the job but they knew talent when they saw it and offered her a position in the all important sales office with the two Basils, Lapworth and Singleton. "I loved it, especially the

Peter Tomelty, Teresa Duffy and comedian Tom Raymond on the Fiddle and Flute set.

social side so I offered my services to serve drinks in the boardroom to all the visiting stars and personalities. It paid off when the next PA job became available and I was offered it." She believes that those early days behind the scenes stood her in good stead. "They taught me more about television than anything else could, timing live programmes, working throughout the day, moving from one show to another, magazine, musical, news and sport - all live. Learning to read a clock and the stopwatch and getting everything to come together at the right time was one of the hardest things, although the paperwork was a headache too. Everything had to be 100% accurate, budgets, music returns, film request forms all had to be filled in by the PA. Imagine the budget for the musical show *Fiddle and Flute* was £100, that paid the artists and the musicians and all the props required." It was a hectic life but a stimulating one. "Although everything was slightly difficult at the beginning this made it even more challenging and exciting."

Gertie Wine and her husband, the much loved tenor Peter Tomelty, starred in *With a Fiddle and a Flute,* shortened by us to *A Fiddle and a Fart!* Talking to her from the Tomelty family home town of Portaferry, she remembers meeting Peter in the studio, falling in love, the fun and the fee, the princely sum of £5 for each show.

"It must have been 1962 and we were booked for a 13 week run, Teresa Duffy, the Gallowglass Ceili band, known as Ireland's greatest ceili band ever with Peggy Keogh on fiddle, Peter, Frank Carson, a whole lot of us, we were all there. There was a real party atmosphere with dancers enjoying the sets and the reels, the jigs and the polkas." There was also a man called Frank McIlroy. "I don't know who he was, no one did. He just sat in a rocking chair but he never opened his mouth once. The show ran for seven or eight weeks, breaking the ratings, even beating *Coronation Street* with viewing figures but Frank still didn't speak! Then there was a big strike and that was the end of it." Frank Carson recalls, however, that Mr. McIlroy did once take them by surprise and at the end of the show, stood up and sang *How are Things in Glockamora?*

Gertie was only two and a half years of age when she first appeared on stage. Her Shirley Temple act took Dublin's Gaiety Theatre by storm. "But I was afraid of the mic so one day I threw it down and so developed my voice and learned to project. We moved to Cork when I was 12 and the Opera House became my stage, first in *Red Riding Hood,* then I graduated to fairy queen and reached the heights of pantomime when I became principal boy!"

Her mother Nancy Cavanagh and her auntie Eileen ran dance schools in Cork, Eileen for the younger children and Nancy for the older girls, *The Shandon Bells*. "So I got all the support from the family. I was touring when I was 15 with Ruby Murray and Billy Livingstone." In her early 20s she was top of the bill in clubs through the country, appearing on television and booked for *Teatime with Tommy*.

"I remember Peter brought in the music for *Lovely Derry on the Banks of the Foyle* and Tommy saying, surely it's Londonderry." Shades of BBC correctness of the time. "Peter just said do you want me to sing Londonderry. He sang *Lovely Derry*! Tommy was great, everyone loved him." She laughed, "You know, we called him knuckle dusters."

Gertie is still on the go. She was 75 in August 2009 and planning the Portaferry Panto. She teaches tap and choreographs and loves her memories. Like so many people she misses Peter Tomelty who died 2007.

"I still can't play his CDs even yet. It's too soon. But I have those days to look back on, it was great fun in the studio, Peter and Frank and the rest, Gloria Hunniford was working on the programme and Mike Kent was the director, I remember him!"

The pot of memories is stirred. "There was one programme I'll never forget. I was singing *Paddy McGinty's Goat*. I was half way through when something began poking me in the back, I turned round and it was a live goat! No one had told me, I nearly had a heart attack!" And she wasn't even wearing a bolster underneath her petticoat as did the young girls in the song. That was the fun and the challenge and the jokes in those days packed full of

Brigid Macgregor with director Mike Kent.

Pat McBride

energy.

The excitement and the challenge continued for Gloria. From behind the scenes at UTV to a microphone at Radio Ulster and from radio back to Ulster Television presenting the teatime magazine and news programme *Good Evening Ulster* and then the leap across the Irish Sea to become the first woman to have a daily radio show on BBC Radio 2. Soon she was back on television but this time it was on network hosting many important programmes - *Open House, Heaven & Earth, Sunday Sunday, Cash in the Attic* and *Castle in the Country* with John Craven, all different and all hits. And this is only a handful of her successes. She's a much sought after guest on television programmes and her down to earth opinions and advice had helped many people, as have her two books written in memory of her daughter Caron, *Next to You* and *Always With You.*

Anne Gregg was the first woman from Northern Ireland to broadcast to audiences throughout the United Kingdom and Ireland, then Gloria and in 2009, 29 year old Christine Bleakley from Co. Down followed in their footsteps presenting BBC's *The One Show* with Adrian Chiles and blossoming into other areas of programming. These women, like others from Northern Ireland who have gone into news and current affairs, have one thing in common. They have the ability to engage with their audience, no airs and graces, hard workers who realise they are a small cog in a very big wheel as broadcaster Audrey Russell put it to me so many years ago. And they have generosity of spirit, they have time for charities and never forget their roots.

I think one of the loveliest things about the early days of Ulster Television and the people who were part of that adventure, is the fact we have all remained close friends with fond memories and a special bond.

Many have died over the years and we seem to meet at funerals more often these days than at parties but the hard core is still around and when we get together the craic is mighty. And we talk of old times.

The first production assistant was Brigid Macgregor, and when I was appointed production assistant a couple of years after the opening, my fellow PAs were Gloria Hunniford, Jean Clarke and Pat Windsor. Jean Clarke was an example to all the girls, beautiful, efficient and kind, we looked up to her, the only one of us married at the time, and we tried to emulate her poise and manner. She was working in a senior management position when she was diagnosed with Alzheimer's and within a comparatively short time died as a result of the disease. Often when we meet, Jean's name comes into the conversation as we look back to the time she gently took us all under her wing. Indeed, it was she who took control of my life when I was first put in front of a camera in October 1982.

Lifestyle, - my co-host was Gerry Kelly - was a new idea, a social action programme, a weekly half hour which was to find its feet and develop into an important area of broadcasting. I'd been

Jean Clarke

approached to present and this was the vehicle. At the time I was working in the theatre, had a programme on Radio Ulster and another with the World Service. After much thought and discussion within the family, I accepted. For me it was training on the job and it wasn't easy. There was tension in the production office. The only one who knew of my unhappiness was Jean. Life, I told her, was too short. I was content to leave and go back to working as publicity officer with the Ulster Actors Company at the Arts Theatre and the several other clients in my portfolio, perhaps the BBC again. She swung into action, insisted I talk to assistant programme controller Derek Murray, pushed me through his door with the advice, 'think like a man', and waited outside until we'd done. At the heels of the hunt, Derek surprised me that afternoon by saying he knew what was happening and wanted me to move on, offering me my own ten minute programme saying, "If you're half the girl I think you are you'll make something of it." A challenge I accepted with relish.

Advice with Anne Hailes grew to *Ask Anne*, a half hour programme every Monday evening, then the medical series *Anne Hailes' Casenotes.* When the company took the mean decision to drop credits from programmes I was quids in – for some reason the titles management gave the programmes I was producing and presenting all included my name!

The fourth PA was Patricia Windsor from Carrickfergus and what a life she has had since those days.

Pat joined Ulster Television around 1962, but soon married local man Maurice McBride and left to live in India when Mackie's Engineering posted him to Calcutta. We loved getting her letters, always written in green ink, telling us of the heartbreak of street children and women trying to bring up their families in poverty. There was also the high life of embassies and functions which didn't sit comfortably with Pat who has always championed those without a voice. After six years Maurice was transferred to the company's plant in Lille, France where she still lives.

When they took up residence in Lille, the couple realised that English-speaking people needed a centre to meet and make contact. Many of them were from Ireland, many working in textiles, linen and engineering. They found a former Anglican Church in the city and there they opened the British Community Association which, despite the name, attracts men and women from countries around the world. All have one thing in common, their first language is English.

The church too began to thrive and in recognition of her work with her husband, Patricia became British Consul and the bishop's lay assistant. She plays host to thousands who come every year to visit the war graves. Through her work with the veterans she became involved with the *Westhoeck*, Belguim's soldiers, seamen, airmen and members of the resistance and also with the Belgium Prisoner of War Association, the national federation of Belgium war volunteers, who incidentally trained in Carrickfergus during the Second World War.

As a thank you for her work with these ex-servicemen she received a prestigious honour in 2004.

It has pleased His Majesty Albert 11, King of the Belgians
in recognition of outstanding services to the country,
to award the insignia of Knight of the
Order of Leopold 11 to our Member
of the British nationality,
Dame Patricia McBride-Windsor MBE.'

Her award was presented in Brussels in the presence of Queen Paola of the Belgians and the Belgium veterans sang their 'regimental' song – *When Irish Eyes are Smiling.* Such was the emotion and their love of this modest woman from Carrick that the tears of remembrance caught up with them and they couldn't finish. So guests, including the Queen, joined in. Widowed in 2000 and now remarried, her husband Peter Hawkins has the same deep commitment to her work especially with the Commonwealth War Graves in Ypres.

The production assistants still keep in touch. Brigid Macgregor, as the first PA has a special place in the history of the company. Jenny Bennington who left us to go abroad to Africa when she married. Her late sister Fiona also worked in Ulster Television. Maire Browne had grown up in Ceylon - now Sri-Lanka - and Calcutta, when her father worked on tea plantations as a member of Sirocco Engineering staff. She brought so many stories with her and Zandra Smyth, the most glamorous of us all. And so many more over the years, all special and talented with interesting life stories to tell and some, like me, who had to move on because they fell in love and married 'within the company'.

John Cooke, the man who kept audiences laughing throughout the 60s and into the Troubles of the 70s and beyond.

8
The Lighter Side of Life

"Paisley is invited to a mixed marriage and sits beside the local priest."
He's off. "At the reception a guy comes round with a glass of wine.
The priest accepts but Paisley says 'take that awful stuff away.'
Alcohol has never passed my lips and never will, I'd rather commit adultery.'

'Oh,' says the priest to the waiter, 'Would you take mine back,
I didn't know there was a choice.'"

So many people have their own memories when it comes to 31st October 1959. In Belfast Eric Montgomery stopped work early to return to his sister's house. He and Ruby sat down to a cup of tea in Omeath Street off the Cregagh Road and waited. They'd some insider information! Her husband had been working in Havelock House as a heating contractor and he'd tipped them the wink that the phone on the announcers desk wasn't connected up – it was a prop. Eric was 25, working in the building trade as a brickie and was doing up his sister's house in the evenings. But that evening not a paint pot nor a brush was touched. It was Richard Greene and Robin Hood. Eric joined the Salvation Army when he was 56 and became a soldier but he has never forgotten the excitement of the drum roll that heralded Robin and his bunch of Merry Men.

Friday night was bath and hair night for Marion Gibson. Then the family would sit round their new television which received two channels, an improvement on her granny's set which could only receive BBC. She remembers at the age of seven, two favourite programmes, *Romper Room* which she loved and *Dr. Kildare,* her first childhood crush. It was interesting to read that this handsome man, actor Richard Chamberlain, who starred in high octane romances with Holywood's most beautiful women, decided to 'come out' at the age of 69 speaking movingly in his biography *Shattered Love* of hiding his homosexuality to retain his matinée idol image.

Theatre designer Houston Marshall remembers the beginning, the excitement of knowing his family owned a television set that showed *Robin Hood.* "Even though I was very young, I had a great feeling that something was happening, I always associate television with teatime and sitting watching as a family. My aunt and uncle usually came from Holywood to Dundonald to watch with us. It was an old Ferguson television set and on the opening day, everything stopped in our family for this new station. I remember cows being herded down the Castlereagh Road to the markets in those days but even they seemed to take the day off. My only sadness is that Miss Adrienne never saw me in her magic mirror."

As a teenager, Roy Heayberd, became fascinated with the set designs and he credits Roy Gaston for instilling in him a love of design, graphics and ultimately directing in both theatre and television.

One local man became even more involved, quite literally as he ended up appearing on *Teatime with Tommy* and became a regular on television thereafter.

Candy Divine.

In 1960 John Cooke was working in Short Brothers assembling aircraft, the *Belfast* and the *Britannia*. He was there when the SC1, the first vertical take-off plane in the world, was being developed under a cloak of secrecy.

It all began when his mates in the engineering section in Shorts entered him for a talent competition. He sang *San Francisco* and won. From there he developed his compering, threw in a song and few jokes and when Mary Wallace, Belfast's Vera Lynn, asked him to join her in cabaret with The Big Band he jumped at it.

We were talking in Deane's Deli in Bedford Street in Belfast city centre. John is a handsome man immaculately dressed in a dark suit, more the successful businessman rather than the typical comic. Until that is, he tells his story.

"In the sixties Belfast was a swinging place, plenty of work although I think the fact I had a car was a help. We toured clubs and church halls and it was a great grounding for me. Those were the days before the Troubles when Belfast was alive with entertainment. The Abercorn in Corn Market, Piccadilly Line in York Street, Intercontinental in Royal Avenue, Club Orchid Castle Street, Tito's where Candy Devine was the first compere."

When she arrived in Belfast, this beautiful Australian diva was immediately a star. There followed theatre work North and South, her own television series on RTE and appearances on Ulster Television's *White Line* with pianist Billy White. I asked her for her abiding memory and she doesn't need to think twice. It's not appearing in *Skippy the Bush Kangaroo,* it's not even her ground breaking programmes on Downtown Radio but her appearance at Sydney Opera House when, in amongst the sophistication of her style of big band singing, accompanied only on piano, she sang *Danny Boy*.

"Candy was a great favourite, so was Roy Walker in the Talk of the Town. Then there was the Trocadero in Cromac Street facing the Gasworks and Mac's Cabaret at the top of the Newtownards Road, the last bar going out of town. We'd be up and down the Shankill and the Falls seven nights a week. Many a time you'd meet yourself coming back." The memories begin and you realise just how vibrant Belfast was in the 60s, plenty of work for entertainers and plenty of entertainment for the public. "I remember seeing Ella Fitzgerald and Oscar Peterson in the Ritz in Belfast, there was an aura around her, talk about charisma. She said, 'I believe your transport finishes at eleven so I'll be sure to get through by then.' The place went mad with people shouting 'No.' 'No.' We were happy to walk home." Margaret McKee who worked as a floor manager in the BBC was there too. "She really had such presence. She looked wonderful and what a voice." Margaret eventually headed World Service programming in Broadcasting House in Belfast and taught me a lot about broadcasting on radio and television. And it was television that changed life for John Cooke.

"It was very exciting but frightening too, everything was very precise, had to stick to time, very different to doing a gig in the halls which was great fun and it was anything goes. I remember Gloria Hunniford singing on the circuit always looking immaculate in evening wear and long white gloves. Then we would meet up again in Ulster Television when she was timing the programmes and handing out the contracts. It was great and some laugh! Tommy was known as an accelerating pianist which was his downfall the day he did a long roll up the piano and fell off his stool. They just cut away to something else and he got up and got on with it." It was after that appearance that Cookie realised the power of television.

"I was in Boots the next day and the manager came up to me and thanked me for shopping in his store and gave me a basket and accompanied me round as I shopped. Either fame came very quickly or he thought I was a suspicious character." When colour arrived 10 years later it was another red letter day for Ulster Television viewers. "We were so excited. I took a night off to be at home and mother put on her new dress. We had dinner early and sat down to watch the programmes and imagine my mother's disappointment when they were still in black and white. She just thought I was wonderful when I went over and very slowly turned up the colour knob and the picture jumped into glorious Technicolor."

It was on the halls that John perfected his comedy routine, filling in between songs and entertaining his audience, something he did years later when he warmed up the audience for Ulster Television chat shows.

He loves colloquialisms and builds them into his routines. "For instance, the wee woman who said about her friend, 'She put her head through our front door when I was sitting in the middle of my dinner.' We know what it means but would any one else? When I was in Canada I planned to go sightseeing with the next-door neighbours. We'd had a late night and the lady said she'd find it hard to get out of bed so early the next morning so I told her not to worry, I'd knock her up! I'd a lot of explaining to do to her husband. But, if you listen, you hear wonderful things every day. Paisley is invited to a mixed marriage and sits beside the local priest." He's off. "At the reception a guy comes round with a glass of wine. The priest accepts but Paisley says 'take that awful stuff away. Alcohol has never passed my lips and never will. I'd rather commit adultery.' 'Oh,' says the priest to the waiter, 'Would you take mine back, I didn't know there was a choice.'

"You see, we're not afraid to laugh. Even at ourselves, like the old man at the post office who offered to take his friend's pension because 'she just lives up my back'. It started the day I got a taxi to the Europa and the driver explained that while they were renovating the building the front door was at the side."

Throughout the Troubles his humour cheered people on all sides. In the 60s he was asked to play a club in Catholic Ardoyne no later than 11.15pm because the bus taking the pensioners back to the Protestant Shankill left at midnight. That pleased him, although around the same time he was prevented getting to a club in east Belfast because of burning tyres across the road.

"I was trapped, couldn't get backwards or forwards. Then a guy with a hood arrived at my window, 'Hello Cookie, hang on a minute'. He kicked the tyres away and waved me on." That pleased him too, until the night soon afterwards when a well dressed businessman approached him in the Europa Hotel and said, 'you owe me a drink for getting you through that barricade.'

I feel it's time I contribute.

"Did you hear about the American visitor who asked his taxi driver why they built Aldergrove airport so far away from the city? The driver's reply displayed superb logic, 'Because that's where the planes land'".

John: "Did you hear about the two women waiting to cross the road at the City Hall when a cat comes from nowhere and dashes in front of a car. One woman says to the other, 'If that cat had been our dog it would have been a dead duck'. And what about during the war the old couple in bed when the air raid siren sounded. As grandfather jumped out of bed his braces caught on his heel and then hit him on the head. 'Run you on', he says to his wife, 'I've got a direct hit.' Half-way down the stairs she turns back in panic, 'I've forgotten my teeth'. 'Hitler's dropping bombs', shouts the old man, 'not ham sandwiches'".

Me: "Which members of an orchestra can't you trust? The fiddlers."

Him: "What do you get from nervous cows? Milk shakes".

Me: "OK. Doctor, doctor, I have a bucket stuck on my head. I thought you looked a little pale - Boom Boom." By now we were almost under the table laughing. "How do you start a pudding race?" I don't know. "Sago." "What has a bottom at the top?" Thinks. "A leg of course."

All good clean humour and that's what has kept Cookie a firm favourite for all these years. Not always easy. Often very difficult, but a great kindness and genuine talent has kept him going. Hang on, he's off again.

"The Americans, the English and the Irish are sending a man into space. The Americans send their man to the moon. The English send theirs to Mars and when the Irishman was asked where his spaceman was going, he announced the sun. 'Sure he'll get burned up in no time'. 'I've thought of that,' says the Irishman, 'we'll be sending our man up at night'.

I've a good one to throw back.

"Did you hear about Mick from Dublin who appeared on *Who Wants To be a Millionaire*? He'd already won £500,000 and Chris Tarrant was encouraging him towards the million. 'You've only one lifeline left,' he told the excited contestant, 'phone a friend. This is the question for a million pounds, are you up for it?' 'Yes Chris, I'll surely have a go.' Tension mounts. 'Which of the following birds does NOT build its own nest. A. a sparrow. B. a thrush. C. a magpie or D. a cuckoo.' 'I haven't got a clue Chris, can I phone Paddy back in Dublin?' 'A sure Mick that's simple,' says his friend, 'sure it's only a cuckoo.' 'Are you positive?' 'Sure I'm positive Mick, it's a cuckoo for definite.'

Mick gives the answer, his final answer. Cuckoo. There is uproar, it's the correct answer. 'Mick,' says Tarrant, 'you've just won one million pounds.'

Next day Mick invites Paddy to their local pub to celebrate. 'Tell me Paddy. How in Heaven's name did you know it was a cuckoo that doesn't build its own nest?' Paddy looks at his friend in surprise. 'Sure everyone knows that. A cuckoo lives in a clock.'

It's fun having coffee with John Cooke.

"You know," he's thoughtful for a moment, quite serious, "If

And what about a chocolate Titanic! 2006. A chocolate emporium in Berlin. Rausch Plantagen Schokolade displays a 5' long chocolate model of the Titanic. Apparently the hydraulics used in the launch were made in Germany.

the Lord God came down and said, 'John, do you want to change any part of your life?' I'd have no hesitation in saying no, keep it the same. The bad parts only make the good parts better."

This is a book of memories based on a firm foundation although, like all good stories, some events may have become exaggerated in the telling, some of the people more colourful than they really were but, in truth, as John Cooke can vouch, it all happened in those formative years and it was fun.

Life in Belfast was bustling especially in the Markets. One of a series of photo essays for Ulster Television by Kenneth McNally.

Roma Tomelty

9
Naughtiness and the Big Freeze

As an actress Roma didn't make a lot of money with the Young Irish but filling in on holiday relief for announcer Brian Durkin opened her eyes to riches of television. She earned £25 which was more than she would make in a week.
Almost as tempting was another invitation that summer. "A well spoken man rang late one night when I was on a break and said a group would like to meet me and, if I would agree to jump out of a cake – naked - there was £25 in it for me.

Roma Tomelty was the youngest announcer in the country when she filled in as summer relief in 1962 at the age of 17. Although tempted to stay in the industry, she preferred to fulfil her ambitions to be an actor, writer, and director following in the footsteps of her famous father Joe and her sister Frances. Laterally she has been a role model to young people through Centre Stage Theatre Company, a company which tours throughout Ireland often liaising with education departments to work with school children, conducting summer drama courses and promoting new writers. Through Centre Stage, Roma and her husband Colin Carnegie have given hundreds of teenagers confidence, the ability to work together and accept the challenge of getting the job done to the best of their ability. The experience of Centre Stage has also given a grounding in theatre to those who decide to take that rocky road and make the stage their chosen career. She has no regrets that she made her decision to follow her instincts and put her efforts into live theatre.

When she was a teenager, as a member of the Young Irish Theatre Company, Roma had been appearing in *All Souls Night* in the Eblana in Dublin alongside Stephen Rea when her drama teacher, May McHenry, told her Ulster Television was advertising for front of camera staff. 'You should go for an audition at least,' she suggested to her less than enthusiastic pupil.

"I agreed although I'd actually been in the studios before to be interviewed by Ivor Mills about the J.M.Synge play *The Tinkers Wedding* which our company claimed was a premiere performance for Northern Ireland. 'But surely Queen's University performed this play in 1950?' He was very condescending and obviously trying to catch me out but I was able to correct him. 'I think you will find they did it illegally.' I was only 16 and very haughty. 'The rights were not available at that time and Mary O'Malley assured me there had been a problem with copyright so indeed ours is the first PUBLIC performance.' Our verbal tussle was a good learning curve and prepared me to be ready for anything. Jimmy Greene was very helpful and Diana Bamber was wonderfully kind and reassuring and we remained friends until she died. There was a bond between us and often on an opening night somewhere, a bunch of flowers would arrive with a good luck note and a reminder of her phone number."

As an actress Roma didn't make a lot of money with the Young Irish but filling in on holiday relief for announcer Brian Durkin opened her eyes to the riches of television. She earned £25 which was more than she would make in a week. Almost as tempting was another invitation that summer. "A well spoken man rang late one night when I was on a break and said a group would like to meet me and, if I would agree to jump out of a cake – naked - there was £25 in it for me. I turned it down."

She took to the theatre of television. "Once I got the hang of it I loved it and I began to relax and enjoy talking to the viewers. I liked to say good night and then the national anthem would play with the Queen on her horse taking the salute at Horse Guards and I'd wait a few moments and then bring the mike up again and say in a sexy voice, 'don't forget to turn off your set.' I took a chance one night and scolded the viewers in my schoolteacher voice, 'Are you still listening to me?' I barked down the mike, ' Well you shouldn't be, you should have switched off by now and gone to your bed.'"

Years later, Roma Tomelty's daughters continued the acting tradition. One bitter cold night in 1995, President Bill Clinton arrived at the Belfast city hall to turn on the Christmas tree lights. What wild excitement. The town went mad. As it happened, I was visiting Roma and Colin that evening and as we sat round the fire chatting, 13 year old Rachel came in and announced 'I'm going to see President Clinton. Back later.' Her mother poured cold water on the thought. 'There are thousands there, you'll never get even close.' 'We'll see.' Came the mysterious reply.

A couple of hours later, as I was preparing to go home, she arrived back. "Shake the hand that shook the hand of President Bill Clinton." How come? She'd gone to the props wardrobe in her home, taken out a false leg plaster of Paris and two crutches and once at the city hall, put on the plaster cast, a pained expression and limped towards the Christmas tree. The police cleared a way for her and she bravely made her painful way right up to the President of the United States of America and shook his hand.

Enjoying the sweet things in life,
Adrienne McGuill and Diana Bamber.

*

Roma mentioned Diana Bamber. Diana, one of the first continuity announcers at Ulster Television, died in March 2007. She had a spark about her that appealed to her colleagues and the viewers alike, feisty and full of fun. Adrienne McGuill remembered the young girl from Ballymena arriving at the studios fresh from Guildhall School of Music and Drama in London and a career as a model.

"My lasting impression was our trip to ITN in London to learn about news broadcasting with Ivor Mills, Ernie Strathdee and Jimmy Greene, all young and enthusiastic. We went off to a nightclub in Soho, then to Covent Garden where Diana decided we needed flowers for our hotel room. We fancied we were straight out of *My Fair Lady."* Of she went on her mission into the heart of Covent Garden. Eventually Adrienne went looking for her. "I found her standing on a table in the middle of the flower market with the traders dancing all round, three in the morning and there she was looking gorgeous in a red dress, singing and twisting to a most appreciative audience."

Diana was earthy, beautiful and vivacious, and although always nervous, she blossomed on television screens and had a legion of loyal admirers.

Whenever a 'star' visited Studio One, the observation room 'Obs One' was crowded and if by any remote chance the drinks cupboard had been left unlocked, there was a real party. The small narrow viewing gallery above the studio was also a private

As time went by, more 'faces' joined the family. Diana Bamber, Tommy James, Adrienne McGuill, Brian Durkin, Denise Brady and Ernie Strathdee. Jimmy Greene was in the studio when this picture was taken.

romantic spot for clandestine meetings, as was Tommy James' office when he was off being Mr. Music!

We were such a comparatively small but growing company, everyone knew what was going on. I don't believe there was any serious jealousy between departments. We celebrated when sales figures were good as they inevitably were in those halcyon days, when props dressed a beautifully designed set it was applauded

Adrienne meets her match, Sonny Liston, professional boxer who became world heavyweight champion in 1962 by knocking out Floyd Patterson in the first round.

and even though a star was destined for the studio, they always passed through the canteen so everyone had a chance to say hello and get an autograph. Cliff Richard's book *Which One's Cliff* inscribed – To Anne, luv! Cliff Richard – is just one memento I prize.

When it came to Christmas there was so much to look forward to, the exciting company dinner in Thompson's Arthur Street Restaurant, outings to shows, partying around our houses and flats. The delight of carol singing in south Belfast and the surprise on faces when people opened their front doors to be confronted by Ivor Mills or Adrienne McGuill requesting a donation for charity.

The canteen was the meeting place, mid-morning, lunchtime and for afternoon tea and it was where we got to know each other. Soon after I joined the company, my 'boss' in the presentation office, Mary Hunter, was not only my friend but also my minder.

When one of the engineers intrigued me with his talk of black magic and invited me to a séance in his flat, Mary didn't share my excitement and just put her foot down and said "You are not going." That was enough for this innocent abroad; I declined the invitation. She saved my bacon many a time.

Mary and I enjoyed the less sophisticated things in life and one day in December 1962 we decided we'd go into Belfast and do some shopping with a mad idea of heading to Robb's department store in Castle Place and queuing to see Father Christmas. At about midday, on the 26th, it started to snow, gently at first but by lunchtime it was a full scale blizzard. It was the beginning of the

Birthday Dinner. Fred Corbett, Sean Macgaffin, Adrienne McGuill and Colin Lecky Thompson

Big Freeze.

January 1963 was the coldest month of the century. In February over four feet of snow blanketed the province following what was described as a phenomenal snow storm over the two days of the 6th and 7th. St Valentine's Day saw a slight thaw and then it started snowing again. Although the record breaking Big Freeze officially ended at the end of March, snow lay in some places until April 22.

We could hardly believe it as the snow continued to fall for weeks and life was severely disrupted. Plenty of good stories and dramatic film but for families, especially in the country, it was a time of distress. The town of Castlewellan in Co. Down was completely cut off and helicopters had to deliver food, a major event in those days. Lough Erne was frozen over and one foolhardy driver took his Mini across the ice and this was captured on film. Early in January children were filmed playing on the frozen Bog Meadows in Belfast. Surprised swans and gulls were recorded landing on a solid River Lagan. One of our number, writer Sheila St. Clair took out her skis and skied down the Malone Road in Belfast and was surprised at the amount of attention she received.

On the Glenshane Pass the snow was so deep sheep were frozen to death and their bodies lay along the side of the road and, for the first time since 1947, ice on the Mill Lake in Enniskillen was thick enough for people to go skating. Nor did we escape the chill in Havelock House. It was impossible to get out of the building at one time, the canteen ran out of food and children and their parents who'd been in the studio for *Romper Room,* were stranded. Office and boardroom curtains were taken down to wrap the children and keep them warm. No one got away until late the next day.

One of the cars used for filming, was parked outside the building. Cameraman Sean Macgaffin knew exactly where it was so he began to dig it out, all round the wheels starting at the front and working towards the back. The green paintwork confirmed it was his car. Except it wasn't! After hours of labour he uncovered a green Ford and not the Morris Oxford he thought it was. I'm sure the Ford driver was delighted.

Adrienne remembers getting up the Antrim Road in her car and turning into Old Cavehill Road only to be blocked by a motor across one of the smaller avenues. The woman driver came running over for help calling out, "I'm pregnant and my husband has a wooden leg."

It's said that the managing director picked up a new car at that time and travelling from Aldergrove to Belfast in a snowstorm, he pushed the wrong button and the sliding roof opened and wouldn't close!

The UTV photographer's pictures of the snow scenes were made up into a three minute 'filler' with music and clever studio camera work, using a zoom lens and slow movements over the picture. Ken McNally's sequence, for which he received 2 guineas, was shown 22 times over the Christmas holidays. So popular was this interlude, that Ken was given his own mini-programmes of black and white essays set to music. They were cameos of life captured on a still camera and they were a gentle pleasure to the eye and ear. Ken's career with Ulster Television began when he submitted a poem which was accepted and read by Brian Durkin as part of the Epilogue. "I was rich, paid three guineas and I thought I'd never have to work for weeks." In fact he's never stopped working and his books are a visual record of our local history.

My abiding memory of the Big Freeze was of walking to work and home again when transport was impossible. My poor father battling through the snow when able to get me to Ormeau Road and himself into his office in town. Standing at a bus stop in the hope of a trolley bus arriving and a snow flake landing on the black overcoat of the man beside me. It sat on his arm, so big it was possible to see the structure of the delicate flake which was beautiful but, with its colleagues, had brought Northern Ireland to a virtual standstill.

Needless to say, Mary and I never got to see Father Christmas!*

Mary Hunter was my mentor. Coming straight into such a place of business was a great thrill for a girl of 17 and I needed an older sister. At the ripe old age of 20 Mary was worldly wise and experienced and filled the role. She joined the staff in May 1959 when UTV was working out of a small office in Donegall Street, Belfast. Upstairs were offices, downstairs the *TV Post* empire, the *Radio Times* of the local independent television station. She was the fifth member of staff following Mr. Henderson, company secretary Barry Johnston, Valerie Johnston and Brenda Adams. They were soon joined by Gordon Duffield, journalist with the *Belfast Telegraph* who headed up the publicity department.

From Donegall Street, the caravan moved to Havelock House to set up an entirely new system of working from filing to programme scheduling all created on the smart Adler typewriters. "We worked most evenings until 9.00 p.m. and in return we were issued with a meal voucher for sausage, baked beans and chips in lieu of overtime."

Mary lived in Carnaughliss in Co. Antrim. Her journey each day began in the heart of the country near Dundrod when at 7.30 a.m. she set off to cycle a mile and a half to the green bus which took her into Smithfield bus station. Then a red bus from Royal Avenue to Botanic Avenue with a ten minute walk to Havelock House.

Everyone was in the picture when it came to a party. Romper Room's first birthday was celebrated by children, presenter and crew.

"The thing that sticks in my mind is that it could be difficult to look smart. Many a day I would set out in dreadful weather wrapped up in my heavy tweed coat and flat fur lined boots. By lunchtime when I headed into the city centre, the sun was shining and there was I still wrapped up while everyone else was out in their figure.

"We were intrigued as we watched the technicians arriving from England – a completely new breed compared with those I'd worked with in my previous job in the long established linen industry – not only were they much younger, but they had an entirely different vocabulary. My education had only begun!"

As the Heads of Department were appointed, Mary became Secretary to Head of Presentation, Colin Lecky-Thompson who later became Programme Controller. He was fresh in from Manchester with all the low down on ABC, one of the first television studios to be established, so different from our small set up.

In a commercial station people work to the second and the programmes have to fit round the advertisements, they were and are priority. Colin Lecky Thompson laughed when he told us that on his first day at Ulster Television he and Chief Engineer Frank Brady were being shown round the building. "Clocks everywhere, vital in a building which runs to the second but there was something missing on every one, a second hand." They all had to be changed immediately because even one second can be the difference between success and failure.

Back in 1959 where Mary Hunter remembers that the huge volume of work required the help of a junior clerk. "I will always remember the day interviews took place," she said. "After seeing some very efficient girls, Colin Lecky-T selected a young 17-year-old who he said had that special quality which would take her far in television – Anne Shaw. And how right he was! I don't think I taught her anything, except perhaps a little spelling. We worked well together, but it wasn't long before she became a Production Assistant and Gill McKinley replaced her to work with me in the Presentation office."

Mary Hunter made her mark on the new station not only planning and scheduling programmes. She eventually made an impression on screen too.

"I was quite chuffed when my hands were chosen as the Praying Hands to introduce The Epilogue – my one claim to fame."

Brian Feeney. Bar tender, politician, author and columnist with the Irish News.

10
The Long Walk Home

One night passing the gasworks, the noise of the buckets squealed as they rose and fell bringing the coke to the boilers, it was drizzly and cold. At the junction of Ormeau Road and Ormeau Avenue, I was aware of a man following me, a big man in dark clothing.

The gasworks played a big part of my early days with Ulster Television. They had dominated the Ormeau Road since 1822 and for over 150 years the gas was the central power source for the city, feeding factories, homes and even the street lights manned by the lamp-lighter who went round with a long pole, knocking the little lever to allow the flame to fill the mantel. I feel so old when I remember seeing him at dusk going about his important work in Donegall Square West at the side of the City Hall as thousands of chattering starlings swooped and circled overhead.

Another era. A time when children with whooping cough were taken to the gasworks. I recall my mother telling me how she and her little sister Joan were held over the edge of big vats and forced to inhale the gas fumes. Irene McMinn was given 'cinder water' which was a well known remedy for congested chests. "Burning hot cinders were taken from the furnace and plunged into cold water which was then drained through muslin and given to children with asthma or a bad cough."

Journalist David McKittrick's grandmother told her children that they must behave because the gas pipe in their Shankill Road home went all the way across Belfast into the gasworks where her husband, a store man in the complex, was able to watch what was going on in the house.

Brian Feeney, columnist with the *Irish News*, worked in the Ivy bar in Donegall Pass earning a few extra bob in his student days. Although there was a gas workers club in Donegall Pass which opened 24 hours a day to facilitate the shift workers, the Ivy was their pub. Payday was Thursday which meant an early start for the bar staff preparing for the men who liked their Guinness. You may remember that this traditional drink was brought to a new audience during a 1994 advertising campaign, featuring the relatively unknown Irish actor Joe McKinney dancing to *Guaglione* by Perez Prado. In the ad he pranced around as his pint was drawn and he waited for it to settle. It became a talking point in Ireland and the UK. The song was number one in the charts for several weeks. McKinney became such a familiar face that he claimed no one in Ireland was willing to offer him acting jobs so apparently he left the country to seek work elsewhere. But he had a point, drinking the 'black stuff' at exactly the right moment is crucial and drawing a pint of porter is an art as Brian Feeney described.

"It was complicated and involved two barrels, the 'high' and the 'low'. From the high came the foam which was poured in first and then the flat was added from the low and the mixture was allowed to settle". The skill was ensuring a creamy top was sitting perfectly on the black stuff beneath and it had to be right because a bad pint could turn the tummy inside out. "We'd line up the pint glasses along the bar with the high already in just waiting to be topped up. It took all afternoon but when the men came in at 4.00 o'clock, the whole lot was cleared in ten minutes and we were working like cartoon characters in the *Beano* or the *Dandy* pulling pints non-stop until about nine at night."

Keep that glass dirty, was the instruction.

In those days a pint cost 11d in old money. As well draught, there was bottled Guinness. Barrels came from St. James's Gate brewery in Dublin by train to bottling plants in Belfast although the Stagecoach Inn in Dunmurry on the outskirts of Belfast bottled their own. In Belfast, Guinness was often referred to as 'porter' or 'stout' when drawn from the barrel. In Dublin it was known as a 'pint of plain'.

"The men from the gas works were characters and they made a good wage," Brian remembers, "especially men working inside the building renewing the brickwork in the kilns. And they got thirsty! It was likened to the Klondike Gold Rush as men clocked off and raced across the road to wet their whistles. I remember one who made big money so he always had a lot of friends who liked to drink with him. He was no fool. He began to make a detour past his house on payday. He'd whistle to his wife who'd open the top window and catch the wad of notes he'd throw up so he could legitimately limit his spending."

Even in those days, management was very aware of the rolling contract. Men were employed right up to Christmas week then laid off so they weren't entitled to a Christmas bonus. Then they were re-employed in the New Year and again the buckets went round like a giant Ferris wheel filling the furnace.

By the 1960s, electricity had taken over and production of gas had declined and came to a halt in 1985. Obviously the site at the Gasworks was contaminated but it was eventually cleansed and turned into a modern business park with the planners retaining the red brick perimeter wall and some of the more historic buildings. The clock tower still stands a reminder of the summer days in the 60s when a camera would be put on the roof of Havelock House and the announcer would make the links and update the time using the gas works clock in the background.

Until it closed in the late 90s, the Ivy Bar changed little. This was where Brian worked as a student, walking home up Sandy Row to West Belfast late at night, much to the concern of his mother. This is where he closed the door at 10.00 p.m. on the dot refusing entry to any latecomers including a big woman with a black beehive hair-do and a beige coat. "It was 10.30 and I kept shouting we were closed. She kept banging on the door. I kept refusing her entry until the manager arrived to see what the noise was all about. 'Who was that?' I told him about the persistent woman outside. 'Never ever refuse that woman,' he commanded and opened the door, ushering her in with a warm welcome. Transpired she ran the local brothel, always paid cash and her minimum order was half a dozen bottles of whiskey a night. I then realised who the women were who came in with customers and sat in corners supping their drinks."

And Brian's blushes weren't spared on the day he was walking into Belfast with some of his Queen's University friends. "It was 5.30 in the evening when we came across two women obviously doing business on the railway bridge at Bradbury Place. As we drew level I was singled out. 'Hello Brian.' 'How'ya Brian.' I'd a bit of explaining to do!"

I too walked home many evenings from Ormeau Road to Fortwilliam Park – in high heels. One night passing the gasworks, the noise of the buckets squealed as they rose and fell bringing the coke to the boilers. It was drizzly and cold. At the junction of Ormeau Road and Ormeau Avenue, I was aware of a man following me. A big man in dark clothing. With all the arrogance of youth I rounded on him and told him in no uncertain terms to stop following me and go away home. I could hear my voice echo up and down the road. He was so taken aback he stopped. I continued, nose in the air, clicking my way along Cromac Street and home.

I thought I was very brave and boasted next day in the canteen how I coped with my stalker. At lunchtime Brian Durkin, a dear friend, big and handsome, came to me with tears in his eyes and, in front of everyone, told me how hurt he was, how I had shouted at him, snubbed him and told him to go home when all he wanted was to keep me company as I walked into town. I was mortified. All afternoon I kept apologising. Just before we went into studio for the evening programme, he couldn't keep it up any longer and confessed he was joking; he'd been nowhere near the Ormeau Road.

It reminds me of another joke played on me years later by broadcaster, Walter Love. I was working on his BBC programme *Day by Day* answering questions sent in by listeners, which developed into *Ask Anne,* first on radio, then on UTV and in *The Irish News.*

The producer, Harry Adair, was running through the programme content before we went into the studio at 10 o'clock and Walter asked me what I was leading with. I told him a letter from a lady who wrote that one of her breasts was much bigger than the other and she couldn't find a bra to fit - could I help? I explained to Walter that this is often the case with women. I was going to suggest she bought two bras, one in each cup size, cut them in half and sew the two different cups together then she'd have a comfortable and supportive bra. He was very doubtful about this subject being voiced on the radio! Even as we settled down to my section on the programme, he said, "I don't think you should read that letter." I argued I should. He played a disc just before introducing me and literally pleaded with me not to read the letter. "This lady needs help Walter. Give me one good reason why I shouldn't give her my idea?" His eyes twinkling, he cracked, "because I wrote the letter!"

Back to the gasworks and the 60s.

I always wondered what went on behind the high walls but it was that squealing of the buckets that remains in my mind. For

The atmospheric and tragic Jewish graveyard in Warsaw.

some reason, as I walked past, I was horrified by the noise. It made me think of little children in concentration camps during the war. Why I don't know, but it came back to me years later when I visited Auschwitz to make a programme for RTE.

We were filming in a Jewish cemetery in Warsaw. It was November, there was snow on the ground and the sun was low in the sky. The trees had no leaves and their skeletal branches dipped down to touch the rows of stone tombs, vaults and headstones. It was very atmospheric. There were crows in the trees but not a sound came from them. It was as if the whole graveyard was holding its breath. In the centre, surrounded by white stone markers, was a large bare area where, during World War II, thousands of men, women and children had been murdered in the streets and thrown naked into a pit and covered over with clay. Five of us making up the filming team stood, heads bowed for a few moments, before moving to one corner of the silent

Auschwitz, Poland.

cemetery and a large statue of Janusz Korczak, a doctor who established orphanages in Warsaw; he was standing proud in bronze with a group of frightened bronze children clinging around his legs.

*

In the stillness of that Friday morning, standing in front of the statue, we are suddenly aware of a man who appears as if from nowhere.

He is dressed in a long black greatcoat, a blue woolly hat, his hands deep in his pockets. He's about 80 with an expressionless face. His breath comes in short puffs into the cold air. He seems to glide past me to stand in front of the statue. I stand beside him. I ask him if this statue was special. He has no English for me and just nods. "Did you know him?" No reaction. "Was he a brave man?" He seems to relax his body, "Yes," he says "Brave." "We are going to Auschwitz tomorrow." I say. He pulls back his sleeve to reveal a tattooed number burned into the skin on the underside of his arm. "Auschwitz," he whispers. He looks at me so sadly, nods and walks away down the snowy path to disappear into the trees, swallowed up by the mist.

*

It was a deeply moving moment, frozen in time. Who was he? I don't know but I feel he was one of the children Janus Korczak accompanied to the concentration camp to die, one who escaped and had come back to pay homage. Or did he actually exist at all?

It was surreal and it encouraged me to research the life of Korczak. His writings became the basis for the United Nations Convention on the Right of the Child. He believed every child should have the right to love and respect, to enjoy the best conditions to grow and develop. The right to live in the present, be himself or herself. To make mistakes and to have the right to fail. The child should also have the right to be taken seriously, to desire, to claim, and to ask. The right to have secrets and to have respect for his or her possessions – however small. The right to a court of his peers, a defence, to commune with God, to education, even the right to resist education and the right to protest.

The statue of Janusz Korczak with the children who went to their deaths.

The irresistible Frank Carson – A real cracker!

11
A Comic Genius

"And I'd go to Frank Daly's the barber in Great Patrick Street at nine on the Saturday morning for a shave before going to the studios. I used to say he was the best in Northern Ireland. After he finished he gave you a glass of water to see if you were leaking."

Major-General Sir Henry Havelock KCB gave his name to Havelock Street and Havelock House which dominated the area. Sir James Outram gave his distinguished name to the nearby street where, we were told, our typical family lived. Both men were leaders of the British army during the Indian mutiny in the mid-1800s so it was appropriate that the building which would one day house a television station had a military background. It was taken over during the war by the Pioneer Corp, as a certain Belfastman remembers.

He was one of the first locals to appear on television in 1959. In those days he was playing the halls, appearing in the many theatres in Belfast and building a following. His big breakthrough came the autumn the station went on air. The Ulster Bank wanted to make a commercial. These were live or on film and in between the programmes, up would pop an actor, a comedian, maybe a footballer to extol the virtues of sausages or bread or in this case, a bank.

I remember hearing of a conversation in the sales office where an advertising agency executive asked the head of sales, Basil Lapworth, if he had any idea who could represent the Ulster Bank and cope with filming a commercial for television. Basil had been manager of the Royal Belfast Hippodrome Theatre, a flamboyant man who wore red braces and had the air of the ringmaster about him. He was well known for joining the queues outside his theatre and chatting with the audience before they took their seats. Now he was a front man whose audience was the captains of industry in Northern Ireland. As the head man selling advertising, he got rave reviews.

Lapworth thought for a moment. Someone who could handle this new technology and wouldn't be fazed by takes and re-takes? Such people were not ten a penny. Then he remembered a young man who'd brought the house down in the Hippodrome, easy to work with, personality plus and could cope with anything. His name was Frank Carson. Almost immediately Frank did a memorable audition and was booked to film the Ulster Bank commercial.

"I was lying in bed in my pyjamas when two robbers came into the house." I'm interviewing him in a Lisburn road restaurant and an appreciative audience is hanging on his every word. "They couldn't get into the safe," the audience holds its collective breath, "and one says to the other in a panic, 'We can't get the money - what will we do for money?' Then I sit up and ask, 'Will you take a cheque?'"

At that the audience start laughing and clapping! "I got 75 guineas for that and it became a catch phrase."

Like so many others which were born in the studios of Ulster Television.

"But my memories of Havelock House, go back to 1941 when I was 15 years old. It was during the war when it was a base for the Pioneer Corp. In order to protect the shipyard from the blitz, drums were filled with crude oil and placed on roadsides. They would get a warning of planes coming over and with a little petrol on a rag they'd light them up. Obnoxious smell and smoke. Soldiers would stand in the dark and we youngsters would walk past and salute them. Then, if we timed it right, along would come a bus with soup and bread – Rinty Monaghan, he became world champion fly weight boxer, would be up there with us eating bread and soup.

"I knew all the soldiers, I remember two. Sandy Douglas was one and Jimmy Lyle the other, he did an impression of Adolf Hitler I remember. He took a half an hour to get ready, Brill Creaming his hair, rubbing his hair down, putting on a moustache and makeup then he'd come out and go *Heil Hitler*! Their captain was Humphries, nickname Dungannon. He sang *Danny Boy* and the *Green Glens of Antrim*. It was all right a couple of times but every night for two years?"

In those days the young Frank walked from his home in Little Italy, Belfast. His family were of Italian descent, his grandmother was from Sicily. He came from a colourful area off York Street, close to the docks, where Italian families settled and loved to sit with their neighbours at the crossroads on a summer evening, singing and playing accordions as the children danced in the street. The Italian immigrants who came to Belfast were industrious, some opened ice cream parlours, others fish and chip shops and there were many skilled craftsmen working in mosaics and laying terrazzo floors.

I once interviewed a woman in Clifton House old peoples home and she was very proud to tell me her man was a 'tras-a-man' who laid floors in Sawyers fish shop and many of the city churches. He probably worked in Clonard monastery, in west Belfast or Holy Cross in Ardoyne two of many examples of Italian craft work. Going back some years it was such craftsmen who worked on the marble staircase and floor of the City Hall. Even the Titanic boasted this unique Italian skill carried out by these men who returned home each evening to their families in Little Italy.

After school at St. Patrick's in Donegall Street, Frank was apprentice to a plasterer and then an electrician. Although always a comic, he was a tough man too, proud to say he was a member of the Parachute regiment in 1944 serving in Palestine for over two years. "I was superbly physically fit and mentally attuned to jump out of an aeroplane on 29 occasions. But these men based at Havelock House were not fit to fight, below par for some reason, flat feet or asthmatic, so they were given jobs at home. They might have been shoemakers or bricklayers; the pioneers were building walls and digging trenches, stitching soldiers shoes or jackets, important work."

Years later Frank passed through the portals of Havelock House into the glitz that was Studio One. He'd been working at the Wellington Park Hotel for a fiver a night when Ernie Strathdee told him that producers in UTV were looking for acts.

He auditioned and became a regular.

"When I was on *Fiddle and Flute* I got 10 guineas for each of six shows but I didn't make much of a profit as each week my wife bought me a new pullover at the market at £6 a time. And I'd go to Frank Daly's the barber in Great Patrick Street at nine on the Saturday morning for a shave before going to the studios. I used to say he was the best in Northern Ireland, after he finished he gave you a glass of water to see if you were leaking. I did the show with Bridie Gallagher, Peter Tomelty, Gertie Wine, Tommy Moran and Bridie Ward, one of the funniest women I've met. Tom Raymond and Marjory Rea, it was a great cast. You know," he adds, "in those days the pubs closed at 10 o'clock and the show was on from 10 until 10.30 and by closing time there wasn't a sinner left in the pub, they'd all gone home to watch the show."

Frank also made regular appearances on the evening programme *Roundabout* with Anne Gregg and Ivor Mills, singing a different song each weeknight. He also appeared on Tommy James teatime programme.

Frank laughs about two of those programmes, once when he sang *Messing about on the River*. "Do you remember that big props man, smoked woodbine?" I did, he was talking about Isaac King. "As I was singing, sitting at the end of a mocked up pier, he was up a ladder with a bucket of water and supposed to sprinkle it on me as if the water was splashing over me!" But Isaac had a wicked sense of humour. "Ah, he certainly had. He upended the whole bucket over me on the last line!"

The other song was *Speedy Gonzales*, the 1963 hit sung by Pat Boone. "Now this required a donkey. I eventually tracked one down in the Pound Loney on the Lower Falls. So I went up to a house off the Falls Road and found the man with the horse. 'You have to pay,' he says. The fee was a tenner a programme and he wanted a fiver to bring the animal down to the Havelock House and a fiver to take it home! Isaac took charge of it and when I arrived for the show he was feeding it cornflakes. 'Don't do that

The Fiddle and Flute regulars: Teresa Duffy, Gertie Wine, Teresa Clifford, Jim Orgin and Frank Carson.

before the show,' I told him, 'you know what will happen.' Well, the show went all right, the donkey with a hat on and my two sons on either side holding its head, but the minute the director faded to black, the donkey decorated the studio high up and low down and the William Tell was horrendous."

By this time the restaurant on the Lisburn Road is in stitches. It's a mile a minute with Frank Carson. He hardly draws breath. As Spike Milligan said: 'What's the difference between Frank Carson and the MI? You can turn off the MI!' But Frank got his own back in 2009 when he supported 30 members of BT staff who were suspended for telling an Irish joke. "The ridiculous thing about this crackdown on Irish jokes is the claim that they are offensive to the Irish. What a load of old shamrocks.

"Anyway." He's off again! "Mervyn Solomon was standing at the side of the studio with a man who said, 'I love your *Speedy Gonzales*, it's so funny.' I replied that whoever wrote it was a genius, clever, lovely words, a great song. 'Thanks,' he said, 'I wrote it, I'm Buddy Kaye.'"

The laughter continues as he talks about magician Leslie St. Clair and his Vanishing Duck trick. The Great La Vant and his magic trunk. How Roger Whittaker came to join the stage show of *With a Fiddle and a Flute*. "Good singer, great whistler, wonderful but no stage craft. I spent hours teaching him to walk on and off and when my straight man, Danny Small was sick, Roger stood in for him. He was great, one of the greatest straight men I've ever had, he was wonderful."

There's no stopping him, he is a genuine funny man who can recreate a situation, embellish it and you're living every minute.

"Was it *Tommy's Tavern,* the show with the bar and the customers, all people who applied and came in to be the audience? I think there was only beer for them, probably one bottle each because it was free! Do you remember Chalky White the traffic policeman at Shaftesbury Square? Everyone knew him. Well, he told me there was a big argument in the police station at Donegall Pass. 'Come on Frank, let me into the secret, where's that pub?' I told him. 'Is it seriously in the studio!' It was a very realistic set but sometimes the pillars started to wobble and everyone grabbed one and stood by it holding it up as the cameramen got their shots and the floor manager, Miles Scott, got us all under control. There was a parrot, a big green Macaw, involved on one show but it escaped from its cage and flew into the lighting grid, arched its back and proceeded to crap all over the artists. Billy Venard and Jimmy McQueen were up trying to get it down! The bar maids were the two makeup girls in fishnet tights and the audience didn't realise this was a set and they were going up and ordering vodkas and hot Mundies."

It's the way he tells them!

This is a man with a staggering memory who loves a laugh as well as making others laugh. When he was working in Great Yarmouth he read the lesson in church every Sunday. So, when the company decided to hold a 'vicars and tarts' party, Frank was able to get vicar's gear for himself and for singer Matt Monroe. "We wore them along the sea front and a very drunk man came up to me and said: 'Excuse me father I am a sinner.' I said to an equally full Matt, 'Father Munroe, will you hear this man's confession.' 'Forgive me father for I am a sinner,' he asked again. I said: 'Father Munroe, will you please give this man absolution.' Matt could hardly get the words out: 'I absolve you from your sins my son' he said and added, 'and lay off the liquor.'"

The way Frank tells it conjures up a picture of two inebriated vicars holding each other up and a wee sozzelled man looking up at them in blissful gratitude.

Frank's memories are riddled with local names. In the plastering trade he worked with Mickey Matthews and his wife Rosie. Albert McMaster one of four brothers, the greatest brick layers of all time. Friends Danny Trainor and Gerry Fitt. Sean Connery and Pierce Brosnan make an appearance in our conversation as did Liam Neeson. Frank, once the Lord Mayor of Balbriggan in the Republic of Ireland, knows them all and makes no difference between them.

It's sad now looking back to that evening in the Lisburn Road restaurant and his memory of Liam and his actress wife, Natasha Richardson. Little did we think she would die in a tragic skiing accident some months later in March 2009.

"Natasha was with Liam when we met and she said she was glad to meet me because, she said, her daddy, producer Tony Richardson, loved my humour. She said he was always saying, 'it's the way I tell them.'"

In the restaurant, a little girl approaches for an autograph. He chats away, signs a photograph, "I only have eleven thousand left so you're lucky," he tells her. "Take it to the chemist and get it made up. Or put it under your pillow and you won't sleep for a week."

We wander backwards and forwards through the years, from the early days and how as his career ricocheted into the stratosphere.

He was awarded one of the greatest honours in the Catholic Church when he was knighted into the Order of St. Gregory during a private audience with Pope John Paul II. The springboard to success on *Opportunity Knocks,* his appearance in the *Royal Variety Performance*, his charity work and the £130,000 he raised for the children's cancer ward at the Royal Victoria Hospital.

He is loved at home and abroad and he is loved by his colleagues in show business for his genuine talent and his kindness, he makes no difference between anyone.

"The beautiful thing about showbiz is there are no stars amongst the stars."

Thomas Turkington who hailed from Cookstown, often visited Havelock House with musicians Doris Crawford and her husband Alex.

Brum Henderson was the ultimate showman. He loved an audience and never failed to entertain.

A man of many guises, actor, interviewer and character, Charles Witherspoon

12
Picture Perfect

She would brush a dark beige loose powder all over his hair and turn him into a dark blond for the duration of the programme.
But he didn't mind as he enjoyed having it washed off again and his hair blow-dried and styled as a treat afterwards.
Clergymen of all persuasions had to wear blue dog collars and all men were asked to change a white shirt to a blue one before going into the studio.

Television was in its infancy in 1959. No one quite knew how to respond to it, some contributors were naturals, often schoolteachers who were used to standing up in front of a class and expounding on a subject. Bringing this to a level of a mass audience, making it visually interesting and above all entertaining, was a challenge.

Denis Ireland was a man who found that challenge exciting. Patrick Riddell treated it with some scepticism. James Boyce slipped into the role, as he would pull on one of his soft leather gloves. For Charles Witherspoon it was as easy as falling off a bike.

Charlie was an extremely popular presenter. His favourite quote was - *She says to me, she was awful glad she did what she done before she done what she did.* Paul Irwin was sound engineer during a series of short stories featuring Charlie on his bicycle travelling round Northern Ireland meeting people and discovering the history of the area.

"In *Graveyards Tell Strange Stories*, we borrowed a bike straight out of a show room, top of the range, and Charlie took it up the road near Buncrana for a wee practice. We set up the camera and I'd the Negra sound recorder sitting on the sea wall, all was set to go. Lovely day, everything perfect. Charlie got the cue and took off, wobbled a bit, continued head in the air, looking around him - smiling. But no one had tightened the pin which held the handlebars to the main frame!"

Disaster. Blood everywhere. Filming was stopped. An ambulance was called, the cyclist was rushed to hospital and enjoyed a couple of hours surrounded by nurses and patients treating him like a king and looking for autographs.

*

Denis Ireland proved an exciting challenge to the girls in makeup: tall, over six feet, handsome with a shock of white hair. Now that caused a problem. If television in general was in its infancy, then the technology was only being conceived albeit at a fast pace. Lighting and the sensitivity of cameras was a concern.

In order to achieve the best picture possible, the image was 'set up' electronically on an oscilloscope, a black background with thin vertical green lines of various heights across the middle, reminiscent of the Himalayas in profile. Dark images coming from the studio camera showed as short vertical line, bright images reached the heights. The trick was balancing the two, and this was the job of the vision controller, known to us as the racks engineer. In more recent times when I was on television, I would get a ticking off and told to go and change if I wore a white blouse because, thanks to my well defined bosom, the lights bounced off my chest and on to my face causing the tall lines to shoot off the scope and thus unbalancing the picture! These days there are electronic ways of solving these situations but in 1959 it was a problem, therefore the most important man in the studio was the lighting director who actually painted the picture. Bill Brown, Ian Hill, then Tom Reid joined followed by Colin McCallum who arrived in 1960 from Scottish Television. Even after years working in television, it was interesting to talk to him and learn.

"Lighting was crucial in black and white days," he explained, "it literally was painting with light based on the studio photography and how photographers set their lights to highlight the model. The face is the most important and the eyes must have a glint. We once had an interviewee and for some reason her skin just absorbed light and no matter what we did we couldn't get that lovely natural look but that happened very rarely. When there was

Roy Gaston who became a major Irish artist in later years, could design anything from a salon bar to a room in a stately home.

Amending right up to the wire. Ernie Strathdee's secretary Joan McWilliams would type the script but even as Jack Williamson was adjusting Ernie's ear piece minutes before going live on air, Fred Corbett was updating.

a set involved we lit that too, for instance, with curtains the lighting was designed to cast shadows to emphasise the folds and give texture." Somehow, working with set designer Roy Gaston, the lighting boys managed to produce a picture so natural that the viewers felt they could walk into the room and be at home.

Usually the interviewers respected what was required from Colin and his team. "But one day in Studio One, a lady interviewer, I won't say who, came in with some sort of hair piece and I think I caused offence by pointing out that it looked like a dead animal on top of her natural shiny hair. Nothing lights can do about that especially in black and white. When we went into colour about ten years later it was easier although there were still difficulties. Like the time a presenter came in wearing yellow because it was fashionable but under the light lights she looked like a buttercup! She wasn't pleased but agreed to change."

Charlie Witherspoon was a stickler for perfection and if he didn't think he looked his best on studio camera, he'd call for the lights to be adjusted as Colin McCallum remembers. "I'd say, certainly Charles, and ask electrician Fred Hopwood to get the long pole and tap the barn door a couple of times. Then I'd tell Charlie he looked better and all was well."

Tweaking was the byword. If there was anything not quite

perfect someone somewhere would tweak something and everyone was happy. It was teamwork, set and lights, makeup and racks, cameras, sound and floor manager all working together to achieve a perfect studio presentation and making sure the presenters and contributors felt confident they looked their best. And sometimes in those black and white days that meant going to extremes.

Denis Ireland's silvery white hair would have drained his face on screen so the makeup artist had to deal with it. Jill McCord or Connie Larmour would brush a dark beige loose powder all over his hair and turn him into a dark blond for the duration of the programme. But he didn't mind as he enjoyed having it washed off again and his hair blow-dried and styled as a treat afterwards. Clergymen of all persuasions had to wear blue dog collars and all men were asked to exchange a white shirt for a blue shirt before they were made up, eyebrows were brushed and noses powdered then they were ushered into the studio by the floor manager. Make up was a vital part of any performance. It's interesting that the glove puppet Sooty was christened in the 1950s after Harry Corbett covered his nose and ears with soot to make him more attractive.

Because cameras were very basic in those days, lighting and makeup were vitally important. Time was allotted to both. For instance, with an evening magazine programme the day started early. The news room gathered the content, the director sorted out the studio set; lighting, camera and sound had their own head organisers and the technical end was looked after by the senior person of the day who booked the various machines required to get the pictures from the studio floor to the home receiver.

The job of the production assistant, always a girl, was to coordinate these elements. Contracts had to be typed. The head of news, at that time Fred Corbett, gave the list of interviewees. He gave me the list one day including the name A.N.Other of N.F.A. Being a bit green behind the ears and not having come across this before I duly typed the contract, and after the programme tried to find A.N. Other of N.F.A. I expected to find a football chairman or some visiting spaceman but when everyone had gone, I was left holding the contract having found no one to match it to. I went to Fred puzzled that one of the guests hadn't turned up yet no one had noticed. He took a fit of laughing and explained it was an extra contract for someone who hoped to be there but was doubtful. "We would have written the correct name in if he'd showed," Fred explained. "That stands for an other person of no fixed abode." Television talk! As was another piece of jargon which had one wife more than a little concerned. Waiting to pick him up after work, she overheard someone talking about her lighting engineer husband going off on a story and commenting that he'd taken a blond and a redhead with him. Loose words cost lives. It turned out these were the nicknames for two types of lights used in outside filming.

The vocabulary was a mystery including strawberry filters. Most nicknames referred to studio equipment and electronic gadgetry but the strawberry filter was special and much used. This was code employed many a time when children crowded round the cameraman when he was out on a story. Rather than disappoint them, he'd say to the reporter, 'I'll do a strawberry filter,' and to the children, 'can't guarantee this will appear on screen but let's see.' Fair enough, the children were duly filmed waving and laughing, shouting comments and enjoying the fun. In fact, strawberry filter meant, point the camera but don't press the record button.

The first time a camera was taken outside the studio was for the Lord Mayor's Show in spring 1960. The colourful parade coming down the Ormeau Road was captured live although in black and white. Alan Hailes manned camera one, pointing it up over the bridge and following the floats as they passed by, cheered by

The 1960 Lord Mayor's Show.

onlookers, watching as they made their way into the centre of Belfast. It's interesting to note that Alan went on to direct many live programmes with the company's Outside Broadcast Unit costing £500,000 and launched in 1980 - 22 different sports, concerts with a variety of orchestras and choirs, church services from cathedrals to parish churches representing all faiths. So that early experience on Ormeau Road certainly excited his interest.

On the day of the Lord Mayor's Show Adrienne McGuill and Ernie Strathdee were giving a running commentary. This was the man who sealed his place in rugby history when he was part of Ireland's 1948 Grand Slam Championship team and I'm sure he was looking down with great delight in March 2009 when Ireland beat Wales 17-15 to clinch the title after 61 years. How pleased he would have been and how pleased was his teammate Jack Kyle as he watched the match unfold. Jack Kyle, a legendary pupil of my old school, Belfast Royal Academy, and Ernie Strathdee, a great friend of our family who wore his honour lightly and was, as someone once said, a darlin' man. He was a man who made an impression on another legend, Mícheál MacLiammóir, the actor who began life as an Englishman and ended it as one of the most revered Irishmen of all time.

On one particular day the rugby player and the actor repaired to Dirty Dicks between rehearsal and transmission – always a mistake. The craic was great and the two men sparked off against each other.

*

Late afternoon, the light is fading. Inside the pub there is very little conversation from the locals sitting round, downing Guinness before going home for tea. They are watching and listening. The bigger of the two men, jet-black hair and heavy makeup. A thespian of some importance. He is addressing his companion. There is a mocked argument and with much drama, MacLiammóir, twists a ring from his finger and flings it at Ernie – "Take back your ring Ernest," he booms in his unmistakable deep, cultivated voice, "it's over," and flounces out!

There was much speculation amongst the locals and the story was repeated for years to come.

Dirty Dick's, Havelock Arms in the formal list of Belfast pubs, was also known as Studio Three. A second larger studio was built in 1962 allowing a daily news service to be launched and programmes to become more ambitious, but there was still time to kill between the end of rehearsals and the live broadcast or recordings for transmission later. Between time the studio lights were reset, makeup completed, machinery checked and re-checked. So the artists had time on their hands and studio three was the place to relax. It always sounded good to report to visitors that so-and-so will be with you shortly, he's in Studio Three.

It's a difficult thing to shop a person you respect and love. James Boyce I respected and loved and when he arrived for afternoon rehearsal and he didn't seem quite himself, I was concerned. What to do? He was all right in makeup but the heat of the studio is hard to stick at the best of times but it could make a man drowsy after a few jars at a lunchtime engagement. James was a bon vivant, a man who enjoyed good company and excellent wine. And it looked to me as if he'd enjoyed very good company on that day. I was sick with worry but I knew I'd have to mention it to someone. That someone was director Derek Bailey, also a great admirer who wouldn't want to risk the man's reputation. The programme went ahead without the contribution. I lost sleep over that until James and I met up the following week. "Thank goodness Derek advised me not to go on last week. It would have been very unprofessional to show any signs of not being in control." I was so relieved.

*

If you ever see an Irish music programme which emanated from Ulster Television in those early days, somewhere, either featured or in the background, you'll be sure to see Brian O'Donnell.

The ubiquitous Brian O'Donnell, who brought traditional music to the screens of Ulster Television.

The O'Donnell was a Donegal man.

A maker of fiddles and an expert in traditional Irish music. He was the specialist everyone turned to.

I remember so well finding my great grandfather's fiddle, the fiddle Frank played as the ladies and gentlemen danced in the big house in Glenfarne County Leitrim where he was a land steward, probably at the time of the Famine. I can only hope the master of the house, apparently Mr. Harland of Harland and Wolff, was an 'improving landlord' who helped the people in his employ. Frank's fiddle was in a very poor state of repair and I asked Brian if he'd have a look at it in case it was a Stradivarius! Life was full of hope in those days! It wasn't but Brian took it and repaired the damage, restrung the instrument and gave it back to me with loving care, refusing any recompense.

He was generous on another occasion. I was babysitting for Derek Bailey and eventually he and Brian returned home, well the worse for wear, full of fun and giggling like schoolboys. Coffee was required and as this was being organised Brian cornered me and told me he had something for me to say thank you for babysitting. He proceeded to put his hand down the front of his big brown corduroy trousers and rummage around. I was petrified. What does an innocent 19 year old say in a situation like this? He was my elder and better. He was a revered contributor to programmes. I think if he'd looked at me he would have seen a rabbit frozen in the headlights but he was too busy rummaging! Eventually, after much puffing and panting and a gruff 'Ah Yes – got it', he slowly withdrew his hand and in it, to my relief, was a bottle of that rare ould Mountain Dew - poteen.

There were pros and cons to being so young in such a fast moving and glamorous industry. I didn't drink at all because my now 96 year old father is a recovering alcoholic who hasn't had a drink since 1954 and I know won't until the day he dies. Naturally he worried about his daughter being thrown into the mix with all these television types with their high flying lifestyles and as many people thought, dubious morals. Ivor Mills used to get annoyed with me because as he said, "you can enjoy a night without a drink even more than we do with a drink - and you remember in the morning."

Only once was my drink spiked; it was in the Sportsman's Inn, Dunmurry, long gone now. My tipple was orange juice for some inexplicable reason because I didn't even like it, but after one of our regular outings, this time a car rally which ended up in the Sportsman's, I detected a strange taste from my orange drink, later confirmed by one of the more experienced girls to be gin. She let it be known that this was a cheap trick which wasn't appreciated.

*

This was the scene. We worked hard and we played hard. The younger members of staff moved as one; most of us lived in and around Belfast so we socialised together, we enjoyed the heady delights of making programmes, being able to say we worked in Ulster Television and having money to spend in the days when half a crown, 2/6d, (15p) bought cigarettes for a week or filled a car with petrol. Then there were the sophisticates who led a more racy life, or so we believed, and those who worked behind the scenes, the accountants, the sales team, in fact all departments, we all came together on a daily basis to enjoy the dramas and the fun of television, and the canteen was common ground and a grand meeting place.

It was a surprise when the singer Alma Cogan insisted on sitting by herself in one corner of the small canteen which held about ten tables, and a busy kitchen which turned out delicious food during the hours we worked. She didn't talk to anyone, sat huddled in a fur coat beside her manager, didn't even speak to him, went into the studio sang her song and left. It was only later we realised she had cancer and not long after that she died and I felt a sadness that I had misjudged her. Another person who was surprisingly unfriendly was another singer, Frankie Vaughan. He was patron of The Boys' Clubs and when approached to meet with some of the local boys he refused. Probably he had a reason. Years later I discovered what that reason was. He was late for a sound check at the Boom Boom Room where he was appearing a couple of hours later. I soon learned not to be judgemental.

In those days Belfast was an important stop over when a star was promoting his or her latest book or record – singles in those days pressed on black Bakelite. In the late 50s we would go into record shops in the city centre and stand in booths made of yellow sound proofed material studded with little holes, put on headphones and listened before buying. We certainly went wild about a new singing sensation, one Tom Jones with his record 'It's not Unusual.' Little did I know I'd be meeting him and viewing his beautiful bare chest.

The innocence of youth! Anne Shaw, Fiona Bennington and Adrienne McGuill on their round Ireland holiday in 1962.

13
All Part of Growing Up

"I can't cut your lovely hair without your mother's permission."
Without a blink of an eyelid I replied, "My mother sent me."
Big smile and I was in the chair and my plaits were on the floor.

1965 was something of a watershed. Although I was coming to the end of my first association with Ulster Television because of my marriage in 1966, I was in my element. Programmes were exciting and there was a new one every day. If we production assistants weren't scheduled to be in studio we were out filming somewhere in Northern Ireland and occasionally 'overseas' in London. Then came a holiday with my mother to Paris, France! What an adventure. It cost £17 for our return flights Belfast, London, Charles de Gaulle airport. Mummy, of French Huguenot stock, family name originally 'en Hiver' in more recent times 'de Winter', was poised ready, her schoolgirl French polished. One of my lasting memories of that week was Mrs. Maureen Shaw nee de Winter conversing with a member of the Gendarmerie at the Tomb of the Unknown Soldier in the shadow of the Arc de Triomphe. He was gracious and engaged with her but it was obvious he was struggling to keep up with the flow! We bought presents, of course, and nothing would do but we'd find tissue paper somewhere to wrap the more delicate items for transporting home. Tissue paper wasn't included in our phrase book. So, as I stood aside in amazement and admiration, she went into a music hall routine of miming tissue paper. Eventually she resorted to mocking a sneeze complete with hankie, 'tish-you papier', she went, 'tish-you papier', now who wouldn't understand that? Answer – the shop assistant. Bemused is an understatement. We left without the precious tish-you papier.

It was also the week I had my hair cut. At school pigtails were the bane of my life I hated them and it can't have been easy for mummy to plait them against my will. 'Done in two shakes of a dead lamb's tail,' she'd say. One of those bizarre sayings where she knew exactly what she meant, a bit like Ireland Rugby Captain Brian O'Driscoll in February 2009 who replied, when asked to comment on the current England manager Martin Johnston: "Knowledge is knowing that tomato is a fruit, while wisdom is knowing not to put it in a fruit salad." He topped that a couple of weeks later by leading his team to win the Grand Slam Championship after 61 years.

Again on holiday but this time years before in Portstewart, the beautiful seaside town on the north coast of Northern Ireland and at the age of 13, I decided to take matters into my own hands and walked to the far end of the town, almost to Portrush, until I came on a barber's shop. I marched in with my pocket money in hand and demanded a short back and sides. The man was somewhat taken aback. "I can't cut off your lovely hair without your mother's permission." Without a blink of an eyelid I replied, "My mother sent me." Big smile and I was in the chair and my plaits were on the floor. Of course, I got what for when I arrived home but grudgingly the family agreed the short back and sides suited me.

In Paris I went 'gamin'!

Actress Leslie Caron was the inspiration at that time and a hair cut in Paris meant a close crop. It was lovely to wear and easy to keep and I walked taller and felt like a film star as we strolled along the Bois de Boulogne with an independent air and stood in awe at the mirrored ball room in the Palace of Versailles catching a glimpse of the Sun King Louis XIV and I think the ghost of Marie Antoinette who glided by 150 years later. Frenchmen certainly are romantic and attentive and, as they say, I went away a girl and came home a woman, not physically I hasten to add, but in every other way, a good dose of confidence is what every girl needs.

We each bought a new outfit with the money my dad John Shaw and brothers Mike and Johnny, presented us with as we left Belfast. Mine a white lace skirt and jacket and for mummy a cornflower blue dress. Not knowing the first thing about custom and practice, we were so terrified of having them confiscated at the airport that we wore them under our travelling suits until we got to the ladies toilet in London Heathrow, where we stripped off and cooled down.

The upshot of that wonderful experience was to change my life. I had memorable romantic interludes, got engaged and married the following year. All because of a hair cut? It certainly helped.

Appearance is all important as we were to learn from the women who came to the studios at Havelock House. Maureen Martin, for instance, was a regular in Studio One and the envy of the girls, always dressed to kill, always laughing and happy. She was a young glamorous model working for the legendary Stella Goddard who was the epitome of elegance, supremo of the Stella Goddard Model Agency. When it came to fashion in the 60's Stella Goddard was the ultimate, tall and very beautiful; she ran her agency to provide models for show rooms, for trade shows, modelling in restaurants and at venues like the King's Hall during the Ideal Home show. The UTV girls were young and we thought ourselves a gift for Stella's books, so with Maureen's encouragement, one night we went to audition. I think Brenda Adams, the company secretary's secretary, was the only one to pass, the rest were OK but not quite what Stella was looking for; and then it was my turn. Stella had a lovely home near Stormont in Belfast with an especially built extension where she positioned a ramp so the would-be model could walk from a side room, through the arch, onto a platform and down the cat walk. I did this, poised and smiling, every inch a glamorous clotheshorse, or so I thought. I waited for the gasp of delight and a contract. Instead, Stella looked at me sadly, shook her head and said, "My dear, with hips like those I could do nothing." Shades of those childbearing hips again! Undaunted, a few days later the same group of hopefuls went off to audition to be air hostesses at the Wellington Park Hotel in the days when long haul meant a three day stop over in the best hotels in exotic lands! I was rejected there as well!

The fashion icon of the day, Stella Goddard on a visit to Belfast to celebrate her 80th birthday.
Irish News

We all learned from Stella Goddard, directly or indirectly. Poise, walking, turning, grooming, no matter when we saw a Stella Goddard girl, we wanted to emulate her looks. We asked the girls for tips. One layer of foundation, allow it to dry and then apply translucent powder and another layer of foundation on top gave a lovely creamy complexion. To get an extra glow after applying makeup, dab your cheeks with a dampened sponge and Max Factor *Pan Stick* covered spots and stayed in place all day. They bent the end of the mascara wand to give lashes an extra lift, or if using a brush and solid block they always used spit for adhesion and two applications for extra long lashes. The models perfected walking with a straight back by placing books on their heads and under each arm. When it came to bosoms, my friend Sheelagh used socks but the models lined their brassieres with sanitary towels to give upward thrust and separation, remember this was long before Gossard Wonder bras!

Gossard's poster campaign in 1994 featured model Eva Herzigova in a Wonderbra, gazing down at her breasts with the caption 'Hello Boys'. It was a sensation. It caused crashes and traffic jams as male drivers were distracted by the vision! The poster was voted number 10 in a Poster of the Century contest and was featured in an exhibition at the Victoria and Albert Museum. In 2008 Debenhams store asked 3000 women customers for their fashion favourites. The answer was the push-up bra, the greatest invention ever. The first film star sex symbol and sweater girl was Jane Russell, 5' 7" tall, vital statistics 38D.24.36. In her first film *The Outlaw*, director, aeronautical engineer and billionaire Howard Hughes designed the first underwire bra to accentuate her assets. In fact she didn't wear it in the end, she used her own bra, padded with tissue paper and Hughes didn't even notice but his was probably a prototype for the Wonderbra worn and loved by so many of us.

Elastoplast was used to prevent nipples sticking out and bra straps were never allowed to be on show. Before appearing anywhere, the last thing was to check back and front view in a long mirror for straight seams and no ladders. A chemist shop in Lisburn sold a brown liquid which when rubbed onto the skin gave a deep sunburned appearance. A must in summer time.

There was always something theatrical about Stella's shows, especially the Ideal Home show.

"It came about when Sydney Goorwitch of the Goorwitch fashion chain asked around for someone to compere the first Ideal Home after the war. I offered myself and arranged to bring models over from the Lucy Clayton school in London but it gave me the idea of grooming local girls for future shows and so my modelling and deportment agency was born."

Her girls, and boys, were instilled with the principles of punctuality, attention to hygiene, abstinence from alcohol when working and always carrying three pairs of shoes. Amongst her leading ladies were Hilary Palmer, Susan Riddell and Maureen Martin, all with that X-factor and the main man, Brian Massey who went on to produce fashion and trade shows in London.

Because she was the star of school productions in London, with the stage name Sophie Ives, Stella was destined to become an actress and appear in the West End. Theatre was in her blood and her fashion shows at the Ideal Home, under the name Stella Goddard, always had a touch of theatricality about them. She was the first to choreograph her models and use music to enhance the show. It was the days of roll-on corsets, living breathing girdles, and perforated latex under garments known and loved as Playtex, a company which had in the 1960s a contract with NASA to produce their space suits! Yet the girls all looked natural and graceful, although on one famous occasion a black wig was worn elsewhere than the head and a naughty flick of the skirt revealed far too much. Not a Stella moment but no wonder the crowds queued round the balcony for tickets. There were three or four shows each day, six days a week for three weeks.

So successful were they that before long London fashion houses were coming to Belfast to invite Stella's models to their big shows, including one at Olympia in front of the Queen. This really put our local girls on the map and Stella and her partner Denise Lowry into the top contact books.

Sizes were Standard, Junior Miss and Petit ranging from 12 to 16 and if you were over a size 16 you certainly didn't admit to it and you made sure to cut off the label. Styles were sophisticated, skirt lengths to the knee and pencil slim or full and swirling for informal occasions but always with stockings and high heels. Stella made me laugh remembering one show in Ballymena where the owner of the shop wanted to run through the programme. "The clothes were beautiful and the audience wealthy wives. I told him the first round was cocktail wear – 'no, no can't mention alcohol'. Next round was ballgowns. 'No, no, it has to be evening wear'. We were back five years later and he gave me a nudge and said it was now alright to mention cocktails." Presumably ball gowns were still beyond the pale.

On her 80th birthday in 2004 many of her girls threw a party for her in Culloden Hotel in Co Down and she flew over from her home in London to be wined and dined. Amazingly all her models were still tall, svelte and elegant – and I still had my hips.

During those days of slim line skirts, two Ulster Television girls went into town on a new Vespa scooter. Dark glasses, knotted scarves, they set off in style. At traffic lights in the centre of Belfast outside Anderson and McAuley's, they stopped waiting for the lights to change and the passenger looked at herself in the big shop window admiring the picture they cut, big hair, straight backs, their long legs and winkle-pickers. She had rested her feet on the ground as they waited. Suddenly the lights changed, the driver revved up and the bike shot off towards Royal Avenue. The passenger was left standing, legs apart, skirt round her bottom looking anything but elegant and still admiring herself in the window. The shoppers applauded and fell about laughing. I am duty bound not to name names, a promise is a promise!

We loved glamorous singer Dusty Springfield and her beehive hairstyle, a style stiff with lacquer which stayed in place for weeks without benefit of brushing or washing. It was appalling to hear of a woman in Belfast who ended up with tiny insects nesting in her extravagant Amy Winehouse style feeding on her scalp! An urban myth?

There was no mousse in those days, instead beer was used to stiffen the hair into the desired set and often I'd return to work stinking of alcohol even thought I didn't drink a drop. We kept fit by jiving at every opportunity, stiffening our net under slips with a sugar solution so they stuck out as far as possible. My great joy was the can-can slip my uncle, Billy Graham, brought me from London. Layers and layers of pastel coloured net, the envy of all my girl friends although it proved quite hard to get close to your partner during a slow dance.

Another place to show off was the ice rink at the King's Hall and, despite the rumours that would filter through that as someone's fingers were lying at the top end of the rink, we weren't fazed, we believed we cut a dash and could tackle anything! Looking back I imagine we were terrible show offs but I suppose we were blinded by happiness.

The man I lost my heart to and lost my job at the same time! No complaints. Alan Hailes on Vidicon Marconi Camera One during Teatime with Tommy.

(opposite)
Not just a pretty face. Model Maureen Martin went on to build up a model agency which was second to none. The £12 tuition fee she paid Stella Goddard in the early 60s was an investment which paid dividends.

The adventurer and eminent film maker James MacQuitty, the producer of A Night to Remember acknowledged as the definitive story of the Titanic.
Belfast Telegraph

14
Midnight Oil

Whether or not that gave him the right to kiss
the girls I don't know and most of us
avoided the confrontation but
I think, had I known the genius of the man,
I might have thrown myself at him with open arms.

In 2007 UTV introduced a series of programmes looking back at past glories. In *UTV Rewind,* presenter Julian Simmons took the viewer from full colour, interactive, hi-tech television back to grainy, poor quality, black and white, fuzzy pictures and basic technology. It was indeed another era, a time without benefit of recording machines, Nor was there any 'autocue', a device for presenters to read their script as it passes over the camera lens.

Even when recording facilities did arrive in 1963, early machines had no editing facilities. 'Record as live' it was called, so it was every bit as nerve-racking and presented major headaches for the studio team. Some programmes required a series of photographs and these were propped up on a caption board. In the rush to get the correct photo in place for the camera, often the whole heap would fall over and it was back to the beginning. As it was if a presenter got muddled or if one of the overhead lamps would explode with a loud and alarming bang. There was no such thing as 'out takes' in those days, no matter how far you were through the programme, it was a case of doing the whole thing again – 'from the top'.

Midnight Oil and the sequel *Inquiring Mind* were classic productions in every way and it's hard to estimate how important these were, the very first adult education programmes on the network and said to be the inspiration for the Open University. *Midnight Oil* set the pattern.

There were six different subjects with their specialist presenters, 42 programmes in all, transmitted at 10.30 in the evening over the summer of 1962. The producer/director, Derek Bailey well remembers the punishing schedule and so do I. Although there were no scripts as such, there was an outline to be typed, the sequence of rehearsed shots noted, the timings finalised. Those were my jobs. It all came together in the studio, Derek following the presenter's words and cutting up the correct illustrative shots during what was essentially a lecture. Most were pretty basic, a blackboard, chalk and a stand up teacher.

Fortunately these 'teachers' were well selected and brilliant men, and each brought their own personality and academic quirks to the screen.

Andy Crockart, floor manager for the series, recalls how Derek instilled his unique touch to the production and, with designer Roy Gaston, devised a frame for the blackboard giving the impression that the knowledge was flowing out of the studio, through a television mast and into the home. Goodness, we don't even have blackboards anymore let alone 25 minute straight to camera addresses without autocue.

*

Andy had come to UTV from BBC less than a mile away in Ormeau Avenue. The BBC was more formal, a place to learn. He remembers how producers and management would look from their imposing white building towards the renovated shirt factory on Ormeau Road with some envy. "There was such a relaxed technique in Havelock House compared to the more stilted broadcasting of the BBC. They also admired the presentation skills of Anne and Ivor who were good to start with but grew in confidence and ability as they became more experienced."

Certainly the commercial company had a fresh new outlook on the scene in Northern Ireland. When the well-known tenor Peter Tomelty was compiling a list of songs for a recital he was giving on the BBC Home Service, the producer turned down one suggestion, *Lovely Derry on the Banks of the Foyle.* In the BBC lexicon, Derry didn't exist. It was Londonderry or nothing. When I worked in BBC Radio Ulster I was instructed that the first referenced must be Londonderry, thereafter Derry was acceptable. Years later Gerry Anderson got round the dilemma by referring to 'Londonderry-stroke-Derry' and so coined the answer to everything, Stroke City.

Andy joined UTV as a floor manager responsible for the studio through rehearsals and during transmission. Not for long. He displayed an enthusiasm which impressed! "I came back to Studio One for *Roundabout* afternoon rehearsal, I was handed the captions for that evening's programme. There amongst these credits was one that read, Director Andrew Crockart. Without even knowing it I'd become a director during lunchtime!"

Certainly the BBC watched *Midnight Oil* in 1962 and *Inquiring Mind* the following year, with great interest. As did the public. A new and bigger studio was opened that year offering additional facilities and *Inquiring Mind* certainly benefited. There were more visuals than it's sister programme, photographs, maps and film and room to expand the set. These programmes broke new ground in the sphere of education and they featured men who were at the top of their professions. In the *Inquiring Mind* series, James Boyce schoolmaster, writer and raconteur presented *Art with a small A.* During a planning meeting he brought to the production office a

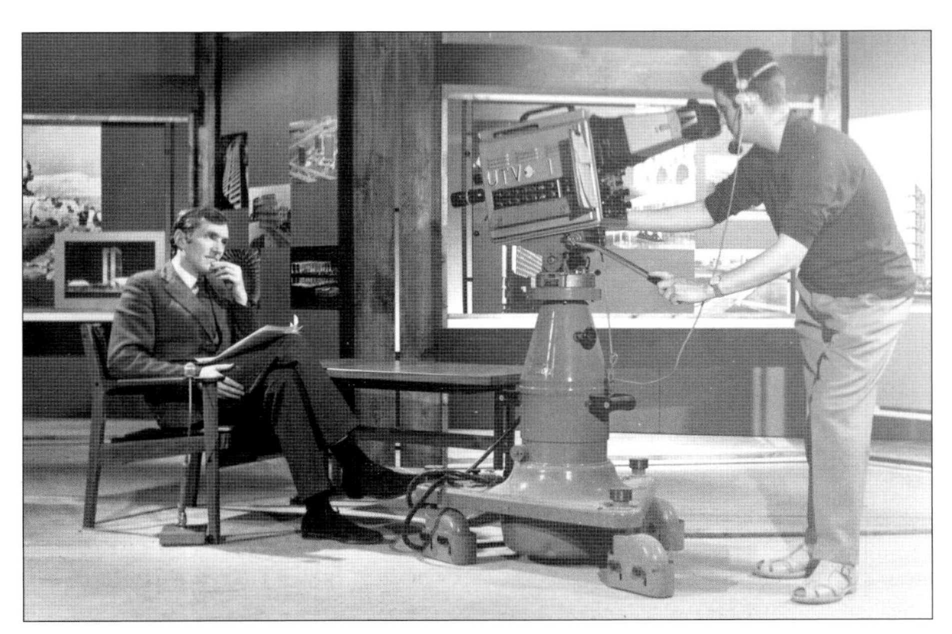

Brian Boyd during his series on architecture. Cameraman Jim Starrett.

painting by Pablo Picasso. It was *Guernica* and to my ill-educated eye, a jigsaw puzzle of nonsense, severed legs, tortured heads, dismembered bulls. Then the story of the Spanish town began to unfold.

The 1937 bombing of Guernica by the German Luftwaffe Condor Legion and the Italian Fascist Aviazione Legionaria was burned in to the artist's mind. Within 15 days of the attack, he produced the landmark painting which toured the world and was destined to hang in Madrid as an anti-war symbol and embodiment of peace.

There were the disasters to cope with too. During one *Midnight Oil* programme, Professor Philip Cranmer illustrated his lecture on music with the use of a grand piano. He was a very exciting character, indeed after his programme was recorded we had a little celebration with a few drinks and late in the evening Professor Cranmer was to be seen cycling around the ground floor of Havelock House singing at the top of his voice. Thank goodness because only hours before, in his enthusiasm for the subject, he had jumped up from the piano seat, smashed his head into the heavy overhead boom microphone and knocked himself out. That was a case of stop recording, clear up the blood, bind up the wound and 'from the top'. He proved to be so popular with the audience that he returned for the second series of programmes.

The Times obituary in 2006 read: 'An accomplished musician and a distinguished musicologist, Philip Cranmer exhibited throughout his life a healthy understanding of the balance required between the serious and the frivolous.' We were fortunate to experience both.

During *Inquiring Mind*, Brian Boyd talked of architecture and, amongst other topics over the weeks, introduced us to Cumbernauld in Scotland. Inspired in 1947 by the French architect Le Corbusier, this city was created in 1956 to accommodate the population overflow for Glasgow and is now part of Greater Glasgow urban area. As Brian explained, it featured concrete as the main ingredient and was planned around a multi-purpose town centre fringed by high density housing. It was before its time, designed so families would be able to walk safely to and from the centre without ever coming across a car. A private transport scheme was restricted to a number of wide roads running through the residential area and we learned that, once finished, the town centre would be the most remarkable feature of Cumbernauld. It would accommodate all the retail, public buildings, commercial offices and leisure needs of a town of 50,000 people, not forgetting a number of penthouse 'executive' apartments. This all sounds very familiar 50 years later when you consider the Titanic Quarter on Queen's Island in Belfast.

Professor Jack Pritchard with his assistant during the making of Inquiring Mind.

For me the series of two have become one in my mind, *Midnight Oil* ended and planning *Inquiring Mind* began, between all the other routine programmes we worked on.

They combined to give me all I had wanted from my school days and didn't get, learning on the grand scale, being taught by brilliant men who knew through their professionalism how to grab their audience. David Keith Lucas, son of the inventor of the first aeronautical compass, brought his expertise in aviation to the studio. At the time he was technical director at Short Brothers and Harland and responsible for many innovative designs. He was also a member of the senate of Queen's University in Belfast. In a written introduction to *Flight*, he talked about the Wright brothers making their first flights in a powered aeroplane in 1903. *"They flew at less than 40 mph. We now fly from Belfast to London at 400 mph......"*

Aviation came a long way in the first 60 years and even further in the next 50. Consider Concorde, a supersonic passenger aircraft which could travel faster than the speed of sound with a cruising speed of 1340 miles per hour.

Then there was war historian, Brigadier Ronald Broadhurst, an imposing man, tall, handsome with military bearing. He'd already experienced the studio when he presented *A Fighting Breed* in 1961, a series recalling great Ulster soldiers. Now his task was to take his audience through the *American Story* in which he highlighted ".... the part played by the Ulster Scots or the Scotch-Irish as they came to be known, played a part quite disproportionate to their numbers. This arose, no doubt of it, from the remarkable qualities of the Ulster Scots, and the greater of these qualities was, I believe, the invincible firmness and independence of their spirit."

He was very decisive, knew what he wanted and scolded me for a misprint in his notes. One day, when I was talking to him on the phone I got a tickle in my throat, probably due to terror. I began coughing and spluttering. "Put the phone down, Miss Shaw," He barked. "Now put it down at once. Ring me when you have recovered yourself." You knew where you stood with the Brigadier!

Another distinguished presenter was Scotsman, George Dick, professor of microbiology at Queen's. During the ten years he held this position, his most innovative work was carried out working with a dedicated team at the Royal Victoria Hospital. Over six feet tall, popular and erudite, he and his team revolutionised both the smallpox vaccination medical programme and poliomyelitis, even trying a new kind of live vaccine on his four-year-old daughter.

We did well for professors! Jack Pritchard, Professor of Anatomy and a man who some years later, appealed for body donation for dissection in the local press saying, "The body is extremely useful for medical research and teaching. We can't teach our medical students without bodies".

This was the calibre of man I was dealing with; what better education could I have had and working with Derek Bailey and his equally dedicated team taught me the value of never settling for second best.

*

One of the men who spearheaded the idea of *Midnight Oil* and the sequel *Inquiring Mind*, was William MacQuitty. MacQuitty was a member of the Board and on the days these worthies met, we could expect a visitation. They would tour the building greeting the staff, somewhat aloof and patronising but nonetheless interested in the glamorous world of television. The girls were advised how to behave almost to the point of curtseying and we hated the charade. They were on the periphery of our creative world although one, William MacQuitty, was way ahead of the game. Whether or not that gave him the right to kiss the girls I don't know and most of us avoided the confrontation however, in retrospect, I think had I realised the genius of the man, I might have thrown myself at him with open arms!

He was born in Belfast and at the age of 18 joined the Chartered Bank of India, Australia and China. So began his curriculum vitae. Later he joined the Auxiliary Punjab Light Horse at Amritsar. He was founder member of the Lahore Flying Club. This was an adventurer who obviously had a great love of life and could turn his hand to most things and his enthusiasm took him into areas he never dreamed of.

When he returned to Ireland in 1939, MacQuitty was set on taking up a medical course in London but after making an amateur film on Ulster farming, entitled *Simple Silage*, he gained plaudits from the Ministry of Information and was at once engulfed by the world of film. He worked with the stars of the day as a producer but it was his most famous film *A Night to Remember,* first seen in 1958, that brought him to the notice of the public. This was the definitive film of the sinking of *RMS Titanic*, a ship the young MacQuitty watched being launched 47 years earlier from the slipway at Harland and Wolff, no doubt standing on the VIP platform with his father who was MD of the *Belfast Telegraph.*

As producer of *A Night to Remember* he left no stone unturned when it came to research and survivors became his personal advisors. It certainly worked. The audience felt the chill of the North Atlantic, shivered as the story unfolded and marvelled at the recreation of the disaster. Apparently director James Cameron thanked him personally for contributing to the inspiration of his own 1997 *Titanic* film.

MacQuitty was drawn to Egypt and was involved in the attempts to save the temples of Abu Simbel. His photograph of Tutankhamun's funerary mask, which was seen all over the world, became a collector's item when it was used as the poster for the 1972 British Museum exhibition. He said that he considered he took full advantage of the Banquet of Life. Derek Bailey met him in Putney as they were leaving the funeral service for F.E. McWilliam, the eminent sculptor born in Banbridge Co. Down. "He turned to me and said, 'It's hardly worth my while going home!'" In fact William MacQuitty lived another 12 years. He died in London in 2004 at the age of 98.

I didn't realise the brilliance of this man and what he had achieved. How sad no one took the trouble to introduce him properly to the staff who would have loved to hear of his exploits and know him better. Looking back, I'm glad he got the better of me one day and kissed my cheek.

*

The name Derek Bailey punctuates this text and no wonder. He was my first boss, an inspiration and a friend since 1960. How fortunate for a young woman of 19 to be working with a man who squeezed the last drop of enthusiasm from life, a man who loved the challenge in those formative years of local television and would only accept the best. What a life. Steeped in music, an actor, a broadcaster and an award winning director and producer.

As a 13 year old pupil at Royal Belfast Academical Institution, known as Inst., he played the part of heroine Rosalind in *As You Like It*. His director was his English teacher James Boyce, destined to become a close friend and confidant and the star of many Ulster Television programmes.

Derek's first taste of broadcasting was as a child when he reported a live, on-the-spot commentary for BBC's Home Service. It was the switch-on of the City Hall Christmas tree lights. The programme was *Children's Hour* and the year 1946. Derek could hardly have imagined that this would lead to an international career.

It began when he joined Ulster Television in 1960 as a floor manager and it was only a matter of weeks before he moved to the production department to direct and produce. It's really nostalgic to talk with him about those years in Studio One and then Studio Two where there was more room to move and create. We talked of John D. Stewart who presented *Sol y Sombra* in which John relived his days as an architect in Spain. In his unique style he took the viewer on a journey through that country, the sights and sounds, the music and the language. Then here was the memorable *Nocturne* featuring concert pianists, and husband and wife, Ivor Mills and Muriel Hay, with their guests including Una O'Callaghan, Janette Simpson, Jim Shaw and Uel Deane. We remembered the programme *Only a Rose* to coincide with the World Rose competition held at Lady Dixon Park in South Belfast.

An all-star cast. Harold Goldblatt played the Victorian writer, clergyman and rose specialist Dean Hole and David Kernan, well known for his appearances in Ned Sherrin's satirical *That Was the Week That Was*, sang the First World War song *Roses of Picardy*, written by Frederick Weatherley, not for a sweetheart at home as many assume, but for a French widow who have him protection in her home!

The programme was presented by James Boyce who told the story of the Queen's Lancashire Regiment. Their cap badge features a golden crown and a red rose and apparently, when young cadets were initiated during the mess dinner, each held a red rose aloft whilst drinking its health, then they were expected to eat the flower. Without batting an eyelid, James told the tale holding a red rose gently in his hand. He raised his glass, made the toast and, to everyone's amazement, ate the rose!

We also talked of Patrick Riddell's moving and very personal series *I Remember I Remember* in which he talked of his life. "He had a cottage at Kirkistown on the Ards Peninsula and we planned it there." Derek recalls that he was very fond of music and was anxious to use a certain record. "It was the first time I'd heard *Fantasia* on a Theme of Thomas Tallis by the composer Ralph Vaughan Williams. A moment I will always remember."

*

Derek left Ulster Television in 1964 to take responsibility for the regional magazine programme for ATV in Birmingham. He returned for a short time in 1965 to pursue a management position and he was also involved in the consortium which unsuccessfully challenged UTV's contract in the 1970s. Probably a good thing it didn't work out in light of the exceptional career which was to follow. When he returned to the network it was to London Weekend Television, where he became senior director for their award winning network arts series *Aquarius,* working with Humphrey Burton and Peter Hall.

A little aside at this point – fate or a divine appointment? I was flying to London in December 2008 to visit Derek. At the International Airport, it all went wrong. When I passed through the security scanner it went mad so I was taken to one side and frisked. At the same time my bag set off another alert so it too was arrested and examined in minute detail. Turned out I was wearing a brooch which the scanner didn't like, and my bag contained a rogue tin of talcum powder. I'd been talking to a young woman as we queued. She was on her way home to

London following a degree course at Queen's University in Belfast. She kindly waited as I went through my embarrassment and we ran to the plane together, sat beside each other and continued our chat. She was studying drama. I boasted of my theatre experience playing mother to entertainer Lionel Blair in *Beauty and the Beast* in the *Grand Opera House, Belfast* and the *Gaiety Theatre, Dublin.* Then we talked about television and the possibility of work for this young actress. I spoke of Ulster Television, she told me her mother had worked as a production assistant with London Weekend Television in the 60s. We swopped phone numbers. As a result I talked to Rebecca's mother, Tina Hampson.

"It was wonderful in those days, the sense of freedom. We were able to follow our instincts, directors and producers were able to push out the boundaries because there were no boundaries! It was all live programming so the excitement was immense." She worked with David Frost, the pioneer of political satire and famous for his in-depth interviews, and on the series, *Upstairs Downstairs.* Then she dropped into the conversation that she also worked on *Aquarius.*

"Derek Bailey?" I ask. "Yes, yes, I worked for Derek." I could hear the excitement in her voice! "My first boss when I became a PA," I told her. "Where is he? How is he? Do you see him? Give him my love."

Now living most of his time in a small village in Suffolk, Derek Bailey continues to produce arts and music programmes.

*

Derek established his London based company, Landseer Film and Television Productions in 1977 but a lot of his heart is still at home. This is obvious when you read down the award winning list of television and film achievements, including ITV's first *Music Prix Italia,* the oldest and most prestigious international competition for quality radio and television, the *London Evening Standard* award for outstanding artistic achievement in ballet, a Prime Time Emmy nomination and the Gold Medal for Cultural Programmes at New York Festival. In amongst his credits, including documentaries on the *Hermitage in Leningrad* with Peter Ustinov and Natalie Wood and another on the beautiful ballerina Natalia Markarova plus live productions from the Royal Opera House and Covent Garden, you'll notice programmes on Northern Irish writers, a 16 part history of music with James Galway, over 20 concerts with the Ulster Orchestra not only with Cleo Laine and Kiri Te Kanawa, but also with Barry Douglas and again, James Galway. Edna O'Brien's *Mother Ireland* is in there too, as is *Heaney in Limboland.* Made in 1970, this programme was included in the 2009 BBC television hour long tribute to Seamus Heaney on his 70th birthday.

More recently Derek has been producing and directing the live TV link-up to the Royal Albert Hall during September's *Proms in the Park,* coincidentally most of them from the grounds of Belfast City Hall where for this talented man, it all began.

In a break away from being behind the scenes, in 2006 the BBC invited Derek to present a series of radio programmes where he chose music which meant something special to him, blending his special favourites with his personal stories.

Belfast Notes was an intriguing programme because, alongside the stars of the world stage, he highlighted the history and wealth of talent in Northern Ireland. There was the rare delight of hearing again the voice of James Johnston singing 'The Flower Song' from *Carmen*. A butcher by trade but an outstanding singer by profession.

In 1945 James had a visitor. The renowned theatre director Tyrone Guthrie arrived at the door one day to invite him to join the Sadler's Wells Opera Company, a great honour. The busy butcher, however, told him he would only consider a leading roll and if granted this, he'd decided whether or not he would join the company after a six week trial. Between the sausages and the kidneys, and I'm sure to some surprise, Guthrie considered, then accepted the ultimatum. The trial was successful. James left his shop in good hands and moved to London.

"At last," proclaimed Sir Adrian Boult in the late 40s when he first heard the Belfastman sing, "a great tenor". The eminent conductor had just heard James sing Pinkerton in a radio broadcast of *Madame Butterfly* and he sent the complimentary message by telegram to the BBC.

Johnston's career spanned 40 years and he was always a welcome visitor at Ulster Television. Down to earth, one of us, talking to him belied his credentials. Principal tenor at Sadler's Wells and Covent Garden and sharing opera stages all over the world with divas including Maria Callas, Dame Joan Sutherland, Victoria de los Angeles and Elisabeth Schwarzkopf.

"He was a very important character on the international music scene even before jet setting was the norm," Derek said. "Jimmy retired early in 1958 and went back to his butcher's shop on Sandy Row. I remember well how he would give an impromptu demonstration of Italian Opera as he was cutting the chops on a Saturday morning and there and then, Sadler's Wells came to the heart of Belfast."

*

When he was invited to break into his heavy schedule to compile *Belfast Notes*, Derek thought it would be easy.

"I was faced with the challenge of how to make programmes of interest to listeners other than myself and friends, to get the right balance of music and avoid boring people with too much 'name-dropping' of artists I have been fortunate enough to work with. And," he adds with a twinkle in his eye, "above all, not sounding too much like an old fogey with far too long a memory going back to my boyhood in Belfast in the closing years of the war!"

Although a classical series, Derek extended the story to include the many other strands of music he knows and loves and the people he has met and directed - Petula Clark, Bing Crosby, Alma Cogan and the great Louis Armstrong whom he filmed on that warm sunny summer day as the Jimmy Compton Jazz Band greeted the great man and his entourage when they arrived at Nutts Corner.

"I have many musical memories to draw on," Derek told me. "I began concert-going in Belfast when I was 12 and the memories began to build. The autograph books I have kept reflect memories of Sir Thomas Beecham in the Assembly Hall, Paul Robeson in the Grosvenor Hall, Sir Malcolm 'Flash Harry' Sargent in the Ulster Hall, Barbirolli at the King's Hall and later experiences with the Ulster Operatic Company, working with Havelock Nelson and Studio Opera Group before film and television took over my life."

Covent Garden, the Bolshoi, Glyndebourne just a handful of the prestigious stages he has mastered. At la Villette Paris he directed the epic 18 hour Chinese Opera *The Peony Pavilion* and from the Royal National Theatre Bill Bryden's *The Mysteries,* a cycle of medieval mystery plays. And that's only the half of it. There can be few, if any, local men who can boast such a list of credits and command respect from the best in the world. And just think, after school he graduated from Queen's University in Belfast with a Bsc.Econ and if he hadn't had the wit to immediately apply for and be accepted into the London Academy of Music and Dramatic Art, he might have been lost to the arts and ended up being an accountant.

When it came to setting standards within broadcasting, Ernie Strathdee was amongst the best. His knowledge and influence and his love of life touched all of us within the Ulster Television family.

15
Setting the Goal Posts

'Jokes built around bible stories, e.g. Adam and Eve, Cain and Abel, David and Goliath, must be avoided or any sort of parody of them.
All such words as God, Good God, My God, Blast, Hell, Damn, Bloody, Gorblimey, Ruddy etc., etc., are to be deleted from scripts and innocuous expressions substituted.'

When he died in December 2003 at 75, there were many tributes to Bob Monkhouse OBE and undoubtedly he was a superb performer.

During the 60s a film crew from Ulster Television went to London to record a series of interviews for a programme called *Heads or Harps,* a tongue-in-cheek look at the English perception of Northern Ireland. The results were of stunning ignorance. But then, it was a long time before the Troubles.

We had arranged to meet Monkhouse at the Paris Studios, to talk to him mainly because in 1949 he had married Elizabeth, an Ulster woman whom he'd met when they were both serving in the RAF. The marriage was dissolved in 1972 and he married his long time secretary the following year.

We arrived on time, he was late. We were hanging around a big studio area with a wide staircase running to a balcony above. Suddenly we heard a door open from on high, then close. We all looked towards the noise but, because of the light from a big window behind him, it was a few moments before we could make out a figure standing at the top of the staircase looking down. It was the man himself. When he got no reaction for his small audience below stairs, the sarcastic voice boomed out, "What's wrong, are my flies open?" I was embarrassed – it was 1963 and men didn't talk like that in front of a woman. He must have been annoyed when his comment went down like a lead balloon as once the interview was over, he left without a word of farewell. So I had an in-built dislike but I must admit through the years the very force of his talent changed that.

His final television programme, when he knew he was dying, was moving. Sitting in his garden, he put himself on record and stripped of arrogance, talked of his life and impending death.

After he died in December 2003, his family allowed a short cleverly edited film to be made and shown during Male Cancer Awareness Week advising men to check for prostate cancer. Featuring effective black humour, it had everyone talking and raised the awareness of this cancer to an all time high. Using a body double, an actor who imitated his voice and computer technology, Monkhouse is seen standing in a graveyard next to his own gravestone talking about prostate cancer.

"What killed me kills one man per hour in Britain. That's even more than my wife's cooking." Before he turned and walked away from camera he said almost as an afterthought, "As a comedian, I've died many deaths. Prostate cancer, I don't recommend. I've paid good money to stay out of here. What's it worth to you?"

Compare his brainpower to some younger comedians and their messy, and to me anyway, unfunny jokes. They should take a few lessons from the master.

*

Television was an education for most of us, especially for me as I'd been asked to leave school when I was 15. A good day's work by headmaster John Derbyshire at Belfast Royal Academy. He realised I was seriously bored, school wasn't grabbing my imagination and he suggested to my father that someone else could take up the academic opportunity I was squandering. I should go, he said, and do something more practical. He was right. Walking down Cliftonville Road on my last day of institutional learning I recall so well hop scotching between the cracks on the pavement and thinking, never-again-will-I-ever-have-to-do-home-work—never-ever-again.

My new classroom was Havelock House.

When television was an entirely live entity there was plenty of room for the 'wow' factor, sometimes good, sometimes not so good. I was sitting watching the screen at home on the night a long time taboo was blown out of the water. Theatre critic and writer Kenneth Tynan broke all the rules when he used that four letter word. It was 13th November 1965 during a live debate when Tynan, commenting on the subject of censorship said, "I doubt if there are any rational people to whom the word 'fuck' would be particularly diabolical, revolting or totally forbidden."

This was the first time the word had been spoken on national television. Someone later called Tynan's use of the word 'his masterpiece of calculated self-publicity,' adding 'for a time it made him the most notorious man in the country.'

In films, bedroom scenes required the male actor to keep one foot on the ground; when it came to romance on television, explicit bedroom scenes didn't happen until Fred and Wilma Flintstone came along, the first couple to be shown in bed together on prime time TV.

Those were the days when the Green Book was still considered the rigid guide to acceptable humour in the BBC, apparently demanding 'an absolute ban on lavatories, effeminacy in men; immorality of any kind; suggestive references to honeymoon couples; chambermaids, fig leaves, prostitution, ladies' underwear (e.g. winter draws on), animal habits (e.g. rabbits), lodgers, commercial travellers.' Extreme care was urged in dealing with 'references to or jokes about pre-natal influences (e.g. his mother was frightened by a donkey); marital infidelity ... the vulgar use of such words as 'basket' must also be avoided.'

So said the good book although in the 50s the guide apparently could not make up its mind about biblical jokes. 'Jokes built around bible stories, e.g. Adam and Eve, Cain and Abel, David and Goliath, must be avoided or any sort of parody of them. All such words as God, Good God, My God, Blast, Hell, Damn, Bloody, Gorlimey, Ruddy etc., etc., are to be deleted from scripts and innocuous expressions substituted.'

And bad news for would-be Rory Bremners of the day, no unauthorised impersonation of elder statesmen was allowed, even Winston Churchill.

And something which people in general would do well to pay attention to today - the Green Book instructs there must be, 'special considerations for overseas broadcasts where humour is limited by different social, political and religious taboos from our own. The term Boer War should not be used – South African War is correct. Jokes about harems are offensive in some parts of the world and jokes like - enough to make a Maltese Cross - are of doubtful value'. Even reference to the MacGillycuddy of the Reeks was to be avoided.

On occasions even the BBC had their moments. Pussy Cat Willum appeared in a children's series called *Small Time* with presenters Wally Whyton and Muriel Young. It was massively popular, 400 letters a week and a huge audience and being live, the two had to ad lib through the commercial breaks if too few advertisements were booked. On such a day, under pressure, Wally announced that he'd been to the Chelsea Owls Ball and Muriel in all innocence replied, 'I didn't know owls had balls.'

On 13 November 1965, I was watching with my parents when Tynan dropped his bombshell. There was total silence, none of us reacted, at least not out loud. I bet like me, their hearts were pounding in their chests. It was not referred to then nor has it been since. Publicly there was uproar.

The BBC issued an apology; the outrage was raised in The House of Commons and Mary Whitehouse, campaigner for morals and decency, wrote to the Queen suggesting that Tynan should have "his bottom spanked." Tynan's television career was finished but in a few seconds he managed to break all the rules of decency with his comment and from that moment the rot set in and gradually standards were eroded until the situation of today where there seem to be few boundaries yet to be crossed. What I wonder would Mary Whitehouse make of comedians Billy Connolly, Jonathan Ross or Russell Brand?

Although on that night Tynan left no room for innuendo, others did, often unwittingly as with Sylvia Peters. I didn't witness this one but the faux pas of all faux pas is widely acknowledged when this pristine announcer, a dancer before becoming the face of BBC until 1959, smiled as she gave her windup.

It happened at the end of one of the BBC's most popular programmes starring one of the first truly spectacular celebrities, Fanny Cradock, a woman who dressed in ball gowns to cook in her studio kitchen set and whose make-up rivaled any pantomime dame. She was a natural personality, married four times, one even took place whilst she was still legally married but when she met Johnnie Cradock it became a working partnership. It's reported that he left his wife and four children and had no contact with them for the rest of his life although he and Fanny didn't marry until 1977 after the collapse of her television career. She'd been a reasonably successful novelist and children's author before turning to restaurant reviews with Johnnie. They presented *Kitchen Magic* where the couple turned theatres into restaurants, cooking on an extravagant scale and then serving these meals to the audience. They packed out the Royal Albert Hall for their Christmas show in 1956.

Their 'act' developed, he portraying the tipsy, hen-pecked husband, she the domineering wife. When their television show reached its peak in the late 50s, it was essential viewing. The chiffon gowns confirmed her belief that cooking is 'a cleanly art not a grubby chore' adding charmingly, 'only a slut gets in a mess in the kitchen.'

She also had a serious side to her work, using wholesome ingredients, campaigning against artificial flavourings and fertilizers and exposing that monkfish was being used in restaurants as a cheaper alternative to prawns.

So it was that one day on television she prepared an elaborate children's party table, and Silvia Peters was watching. Decorations, flowers, cakes, dishes, and, the pièce de résistance, doughnuts. Looking regal, she brought these delicacies to the table, piled high, covered in sugar and the heat still rising; she placed the plate in the middle of the table. Roll end captions. Fade up Silvia Peters looking beautiful and poised in her chair. Cue Silvia's windup to the programme. "Wasn't that wonderful, and if you are planning to make doughnuts for your children's party, I hope they all turn out to look just like Fanny's."

Of course, stories like this are legion in journalism. The newspaper reporting on a royal visit to Dublin in 1900 for instance. Above a photograph of the procession, the headline screamed, 'Queen Victoria pisses over O'Connell Street Bridge.' Only worse was another headline at another time, 'Queen Mary Having Bottom Scraped.'

Again many years ago, an obituary of a very much-loved bishop in the Republic of Ireland read, 'he leaves three sisters and a brothel.'

In a radio phone-in quiz show, a lady in the south of England came to the final question and was hovering on the verge of a sizable cash prize. The question, 'who was the famous Formula One racing commentator who retired last year?' The answer was Murray Walker. 'Oh, give me a clue,' pleaded the well spoken woman at the end of the phone. Thinking of Murray Mint sweets, the host prompted her, 'you can suck his first name'.

Immediately, and getting her sports commentators somewhat mixed, the woman shouted in excitement, 'Yes, yes, I know the answer, Dickie Davis."

An unfortunate malapropism came nearer home. At the beginning of a UTV programme, the production assistant was about to give the instruction to start the Ampex recording machine. She leaned forward, flicked the switch and called out to the operator at the other end, 'Roll Tampax', before slipping under the desk in embarrassment. Remember it was the beginning of the 60s when such things were never acknowledged and certainly not spoken of out loud.

Poor Brian Johnston, the BBC cricket commentator had an equally red face during a commentary which has gone down in the annals of broadcasting history. It was a test match when the English team included the batsman Peter Willey. The West Indian fast bowler Michael Holding was about to run up and deliver. Hush as the fielders took their places just in time for Johnston to remind listeners "The bowler's Holding, the batsman's Willey."

Frequently we had visiting freelance floor managers and directors and I was struck on numerous occasions by the difference between our colloquial speech and theirs. I took an Australian cameraman for a drive along the north coast stopping at Ballycastle for lunch. It was a lovely day, lots of people about and the restaurant was full. "I think we should go on a bit further," I suggested, "there's an awful lot of people waiting to eat." We found somewhere else but on the return journey he asked me, somewhat hesitantly, what was wrong with the people in the first restaurant. I didn't understand. "You said they were awful."

On another occasion, a Cockney director looked up from the evening paper as he sat in the newsroom. "Cor," he said looking puzzled, "I can't believe the way people in Northern Ireland die in alphabetical order."

The Sportscast set with presenters Ernie Strathdee and Malcolm Brodie.

An embarrassing *double entendre* came when I invited a director from the West End of London to come up for a bite of tea and a bit of craic. The light nearly left his eyes, 'a bit of crack?' I'm not sure what he was thinking but it wasn't what I was offering.

For some being funny wasn't a joke. The brilliant comedian Ken Dodd topped the bill at Blackpool in 1958 and began popping up on television. At the time his trade mark 'buck' teeth were reported to be insured for a massive £10,000 but there were conditions laid down: he wasn't allowed to eat seaside rock, ride a motorbike nor play rugby and he was required to brush his teeth three times a day. Life at the top!

Compared to the swingometers and rolling graphics employed in current coverage, the 1965 election results studio was a very basic affair. Nonetheless, coverage was fast and efficient thanks to the men and women behind the scenes including Bill McGookin (news room) and presenters Brian Durkin and Ivor Mills.

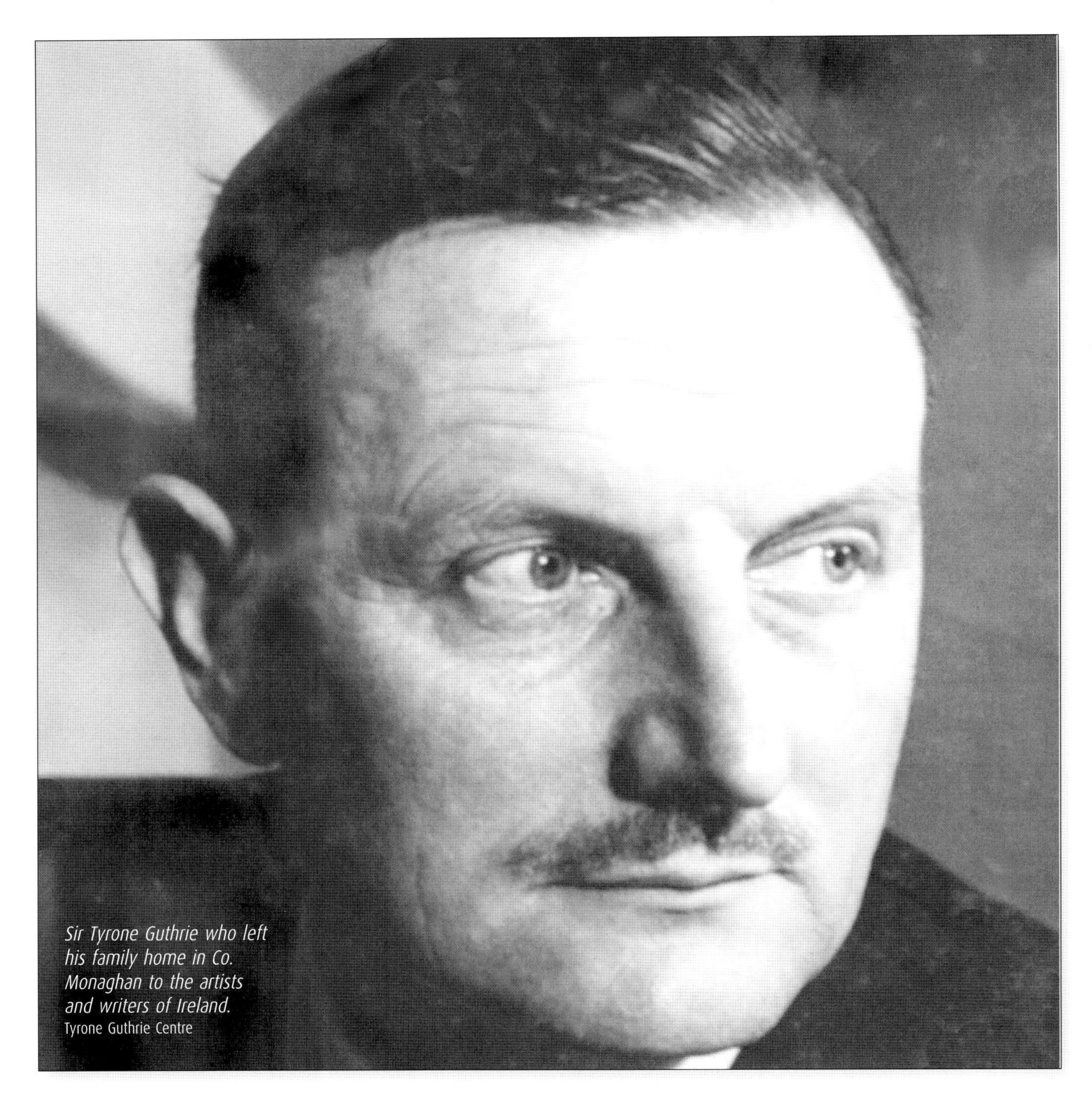

Sir Tyrone Guthrie who left his family home in Co. Monaghan to the artists and writers of Ireland.
Tyrone Guthrie Centre

16
Imposing Figures

22nd April 2009.
Annaghmakerrig. Co. Monaghan.

Early morning. I'm sitting at the bay window overlooking the gardens and the lake beyond. There's the delightful smell of freshly cut grass as Paddy works on the slope outside the front door. The shoreline of Annaghmakerrig Lake is fringed by dark firs and already it's glistening in the sun. I can just see the pointy roof of a little gazebo.

The big Victorian baronial style house is surrounded by trees, lime and chestnut rise between mature shrubs. Rhododendrons are blood red and a warm haze hangs over them. Birds are celebrating the day and the swallows have arrived. There's a constant buzz of bees. My laptop is resting on a round rosewood table with brass inlay. Result? Happiness.

This is the sitting room of Sir Tyrone Guthrie's house at Annaghmakerrig outside the village of Newbliss in Co. Monaghan. This is the table I sat at 45 years earlier with director Derek Bailey, cameraman Sean Macgaffin, Paul Irwin on sound, Lady Judith and Sir Tyrone, one of the biggest men in theatre, both literally and metaphorically. The famous theatre and costume designer Tanya Moiseiwitsch sat opposite, beside her a small animated gentleman, also a theatrical but regrettably I don't know his name.

Tyrone Guthrie was a caring man, and thanks to the urging of his sister Susan, he left this glorious welcoming house to a new extended family, artists from around the world. Today it is supported by both Arts Councils in Ireland under the chairmanship of Brian Garrett and the Centre operates under the caring eye of director Pat Donlon. In April 2009 it boasts 10 bedrooms carefully redesigned to provide working space and lots of light. Outhouses in the farmyard have been converted to self-catering cottages, there's a conservatory, performance space and studios for artists and musicians, all renovated under the direction of architect Fergus Flynn-Rogers. Yet, as we met together, the ambience was still that of a family home, Guthrie's home place. In the main rooms, it seems everything is in place just as it was when I first visited.

The stone steps up to the big double doors, half glass set in a heavy oak surround, a mortise lock and a fancy key are the same. So is the stone slab entrance hall with oriental rugs, the stern staircase on one side with its stout balustrade. The stair carpet has brass runners and the walls are a mellow burnt orange with a dark cream vaulted ceiling. Throughout the house are treasures left in place as directed by the owner in his will. There are literally thousands of books. I notice in my attic bedroom the bookshelf carries *Romance and Reality* by L.E.L inscribed by Guthrie's grandmother, Martha Moorhead and dated November 27th, 1856 and *The Anatomy of Melancholy* by Democritus Junior. Between rests *Sam McAughtry's Belfast* 1981. A late addition!

This is gracious living and the day goes quickly. Writing, walking in the garden, making cups of tea in the big farmhouse kitchen and writing again.

Now the light is fading and the dusk chorus has begun, blackbirds, thrushes and swallows. Almost time for someone to sound the gong in the hall to summon the house to dinner. By tradition, once the gong is struck, the person must bow to the nearby bust of Sir Tyrone in recognition of his great generosity. Also, by tradition, residents change for dinner, candles are lit and the wood stove casts a warm glow. Four Moiseiwitsch sketches hang on the wall and theatrical memorabilia is all around. We are always aware we are working in the place where he lived for many years and then bequeathed to the nation, insisting that artists of all disciplines north and south, and from further a field, would use it for inspiration, peace and productivity. The Tyrone Guthrie Centre is now supported by the Arts Councils of the Republic of Ireland and Northern Ireland and I'm one of about 12 paying guests staying in the house, others live in cottages in the stable yard. There's a sculptor, a movie script writer, an American wood carver and three young men, one from Wales, one from Ireland and one from Romania, working on movement for an arts installation in Dublin next month. There's a television journalist, the rest of us are writers.

It's a case of déjà vu as I look back.

*

One day in the early 60s I went on a memorable journey with director Derek Bailey, Paul Irwin and Sean MacGaffin. Sean was a Belfast Protestant, fluent in Irish, a leprechaun of a man who smoked Sweet Afton and liked his Guinness and a chaser - Irish Whiskey. He filmed from day one in UTV until he retired to his cottage in Donegal on Loughros Point where he tended his vegetable beds and painted – and introduced me to poteen. He came up against many a difficult situation and unsavoury characters during his time filming for Ulster Television programmes but, as his great friend Andy Crockart recalls, he'd come out with a string of threats in Irish and his florid punctuation stopped them in their tracks long enough for a quick getaway.

The famous 'Big House', Annaghmakerrig, Newbliss, Co. Monaghan.

We were off to cover a story in Co. Monaghan. I'm glad I had my best suit on because we were destined for Newbliss and the home of Tyrone Guthrie. Although he was born in Tunbridge Wells in Kent in 1900, this colossus of the theatre came to live in his family home, Annaghmakerrig House, Newbliss, Co. Monaghan at six months of age. After an international career, he died here in 1971.

I was to come to understand just how important this man was although, on that day, he didn't give the impression of being an multi-award winning Anglo-Irish theatrical director who broadcast with the BBC in the early 1920s, first in Belfast and then in London. He was also destined to become a distinguished Chancellor of Queen's University in Belfast but at that time he was listed as 'Actor Manager'.

He took his productions round the world, establishing theatres and directing both plays and operas. He had just been knighted and we were excited when he and Lady Judith invited us to stay for lunch. In a big airy dining room we took our places at a round rosewood table. Fine china plates with hair cracks, heavy uncut Waterford crystal glasses, silver cutlery and a magnificent three panelled screen behind Sir Tyrone which was covered with cut-out faces of all the famous screen stars and actors he'd worked with, including his cousin the Hollywood actor Tyrone Power.

Guthrie was a giant of a man. He once said:

Women to whom one has just been introduced think that it breaks the ice if they scream, 'Goodness, you're tall!" How would they like it if I broke the ice first, by screaming "Goodness, what thick ankles!" or "Goodness what a bust!"

The talk that lunchtime was centred round the jam factory he had opened in 1962 to give employment to local families. With the arrival of stores in nearby towns would the project was threatened? In the end it was a case of mismanagement at local level which caused the failure. To Guthrie's deep sadness, a great deal of money was lost. But that was yet to come. Our day was optimistic and fun.

The small man at the table, he may have been a designer, was telling us about the final dress rehearsal of Wagner's Tannhäuser. Although essentially a love story, at one point, knights with drawn swords rush on to do ill to the hero. Unfortunately, the dramatic effect was lost as they arrived on stage wearing their leather helmets back to front. He had a wonderful gift of description and had everyone laughing.

Tanya Moiseiwitsch grew up surrounded by music and theatre. Her father was the celebrated pianist Benno Moiseiwitsch and her mother a concert violinist. She is credited as being a pioneering figure in 20th century theatre design excelling not only in classical productions but modern theatre sets as well. She served her

Sir Tyrone leaves his retreat one day in 1962, at the height of his career and a jam factory to run.

apprenticeship at the Abbey Theatre in Dublin designing around 50 productions in five years, invaluable experience for a girl still in her 20s. But it was her relationship with Tyrone Guthrie which is best remembered. According to *The Independent* newspaper obituary in February 2003: *They complemented each other extremely well, with her deceptively quiet demeanour contrasting wonderfully with his mixture of barking Field Marshal Montgomery and a giggling scoutmaster, greeting any setback with an unexpectedly high-pitched "Oh, fucky-poo!" before, inevitably, "Rise above. On! On!"*

As the others enjoyed an after luncheon drink and cigar, Lady Judith and I left the big house, crossed the driveway and the fields to walk round the lake. She asked me about my work and was interested in the new television station so recently opened. It was all reminiscent of the Lake Isle of Innisfree, hearing lake water lapping and low sounds by the shore.

When he bequeathed this beautiful house to be a place of creative retreat for artists and writers, Guthrie wrote in his will

".... my said dwelling-house, furniture, pictures and chattels and the income of my residuary estate to be used for the purpose of providing a retreat for artists and other like persons, ... So as to enable them to do or facilitate them in doing creative work."

Since that time, many of the people who have benefited from this gesture are legends themselves, either staying within the house or in the cottages. There is no hurry here, no timepieces to be seen, make what food you want in the big kitchen during the day. The only stipulation is that houseguests meet together for dinner at seven. It means we sit at a long refectory table and enjoy conversation with a glass of wine and delicious food cooked by Lavina McAdoo-Toal.

Yesterday I drove to the church where Guthrie, and the family before him, attended Divine Worship and where he and his wife are buried. It's a large family plot marked out by a low stone wall and a barley stick iron surround.

The daffodils are almost over, the dandelions are thriving and speedwell and violets are struggling against the new grass. Aghabog Parish Church of Ireland is on top of a hill and the wind is making the yew trees moan and sigh. It's very peaceful, no more than 40 graves scattered on the hillside, some going back too far to distinguish the lettering.

Tyrone Guthrie's headstone lists family from James Moorhead MD born in 1761 to his great grandfather actor Sir William Tyrone Power, his daughter Norah Guthrie and her son Sir William Tyrone Guthrie born 2 July 1900 died 15th May 1971.

When I was planning this chapter, I had a phone call from a young woman friend. "What about you?" she asked. "Great, I'm just about to commit Tyrone Guthrie to paper," I replied. "What? You poor thing," she laughed, "that sounds like a horrible illness." She'd never heard of him. By the end of our phone call, however, she knew a lot more.

Now I've returned to the house, I too have learned so much more. In the library Martina Beagan invited me to rummage through deep drawers full of letters, legal documents, photographs, theatre plans and sketches which she hopes to archive, a mammoth task. I notice a faint typed cast list of *The Bishop's Bonfire* including Joseph Tomelty, Noel Purcell, Milo O'Shea, Siobhan McKenna and Kathleen Ryan. Imagine such a star-studded cast of Irish actors all in one play, probably long before they were famous.

I'm grateful for the permission granted to reproduce parts of two letters which were returned to Annaghmakerrig for archiving. He wrote in a large hand with frequent capitals and underlining to emphasise words. Some say he adopted this style as his mother's sight was quite poor and he felt it would make it easier for her. I came across one letter which interested me in light of our dinner conversation over 40 years ago. It was dated October 1965 and addressed to his close friend, Fania Lubitsch, Tel Aviv, Israel.

He relates how he is working on Benjamin Britten's opera *Peter Grimes* which he will produce at the Metropolitan Opera in New York in fifteen months time.

They need the models and drawings a year ahead! We got back from Minneapolis about 6 weeks ago. I have finished there now as director (after 3 years) we hope to go back from time to time to do a play, when wanted. I think it is now a well-rooted tree and will grow – the theatre, I mean. I am now engaged to make a film. It seems odd to want to be the OLDEST THING in the film industry (with the possible exception of Joan Crawford) but there it is! I thought I should have a try while somebody is still willing to give me a chance. The story is an interesting one. He adds. *We'll hope for the best. To change the subject. Can you please HELP ... you know we have started a small jam factory in Newbliss to give employment. It's doing rather well and we would like to expand our range to include MARMALADE. Can you put me in touch with an exporter of suitable type of orange (bitter 'Seville' type) in Israel. We cannot import in very large quantity and can only afford very moderate price. But we should hope to be a regular customer and to import in gradually increasing quantity.*

Unfortunately it was not to be.

When he died in 1971 one of the first letters of condolence was from Fania Lubitsch. Lady Judith replied:

'I'd always imagined that letters of condolence would be weep-making but they aren't. They are stimulating, as you say, 'The Friend is Here'. It was such a blessing that Tony was at home instead of driving the car alone and too fast or flying around alone lecturing in the USA. Which was to have been his next project. And that the end was so swift. And that he didn't have to face a long illness or the problems of retirement.' She added that his heart had been in poor condition but he persisted in over working. *'But, as you know, over working was what he liked.'*

I also discovered something else, Miss Worby, affectionately known as Bunty, the resident ghost. Miss Worby worked as a nurse in Tunbridge Wells in the hospital founded by Tyrone Guthrie's doctor father. When he died, the young woman came to Co. Monaghan as companion to his widow. She then became housekeeper, stern but kind, keeping the housemaids in check and the stable lads in place. In the house there is a hand written cookbook although I can't imagine her pear and almond torte was a patch on Lavina's!

So it happened, when shopping in Cootehill village store, Bunty met and fell in love with Duncan Campbell, a handsome young lad destined to fight in France in the First World War. She was very much in love and he only had eyes for her. One memorable day they took the little boat from the shore and spent the day together on the lake, drifting and talking until sunset. At the end of their lovely day, he broke the news that he was going to France to fight but promised he would be back.

They said their sad goodbyes and she never saw him again.

Miss Worby fell ill and Tyrone Guthrie sent for her brother. She pleaded to be taken home to England to die but he turned a deaf ear. When she passed away he didn't want to spend money bringing her body back to London, so she was cremated and scattered in the garden, under the white rose bush by the side of the house. Now she walks through the house and gardens listening for her dead lover's footsteps, but he doesn't come. She is still a presence, oversees the household, checks out the guests, always accompanied by her little dog Patch. Strange things are reported. Apparently quite recently, a lady was working in the library one still evening when the heavy casement windows flew open. One of my new friends here woke in the night and found she couldn't sit up in bed because of something heavy on her chest. This experience has been reported before and is not an isolated incident. The stories around this house are fascinating but confidentially is important.

Sir Tyrone Guthrie was revered and respected, stretched his artists to their limits and received the very best from them. He delighted audiences with his productions and his presence. His generosity of spirit lives on in this wonderful rambling, inspiring house.

*

Eoin 'Pope' O'Mahony being interviewed by Ernie Strathdee for the series, Look Here.

One of the most imposing figures to grace the Ulster Television studio was Eoin O'Mahony who, when asked what he wanted to be when he grew up replied, "The Pope". Ever after he was known as Pope O'Mahony. This barrister, genealogist, lecturer, raconteur and world traveller as well as being a Knight of Malta, was a welcome guest and the craic was mighty when he sat under the warm lights to expound on any topic thrown his way. I think the programme was *Look Here* and the interviewer Ernie Strathdee. The Pope's cousin, David Tynan O'Mahony, was also well known but by another name, comedian Dave Allen, both brilliant performers who loved an audience.

Then there was a gentleman, child psychologist as I remember who sat in the studio and told the world that children who sucked their thumbs had been deprived at the mother breast. Looking back now I can see the sense but at the time I thought he was barking mad.

*

He looked shyly round the corner of the big scene dock doors into Studio One. Who was this little man in dark clothes? He turned out to be Markey Robinson, a boxer, merchant seaman and painter. He was becoming a collectors item even in 1962 with his very fresh look at painting, geometric Irish countryside in blocks of muted colour. He was being called a naïve expressionist and he was prolific. Apparently, any surface was his canvas whether it was the back of wallpaper, hardboard, packing cases or shoe boxes, he even painted on glass bottles. Robinson's father encouraged this talent which was first recognised at Perth Street Public Elementary School in Belfast and later nurtured at Belfast College of Art. He became known as Markey, a traveller who travelled light to allow room for his paints and brushes. Just as he'd paint on any surface, no matter where he was he'd paint any subject. Still life in the vivid colours in Spain, nudes in France, the greys and greens of Ireland. He's been imitated but a real Markey stands out as unique, a joyful painting and a sizable investment.

Interesting men but none could hold a candle to Tyrone Guthrie.

James Boyce, Derek Bailey and their studio guest Venus de Milo.

17
So Many Characters

One 12th day I was to work in Havelock House.
My path took me to Donegall Pass right at the
time the local parade was marching.
I went to race between the men in
order to cross the road and on to Havelock Street.
A man grabbed me,
'you don't break the lodge wee girl'
he informed me in no uncertain terms.

He was famous, but didn't realise just how famous and this was well demonstrated the day he received a letter addressed 'James Joyce Dublin'. Someone at the post office had written 'Try James Boyce Belfast'. Indeed it was for him and he was tickled pink. James gave me a tremendous appreciation of journalism, the power of the written word even more than the spoken word. He had the gift of the gab, he spoke in pictures, slowly and deliberately, thoughtfully and fluently and this ability was evident in print.

He was a most popular man, loved by his friends. James was always ready for adventure, especially on the '11th Night', the evening before the 12th July processions, when bonfires blaze and loyalist songs were sung. It's the night women begin making loaves of sandwiches for their men to take to *The Field*, in the 60s at Finaghy, in the 21st century in the grounds of Barnett Demesne, South Belfast.

It was good humoured in those days. Once at *The Field* the lodges relaxed after the long walk and attended the open air service giving thanks that the Protestant King Billy defeated his father-in-law, the Catholic King James at the Battle of the Boyne. It was a holiday for everyone no matter their persuasion and many Catholic café owners would sell hot food and supply drinks along the route. That was to change radically in years to come.

There was always underlying tension. One 12th day I was to work in Havelock House.

My path took me to Donegall Pass right at the time the local parade was marching. I went to race between the men in order to cross the road and on to Havelock Street. A man grabbed me, 'you don't break the lodge wee girl' he informed me in no uncertain terms. Chilling. Being very brave and young I told him I had to get to Ulster Television and no one was going to stop me. It was a compromise, he held on to me until there was a long gap between the one band and the next, he loosened his hold and I was off. Although there are aspects of folk festival, it's serious business for two days every July, from 1690 probably to infinity and beyond. It is the highlight of the year for Orangemen throughout the world.

There's an old joke from those days. A woman rings up a landlady in Ramsey, Isle of Man asking for accommodation for a family holiday during the 12th week in July. The reply was short and sharp. "Sorry, in the Isle of Man we only have four weeks in July."

Loyalist Sandy Row was the centre of the 11th Night festivities and legend has it that James Boyce was a neutral leader of the fun. Apparently a group of revellers would cavort from one end of the famous street to the other, in and out the pubs, dancing round the high bonfires. Catholics and Protestants together and those who had no allegiance to any faith. The craic was something else but then it always was when James was around.

He was high profile in the world of the arts enjoying the bohemian life and his home in University Street was the centre of activity, a salon every Saturday morning when his wife Dorothy would make a pot of stew or some such and the people who sat round their table were the cream of the artistic life of Belfast in the 50s and 60s.

I learned so much from him. In UTV, the big production office was the centre of our universe. It was above the Board Room and while the planning and the finances were discussed on the middle floor of the old shirt factory, the creative juices put it all into action on the top floor before it transferred to the little studio at ground level. We had an exercise class, a choir, we put on theatre productions during lunchtime and one day, the girls were developing a competition which was overheard by James Boyce. Each person tried to outdo the other with their word game.

'Rest your head on this feather pillow,' she whispered softly.

'Pass me that knife,' he demanded cuttingly.

'This is lemon juice, I asked for orange,' he spat bitterly.

'Get those babies to keep quiet,' he ordered childishly.

'Why don't you use some wire wool on that dirty saucepan,' he advised harshly?

That was early afternoon. Next morning in the *Belfast News Letter* our game was reported on at length with a few suggestions by James himself. We were thrilled with the recognition but for me there was something else. In that short time, a journalist had phoned in an article and it appeared in print before breakfast next morning. That was the magic of newspapers and I never forgot that realisation.

We loved playing games, in our lunchtime theatre group, *Swish of the Curtain* we guessed books, plays and films simply from a mime, almost ten years before entertainer Lionel Blair's popular TV show *Give Us A Clue.*

And the jokes and quips kept coming. Did you know that in the 1400s an English law allowed a man to beat his wife with a stick no thicker than his thumb? So the saying *rule of thumb*. And in Scotland, a new sport involving hitting a small ball round a field was barred to women, *Gentlemen Only, Ladies Forbidden* was the rule which gave rise to GOLF. Today there is a little more equality! Men, allegedly, can read smaller print than women, however, balance is restored as, allegedly, women can hear better than men.

I became fascinated with these little facts of life; for instance, in Shakespeare's time, horse hair mattresses were tied to the frame of the bed by ropes that had to be pulled tight every night to keep it in place. So the wish *sleep tight* came into being. Thousands of years ago in the ancient city of Babylon, for four weeks after a wedding the bride's father would award his son-in-law all the mead he could drink to ensure strength and wellbeing. Mead is a honey based drink and so those four sweet weeks became known as the honey month or the honey moon. And talking of drink, ale is ordered in pints and quarts and in the olden days when customers had a little too much and became unruly, the landlord would shout, *settle down boys, mind your pints and quart.* This was shortened to *mind your P's and Q's.* And one more. In those same olden days, an ale tanquard was often made with a whistle in the handle so when the drink was drained the customer blew his whistle for attention hence, *wet your whistle.*

*

When television was the new kid on the block, a programme was conceived, rehearsed and transmitted live and was gone into the ether. No trace of it was left except a script and perhaps a piece of film. On the other hand, newspapers lived forever. They lined drawers, they were used as underfelt beneath carpet, were used as 'paper sticks' to light fires, held fish and chips and were stored under the stairs, they could be around in 100 years time with their news and views, and with microfilm, much longer.

Although I was a staff member with Ulster Television for six years between 1959 and 1966, when I married I went into the public relations business and subsequently broadcasting, all the time I was building a career writing for newspapers. I thank James Boyce for that insight one day in 1962 and my great-grandfather, John Shaw, who worked in the *Northern Whig* and wrote a series of books in 1910.

One lunchtime I went into the production office. There was no one there in any of the four small side offices or in the main room, except James. He was sitting at a desk with his head in his hands.

James was happy in any situation be it a live commercial for tea or the most serious of programmes. He was the consummate professional.

He was weeping. I went to him and asked what was wrong.

"I was born prematurely and I will die prematurely," was all he said.

I tried to cheer him suggesting he couldn't possibly know that but I realised he meant what he said. That must have been 1964. James died suddenly and unexpectedly amongst friends in the much loved pub next door to Havelock House two years later. Unexpected from our point of view but perhaps not as far as this dear man was concerned. He was only 57.

Thankfully there are film clips in the archives, like the day he was filming a story with Derek Bailey who, in his inspirational way, discovered on talking to the locals that there were eight pubs in Camlough and none a few steps down the road in Bessbrook. It made a good story with James winding up to camera by confiding, "Now I know the direction any right thinking man would take." The camera followed his feet in the direction of a dry Bessbrook only to be seen turning suddenly and beginning to stride in the opposite direction, then back again and so on until the viewer didn't have an idea to which village James was heading. We were left wondering where this right thinking man ended up!

There were many such gems; as one listing in the Digital Film Archive reads, 'James Boyce was a well known figure on television in the 1960s, specialising in quirky items. This programme features nine items - Fairy tree at Annacloy, a dog cemetery, Downpatrick jail, a straw wedding in Fermanagh, the Belleek Hotel, the railway station at Fivemiletown, Castlewellan Castle, Botanic loo and cycling with Sally.'

His features are still being aired from time to time and still he proves that words well chosen and well delivered mark out the master.

James shared a popular programme with writer and broadcaster Denis Ireland. It was called *The Humour is on Me Now,* a leisurely wander through literature with songs and stories. The script was concocted in Drumkeen Hotel on the outskirts of Belfast by the two of them with Derek Bailey. It may sound indulgent in this age of being deskbound and working to the clock, but their way of doing business produced the most creative and sensitive series of programmes.

*

It always saddens me that I didn't know the background to these erudite men and so fully appreciate their life stories at the time. For instance, Dennis who interrupted his medical degree at Queen's University to join the Royal Irish Fusiliers serving in France and Macedonia in 1914 but was invalided out with the rank of captain and returned home to represent the family linen business. When he retired from this responsibility and all the travelling it involved, Denis became a writer and broadcaster. He had the distinction of being elected to the Senate of the Irish Free State and was the first member of the Oireachtas, the Irish Parliament, to be resident in Northern Ireland. In 1965 news reporter Bill McGookin interviewed Denis specifically about his mail being censured after the 1939-45 World War and asked him what proof he had. He replied that he knew it was happening immediately after the war and that his phone was being tapped too as the information came from within the Post Office. Bill also asked him, as a Protestant Nationalist, what political views he had. Denis replied he would like to see the re-unification of Ireland but not against the wishes of the Ulster people.

Historic figures surely stalked the corridors of Ulster Television in those days, usually on their way from studio to boardroom where subjects of great weight were discussed over a few drinks be it tea, coffee or, more usually, something a little stronger! If walls had ears what treasures Havelock House would have to tell.

*

Patrick Riddell had the reputation of being difficult. In fact he was something of a perfectionist, looking over his glasses and sucking on his pipe he would pin you with his steely gaze and you wondered what he was thinking. He simply wanted the best.

He participated in panel discussions, getting heated just as expected, rivalling Gilbert Harding who was the network 'l'enfant terrible'. I worked on his series *Looking Back* but my memory is limited to one programme. He brought tears to my eyes when he looked back at the life of Madame Gertrude Drinkwater.

The Gilbert Harding of Ulster Television – he might thump his pipe on the desk, roar his disapproval or stop you in your tracks with his glare but Patrick Riddell was a gentleman of letters and a pleasure to know.

I was born in the converted barn beside her big house on the Shore Road between Whiteabbey and Carrickfergus. In those days our address was The Barne, Silverstream, Greenisland. It was colourful and historic. The silver stream was there, it ran through her garden, past the round pond with the bamboo plants protecting it and the bats flying at dusk. The little fairy house stood next to the steps running down to the stream, a real roof, real windows and no doubt real inhabitants. Certainly to a little girl growing up in her own company. The story was that, in 1690, as King William 111 of Orange made his way from Carrickfergus to Fortwilliam Park en route to the Boyne. He halted his entourage long enough to throw some silver coins to children playing by the stream and so the town land became known as Silverstream.

It must have been a peaceful garden for the esteemed singer and conductor to wander around. No one believes me but one lovely summer day I heard Madame singing *Oh What a Beautiful Morning* from *Oklahoma*! It was a rich, arresting sound. I saw her often as I was in and out of her home playing with her grandchildren but I'd no idea of her fame and importance until the day Patrick Riddell gave me his script to type.

A report in the *Northern Whig* and *Belfast Post* Monday May 21 1951 gives an idea of her standing.

Madam Drinkwater's many friends in Belfast, and these are all who really knew her, will be interested to learn that she is at present spending a short visit in the town.

It is a long time since as a girl member of the Royal Welsh Ladies Choir she sang with it in a command performance at Osborne before Queen Victoria and most of the Royal Family. "What a wonderful little girl," the Queen commented, and sending for her, complimented her. There is not the slightest doubt that had Madame Drinkwater pursued her singing she would have ranked among the greatest but the fates ruled otherwise, and what was her loss was Belfast's gain.

No one who saw them can forget her productions for one charity or another year after year of the Gilbert and Sullivan operas, in many of which her pupils' renderings bettered the professionals. It was a delight to watch her tiny figure in the conductor's chair, so magnetic was she, so bubbling over with energy, so feminine a version of Father O'Flynn. For her work in this way she was in the New Year Honours of 1945 awarded the MBE, an utterly inadequate tribute.

We have owed her much and now we can no answer make but thanks, and thanks and ever thanks.

I only have a vague memory of Madame but Derek Bailey still thinks of her as a little white haired lady in a long dress, wearing elbow length gloves and conducting the Ulster Operatic Society Orchestra at the Empire Theatre, baton held in her left hand. I must try to find out more about this fascinating, elusive woman.

Patrick Riddell was a civil servant who wanted to be a dramatist but his addiction to alcohol dominated his life. Although he did adapt plays for radio, sketches for the BBC and articles for the *Daily Express*, his health deteriorated and in 1947 he went through a severe course of apomorphine, a treatment used at that time for alcoholism, more recently for Parkinson's Disease. Eventually he came to realise that his craving was more a matter of association than physical. His book *I was an Alcoholic* highlights two great attributes he possessed, his writing ability and

The little barn in the grounds of Madame Drinkwater's home in Silverstream, later to be restored and the place I was born and grew up. From a sketch by Dan Dowling.

his courage. I suppose it has only become evident to me in researching his life that this man who seemed to have the world on his shoulders was indeed a man of great depth and understanding.

*

In his book, *A Musing*, Dr. Brum Henderson recalls his first meeting with one of the biggest personalities of all, already mentioned, Brian, known to us all as The O'Donnell.

"I was entering Havelock House when a curly dark haired gentleman with a face he would not have minded me describing as being akin to the colour of the red brick with which most of the houses around Havelock House were build approached me to say: "you don't know me but I know you and I wonder if you would ever think of doing some real Irish music programmes".

The two proceeded upstairs to the middle floor and Mr. Henderson's office.

I should explain that I can only speak of this pioneer of programmes during his time as managing director, and later chairman, as *Mr.* Henderson. He was a figure I held in awe and I was never one to get close to headmasters, teachers or members of management so despite his invitation, I can only think of him as 'Mr.' Henderson, the imposing character who first welcomed me to Havelock House.

Little did I know, 46 years later, early in August 2006, I would be writing his obituary for the *Irish News.*

Robert Brumwell Henderson died in Belfast last Friday, the evening following his 76th birthday. His life was one of privilege, adventure, and a lasting service to the Northern Ireland public as he conceived and nurtured Ulster Television, a company that burst into local homes on 31st October 1959. It was an unforgettable night and conducting the celebrations, one eye on the screen the other on his prestigious guests in the boardroom, was the tall handsome man we were to come to know as 'Brum'.

There have always been those who were envious of his abilities and his power to bring impossible dreams to fruition and there are those who thought he could do no wrong and somewhere between lay the essence of this man. He knew how to make money in business and he knew how to spend it building a television phenomenon. In the early 60s 'Midnight Oil' was a groundbreaking education programme, the forerunner of the Open University. 'With a Fiddle and a Flute' and the 'Half Door Club' brought Irish traditional musicians to the screen, plays and musicals from locations around Northern Ireland and hard hitting political debates; under his guidance Ulster Television took chances and as a result became a huge force in public life. He'd a great saying - 'my door is always open' - and he meant it, as staff numbers grew he knew everyone by name and most of their life stories and always made a point of writing to people acknowledging some action he felt deserved recognition.

Educated at Trinity College and a journalist with the News Letter, this imposing man was named after a family friend Sir Brumwell Thomas, architect of Belfast City Hall, and he was born into the grandeur of Government House Hillsborough in the days when it was the official residence of the Governor of Northern Ireland. At the time his father was private secretary and later comptroller to the Duke of Abercorn, Governor at that time, and in their private apartment the young Brum and his brother Bill grew up in the rarefied atmosphere of cooks and parlour maids, butlers and gardeners. He played with the children of the village and so it was throughout his life; he was equally at home in the company of the rich and famous as with the men and women he met in his everyday life. One of his greatest friends was the fiddle maker and player Brian O'Donnell and Brendan Behan travelled to Belfast especially to see him two days before his death in 1964. He persuaded Sir Laurence Olivier to appear on the first evening of transmission and when he was invited to Buckingham Palace to dine with the Queen and Prince Phillip, Brum was only momentarily abashed when she said, "Mr. Henderson, I am told you do an impression of Mr. Paisley. Perhaps you would do it for us now.' Of course he obliged. Both gentlemen were eventually to lose the 'Mr' and attain Doctorates.

Image was important to this 'fine figure of a man' who was 6' 4" by the time he was 18; in later years, with his silvery hair and ready smile, he was immediately recognisable in any crowd both at home and abroad. He also required his staff to adhere to a standard, which meant suits and ties, skirts and stockings – it would never have crossed anyone's mind to wear a sweater or jeans! And RBH was a stickler for accuracy. Every piece of paper work prepared in Havelock House had to be copied to his office and to my shame one came back to me, a couple of spelling mistakes ringed in his red biro (he was the only one allowed to use red biro) and a cryptic note - 'Go to the general office, get enough money from petty cash and buy a dictionary.'

He parted company from Ulster Television in 1990 and in his book Brum, A Life in Television, he adds a footnote to this chapter in his life; 'my departure was marked by some gracelessness on the part of the company' but he didn't go into detail on paper but rather retained the memories of his days of creating television with Anne Gregg and Ivor Mills, Ernie Strathdee, Jimmy Greene and Brian Durkin, all names most likely unknown to today's audiences. But his name will not be forgotten by those who worked for and with him, the many organisations he supported with his good humour and knowledge and the charities he championed. He worked tirelessly to bring peace and reconciliation through Co-Operation North, later Co-Operation Ireland, and at fundraising dinners he would hold his audience spellbound as he recited a long and beautiful grace in Gaelic.

A memorial service was held in St. Anne's Cathedral on 18th August 2005 and he commanded a packed house and the quite remarkable aspect of that audience was the mixture of background, cultures and faiths, all united in honouring this man just the way he would have wanted it, with fine words and good humour.

I'm sure Brian O'Donnell was there in spirit standing in the background as he did in so many of the film stories on *Roundabout* or on the Irish music programmes. The two had become close friends, the man born in Government House Hillsborough and the carpenter from Donegal. Brum was Brian's best man at his second marriage and as he records in his book, the groom married another Mary, this time a Protestent.

"At the reception afterwards at which his new wife's Presbyterian family and his Catholic children met for the first time, was a marvellous demonstration of how a delicate personal relationship surrounded by love, can overcome difficulties of religious background and social aspiration, and a tincture or two helped."

*

Jack Sayers was another distinguished visitor to the studio. I knew a little about this bespectacled man as he sat in front of our family at Carlisle Memorial Methodist Church in Carlisle Circus in Belfast. A 'down town' church recognised as the Methodist Cathedral of Ireland. It was there my father said to me; "That is a special man I'll introduce you to him." And he did. Jack Sayers was the editor of the *Belfast Telegraph* at that time, considered a 'liberal unionist'. He was like a god to a small girl who wanted to be a reporter, even at 10 years of age. When I was vacuuming the house, I would spend most of the time with the plug in one hand, whipping the lead around my legs with the other, as I walked from one imaginary person to another interviewing them for my own radio show. Years later it came to pass.

I must have been about twelve the day I met Audrey Russell, the first lady of BBC commentators, contemporary of Richard Dimbleby and Cliff Michelmore, all highly respected broadcasters.

My mother insisted we met, she always wanted me to enter the world of writing. "Miss Russell," she said to this elegant lady in seamed stockings, low heel black shoes, red suit and little black pill-box hat. "I'd like my daughter to meet you, she's going to be a journalist." We were at a Territorial Army march past attended by HM Queen Elizabeth, the Queen Mother, and the event was being broadcast throughout the Home Service. That meeting is burned on to my memory and I can still hear her voice in my head as she said, "Broadcasting is a very interesting career and I hope you do join this world but remember one thing. You see and hear me and you think, I want to be like Audrey Russell but Audrey Russell is nothing without the men who built that tower I broadcast

J.E. (Jack) Sayers, the Ulsterman with a card mind and editor of the Belfast Telegraph. *Belfast Telegraph*

from and place the ladder for me to climb up. Without all the engineers here and in London who take my commentary and send it out to the home receivers I'm nothing. Without the drivers who take me around and the researchers who help me write my script I wouldn't be here. Always remember the person who gets all the credit for making the broadcast is only a small cog in a big wheel." With a kind smile and a handshake she and her clipboard climbed the ladder to the top of the tower where she had a bird's eye view of the proceedings. I vaguely recall seeing the Queen Mother that day, I just couldn't take my eyes off this wise woman describing the scene below her. I felt I knew her well when, only months later, she was one of the commentators inside Westminster Abbey on 2nd June 1953 relating to the world the breathtaking scenes as Queen Elizabeth II was crowned.

Wireless programmes were the lifeblood in those days. Television was yet to make its mark, few people had sets on Coronation Day but we were invited into William Robb's home on the shores of Belfast Lough at Silverstream, Greenisland. He'd been a sea captain who sailed clipper ships round the Cape of Good Hope and his house was full of magic – globes and maps, telescopes and a television. It was a beautiful day, exciting and historic, and during a break when the adults were toasting the new queen, I sat on the pier at the bottom on the garden. A little silver fish came to the surface, smiled, dived down and then rushed up, jumped out of the water and back down. The water was so clear I was able to watch him swim away, delighted with his display.

*

Memories are made of little events, one leading to another until a picture begins to appear. My picture of J.E Sayers is a modest man singing lustily in Carlisle Memorial. Years later journalist Malcolm Brodie, told me that Jack Sayers had been an officer on the HMS Courageous aircraft carrier which was torpedoed off Mizen Head in 1939. He was rescued and seconded to the Admiralty to become a member of staff in Churchill's map room where his boss was Sir Richard Pym former inspector general of the RUC.

"John E. Sayers was known as the Ulsterman with the card index mind," Malcolm said. "When you got a memo from him you answered it because he would remember exactly when it was sent and what he'd asked."

And there he was in the pew in front of me, editor-in-chief of our leading newspaper, chairman of a BBC radio programme which toured Northern Ireland. *Up Against It* was the lively forerunner of the popular *Any Questions* programme. A team of eminent people visited towns and villages where the public was invited to put questions to them on any subject they wished. The original team was Desmond Neill a Quaker sociologist, J. J. Campbell of St. Mary's Catholic Teacher Training College, J. C. Beckett professor of Irish History at Queen's University Belfast and Charles Brett chairman of the Northern Labour Party, broadcaster and one of the founders of the Ulster Architectural Heritage Society. And all were contributors to Ulster Television programmes as well as 'Auntie', as the BBC was affectionately known.

Mr. Sayers presided over a thriving newspaper operation. The Derry edition was first to leave the *Telegraph* building every weekday morning and Saturday as well. Then came the 4th edition at 2.00 pm, the early 6th, the 6th and eventually at 6.30 p.m, the 8th edition which carried the racing results. In addition to these, every Saturday evening came *Ireland's Saturday Night*, a sports newspaper nicknamed *The Pink* as it was originally printed on pink paper. It was also known and loved by the public as *The Ulster*. After 114 years the paper ceased to exist on Saturday July 26th 2008. Malcolm Brodie, journalist with the *Telegraph* for 60 years, was editor of the *ISN* until 1991 and his by-line is still on the sports pages of the *Telegraph* most nights.

He wrote in that final publication of his love story with *The Pink* and his deep sadness at its passing. The heading was heart felt, *Goodbye Old Friend*.

The city of Belfast is a poorer place with the demise of these papers and the call of the 'boys', some of them in their 60s. They would gulder out, '6th Tallee' and distribute papers from under their oxter, or arm in more polite society, to the man and woman in the street making their way to bus stops and train stations on the homeward journey.

You can see, although the word 'media' hadn't been invented in those days, this was a vibrant and exciting area of life whether broadcasting, the print medium or television. It was a time of close co-operation as well as lively competition.

The Clancy Brothers and Tommy Makem.
Irish News

18
The Music of Folk and Friends

He'd sit, one leg angled over the other as he stitched away at the last, wetting the twine between his lips and holding it up to the light as he passed it through the eye of the big needle. He sang unaccompanied and although he had no shoe and no needle nor thread in his hands, we could see them clearly.

In those days everyone who was anyone came through the front door of Havelock House. One day in 1964, I came down stairs from the production office on the top floor to reception and there was Brendan Behan propping up a wall. He was obviously not well, he was certainly the worse for drink, ill-fitting dark suit, a once white shirt open at the neck, a shambly man looking older than his 41 years but still charismatic. According to Brum Henderson's' book *A Musing*, it was two days before he died and he had travelled to Belfast from Dublin especially to see the managing director.

There are so many stories about the man. One concerned a pub crawl round Dublin with a friend. Everywhere he went there was the same shadowy man sitting in the corner, not drinking, just watching. Eventually at pub eight or nine, Behan couldn't bear it any more and challenged him. "Why the **** are you follying me? You're ****in' follying me everywhere." he asked in his rich Dublin accent. "Will you for f*** sake lave me alowan." With a few more expletives added. The poor man stood up, looked at him somewhat sadly and explained, "Mr. Behan sir, I'm your driver."

But there was another Behan - Dominic. I remember him coming to the studios to be interviewed, gaunt, dressed in dark clothes and with a soulful smile. Dominic made his name as a writer, especially scripts for radio and television as well as plays for theatre but he excelled as a songwriter. He wrote *The Patriot Game*, *Liverpool Lou*, *McAlpine's Fusiliers* and many others but on this occasion he was singing his story of the legendary greyhound *Master McGrath*.

The studio didn't seem atmospheric enough so director Derek Bailey had a brainwave. As he and the McPeake family sat with Dominic in Dirty Dicks that lunchtime, locals and television people gathered round to listen to the stories in this genuine 'spit and saw dust' pub where the locals welcomed these television types and made them feel welcome.

During this impromptu master class, Derek slipped away, arranged for two cameras to be stretched from the studio, their cables out through the scene dock doors, over the kerbs, across the little street and into the dimly lit pub. It was the first multi-camera outside broadcast.

There Dominic sat in the corner of a worn leather bench seat under the etched window, his feet making patterns in the sawdust

Dominic Behan sitting in Dirty Dick's pub singing Master McGrath.

on the floor. The sun was shafting through the window highlighting the singer through the cigarette smoke which hung in the air. The result was a little piece of artistic delight, a Guinness on the round wooden scarred table, untipped cigarette smouldering in the ashtray as Behan began telling the story of the Irish greyhound's famous win. Slowly at first he took us from the start of the 1868 race, building a head of steam as the Master McGrath overtook the field to win the Waterloo Cup for the first of three times. His head thrown back, his arms going like the greyhounds legs, Behan's unaccompanied voice rose to fill the small bar and enthral the people both there and at home.

He died in Glasgow in 1989 at the age of 60 and his ashes were scattered over the Royal Canal in Dublin.

*

The Dubliners were also welcome visitors. If you haven't heard them, do yourself a favour, have a listen! In 1962 Ronnie Drew founded the Ronnie Drew Group which later came to be known as The Dubliners, taking their name from the James Joyce classic book of short stories *Dubliners,* and at his funeral in August 2008 in Greystones, Co Wicklow. It was a measure of the man that the President of the Republic of Ireland, Mary McAleese, led tributes calling Drew a champion of traditional music.

The original line up is now legendary to all lovers of Irish folk music, Luke Kelly, Ciaran Bourke and Barney McKenna and Ronnie Drew but it's Ronnie I remember. I recall him queuing in the canteen, not very tall but very thin, a serious man with eyes like Jesus, at least I thought so. Piercing and all-seeing. He was kind enough to invite me to have a drink with him in the pub across the road, I was due back in studio and had to decline, I'm sorry now because even then there was so much to learn about his life and his music – and he was handsome in an unusual way. He played Spanish guitar and his voice is hard to define, gravelly, full of dark colour and quite unforgettable. The many obituaries following Ronnie Drew's death at 73 were a reflection of the

Ronnie Drew. Irish News

esteem in which the man was held.

The Times devoted a full page to his life, recounting the story of Ronnie's reaction when the bawdy ballad *Seven Drunken Nights* entered the UK charts. Not all seven verses were included as the story of the drunken man returning home to his wife and evidence of another man having been with her, would probably have contravened some ITA decency guideline of the time!

When he was told the news that he was in the charts, he replied in his deadpan manner: 'Is that good news or bad news?' It was good news for his established fans and the subsequent appearance on *Top of the Pops* alongside Jimi Hendrix, the Kinks and The Who, brought the group more devotees and a world tour.

*

I recall Tommy Makem and the Clancy Brothers when they were regulars on Ulster Television in the 60s, the most friendly of men with Tommy, chest out, head up, singing a lusty ballad or singing the beautiful story of the cobbler. He'd sit, one leg angled over the other as he stitched away at the last, wetting the twine between his lips and holding it up to the light as he passed it through the eye of the big needle. He sang unaccompanied and although he had no shoe and no needle nor thread in his hands, we could see them clearly. The last time I met Tommy, a native of Keady, Co Armagh, was in Alexander the Grate, an old building three storeys high near the Gasworks in Donegall Pass, packed every Saturday with fire places, furniture, antique dealers, browsers and all sorts of bric-a-brac. On one such morning Tommy wandered in, found a fiddle on one of the stalls and soon captivated the men, women and children with a spontaneous performance. It was a magical moment, a little cameo.

When Liam Clancy visited Belfast in the spring of 2008 to appear at the Black Box during the Cathedral Quarter Arts Festival, I told him of this memory and he laughed at the thought:, "Typical of Tommy." he said, "typical." Liam didn't remember the last time he was in Belfast but the crowd did as they welcomed this lovable musical rover, writer and raconteur. He received a roaring reception even before he kicked things off with a rousing version of the Clancy Brothers classic *Wild Rover*.

He yarned away like someone sitting by the fireside doing drawn thread work. Each story linking to another interspersed with poems and, of course, the songs which are famous the world over. Next day he and I talked about the old times and at 72 he was still living the memories and still missing his brothers and his mate Tommy.

"We recorded one of our most popular shows 'Live in Ireland' in the Ulster Hall, it's still requested. I remember going on stage, the hall was packed and when I got my eyes used to the dark I could see all round the sides policemen and nurses lined all around," His voice was hushed, "I'll never forget it. But there was some incredible atmosphere that night, an outpouring of enthusiasm, some gorgeous young teenagers and some older people on sticks."

Liam was the baby of the family. His mother was 47 before she had him and as his brothers were in various parts of the world, he grew up virtually an only child. It was only in the mid-50s that the three boys, Paddy, Tom and Liam got together in America and realised they had a special spirited sound and with Tommy Makem they hit the big time in 1961 on the Ed Sullivan Show. They were immediately signed up by Columbia Records and Liam became a close friend of Bob Dylan. The following year they embarked on their first Irish tour including a visit to Ulster Television. Surprisingly, he told me, he never put much thought into a career, "Flying by the seat of my pants." You can't keep a natural talent hidden.

"Belfast is wonderful now," he continued, "everywhere you look men in yellow jackets and hard hats and staying in the Europa these days is relaxing." He laughed at the memories of staying there during the Troubles. "No longer on tenterhooks, not waiting for the bomb like the night when I'd the worst flu ever and in bed with a high fever. At 3.00 am the bomb alert went off, I got out of bed not knowing who I was or where I was and opened the door in my red, one-piece fluffy zipped up jump suit. There was a young man running down the corridor and I shouted to him 'do I have to get out of the building is there really a bomb?' He did a double take: 'You're Liam Clancy,' he said, 'well, I want your autograph for my mother.' 'Is there a bomb?' I insisted, 'Aught, that thing goes off all the time, never mind it, I want your autograph.'

We looked back even further to their appearances in Studio One at Havelock House and I told him my story of the Clancys.

The first time they appeared I was the production assistant on *Roundabout* and I'd phoned their agent to get details, agree a fee and ask who would sign the contract. 'The lame fellow,' he told me. So all that afternoon I followed the group round looking for someone with a limp, I didn't want to ask which one of them was lame. Then it struck me, it wasn't the lame fellow I was looking for but the Liam fellow.

"That's good, the lame fellow," and he laughed. "Then I remember Andy Crockart directing the Irish music shows and Brian O'Donnell would 'advise'."

The O'Donnell. He was much loved and much respected and when it came to Irish music he knew everything and had time for everybody. "That was The O'Donnell," said Liam, "a generous man. He would ring and arrange to come down to me in Wicklow for a confab and great old confabs they were and we'd plan programmes; on one occasion we planned a great series but with the Troubles it had to go on hold and never happened." He paused. "You know, pride of place in my music room above the mantelpiece there's a painting which means a lot to me. There's a story there.

Andy Crockart and cameraman Jim Starrett.

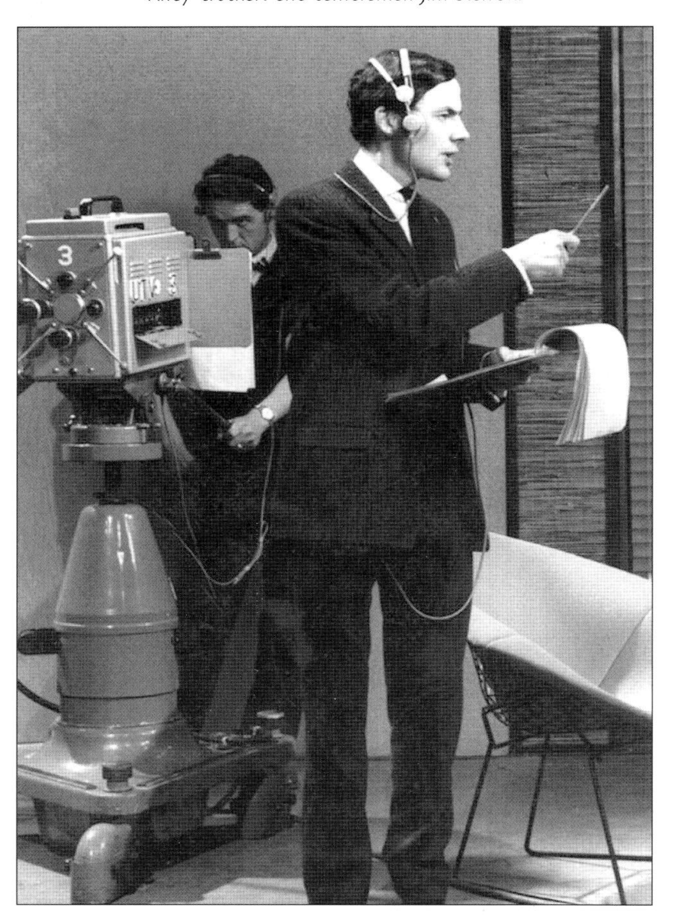

"Brian O'Donnell would be on the phone every day about something, usually he was a bit the worse for wear and I couldn't always make out what he was talking about so I tended just to say 'yes' to everything and see what happened. On this particular occasion the reception was very bad on my windup phone and maybe he'd had a jar too many, anyway, I said 'yes, certainly Brian.' Soon afterwards Andy Crockart phoned to say everything was set for tomorrow, 'see you and Anne Mulqueen about four o'clock.' Now I didn't want to let Brian down so I said 'yes Andy certainly, what are the details?' I called Anne told her we were due in Belfast at 4.00 p.m. and we arrived to a wonderful studio set depicting the front room in Liam Clancy's house and a show to do. I think it was called *Liam Clancy and Friends*.

"After the recording we were invited up to the boardroom and brandy and cigars were plentiful and I was shown a most beautiful painting of Margaret Barry, she called herself the singing tinker lady, Brian O'Donnell, Felix Doran and Johnny Dogherty in the Crown Bar just across the road from the Europa. They asked me if I liked it and of course I did, I loved it. The painting was set aside and we resumed the party. Then it was time to go. I thanked everyone and prepared to leave the room. 'Liam,' says Andy, 'surely you're not going to leave your painting behind you are you? We couldn't afford to pay you what you're worth so we had our designer Roy Gaston paint this for you as a memento.'

And you know, it's there for me every day, it has indeed pride of place above the mantlepiece."

Liam is the last of the Clancy's. "Of course I miss them, I can't tell you how often I go to the phone to ring one of the boys to check on something or I've forgotten someone's name. They were good days."

And it was lovely to catch up. Strangely, only a week later I joined a group of young musicians, including my daughter Susie, in Flanagan's Mill in Sallins Co. Kildare as they played and sang *And the Band Played Waltzing Matilda.* Little did they realise they had Liam Clancy and Tommy Makem to thank for making Eric Bogle's anti-war ballad famous when they performed together in the 70s and 80s.

My first job as production assistant was to time five songs for the following week's *Teatime with Tommy* with singer Una O'Callaghan, a beautiful woman with a rich mezzo soprano voice. We repaired to Tommy James's tiny office on the top floor, he played the piano as Una ran through the songs. Surrounded by shelves stacked with records, all I had to do was start the stopwatch at the first note and stop it at the last note and write down the duration beside the title. Nerves got the better of me. I think Una knew by the look on my face that I'd made a 'hames' of it. Messed up entirely. But the dear lady didn't act the diva and never did. Instead, when Tommy left the room she took my arm, held me back and said, 'I'd like to run over those again, would you mind?' Would I mind? An answer to my prayers. This time I got the timings spot on thanks to her coaching with the stop watch.

On the same day I met Una in Tommy's office I was appointed PA to Derek Bailey, my first and favourite boss. When we met in London one December evening in 2008 sitting outside an opulent Moroccan restaurant, huge overhead heaters keeping us warm, we talked of that day. He had come from working in the Pye factory in Larne as a member of junior management and in 1962 he did the magic of securing the much sought after Pye Black Box record player for my parents to give me on my 21st birthday – the only thing in the world I wanted, this box of mahogany which gave the most superb tone to the old 75 revolutions per minute vinyl records, a three speed turntable and diamond needle. It was people like Derek and Una who gave me my love of classical music, indeed all music.

Una appeared on many Ulster Television programmes and so did her husband Maurice. Maurice O'Callaghan had been one of the original voices to promote the new station using the ITA transmitter. He was an actor and in the 80s I worked with him many times at the Arts Theatre in Belfast when he was one of the Ulster Actors Company and, in Ulster Television days his melodious basso profundo gave authority to many commercials.

Later in life he mixed acting with law when he was appointed Tip Staff at the High Court of Justice in Belfast. His voice would boom through the corridors of power along the marble floor bouncing off the walls up to the arched ceilings and through the pillars to call the trembling participants forward for their case to be heard.

Una and Maurice met when she was only 15 and he was 18. They fell in love and spent their lives talking, singing, laughing, crying and performing together. My lasting memory of Maurice was just before he died in December 2004 sitting by the window of his front room in Rosetta as the light faded on that still winter day, just the three of us, Maurice, Una and me. There was much love in the air, the memories, the laughter. Then Maurice, who had lost his sight in later years, asked for his violin which Una reached to him. He tucked it under his chin, tuned up and began to play. Una joined in singing the beautiful Irish airs they knew so well, *The Last Rose of Summer, She Moved Through the Fair.* Just the three of us. What a beautiful way to remember such a special friendship.

The beautiful Una O'Callaghan who saved my blushes on my first assignment as a production assistant.

Celebrations began with a float in the Lord Mayor's Show. Adrienne McGuill and Anne Gregg with Barney McCool, on-screen personalities who were to become household names.

19
Hallowe'en 2008 – One Year to go

But now in 2008, some sort of corner has been turned and the spiral seems to be downwards. The whole celebrated family of independent television companies is contracting, news is being centralised, small companies no longer need to have their own newsrooms on the scale of a few years ago.

It just happens I've opened up my laptop to write and noticed it's 31st October 2008. It's almost four o'clock and in Donegal the sun is going down, everything is fresh after a deluge of hailstones and the gathering at the pier in Rosbeg is over. The rosary has been said in remembrance of Michael Jack Boyle and young Thomas Moore. They lost their lives in the bay this morning 10 years ago. I shall never forget watching the boats circle the spot that day. The big ships on the fringe had come from Killybegs, the small craft from all round the coast, divers on holiday turned up to join the search and, as has been played out over the centuries, fishermen gathered on the pier silent and grey, the women a little further back huddled together. Then the sad retreat from the sea when hope of life had gone.

The other memory is this afternoon 49 years ago.

Ulster Television has just gone 'on air', the point of no return has been reached and passed and we are on the road to success. Mary Hunter and I are about to head home to my house to get changed for the party of celebration, horrible new coat bought by my mother in Frances Curleys High Street, beige Danimac with chocolate brown fur collar. After a quick tea which Mary remembers was a celebratory fillet steak on a willow patterned plate, there's a lot of leaping as my brothers Mike and Johnny bombard us with squibs and crackerjacks as we run to get into my father's car and he kindly brings us to Havelock House to join in the fun.

What changes there have been since that night, progress,

experimentation, advance technology, satellites, microchip and outerspace. But now in 2008, some sort of corner has been turned and the spiral seems to be downwards. The whole celebrated family of independent television companies is contracting, news is being centralised, small companies no longer need to have their own newsrooms on the scale of a few years ago.

This was predicted by Ken Hamilton who once worked in the sales department selling air time. I bumped into this league cup footballer and dedicated salesman early in the 70s and laughed when he said one day UTV would be a relay station, all material would come from the network, we'd have no local entertainment programmes, religious broadcasting, farming or fun, just regular local news bulletins. He also said there would be many more methods of broadcasting and UTV would be vying with others for a share of the advertising market. Surely impossible. In the 1960s this company we loved was coining it, advertisers were queuing up, we had hours of creative homemade programmes many in the top ten. We were a region to be envied and admired. But he was right. Slowly but surely the local aspect of commercial television has been whittled away and advertisers are looking at other means of getting the message across, more often these days via the Internet and on-line broadcasting. There's Sky and a multitude of other stations. The 'Ulster Television' legend doesn't exist any more, 'UTV' is now known as 'Your TV'. Here in Northern Ireland there is no story any more, it's perceived that the Troubles are over so the media circus has moved on.

In the media in general, men and women who have worked through good times and bad are discarded, young people with growing families made redundant; in a climate of change this has to happen but there seems to be a harsh disregard for people's feelings and an inability to communicate with grace.

The culture of television has also taken a dive downwards. This week as I write in October 2008 has seen the fall of two arrogant giants of broadcasting, Jonathan Ross and Russell Brand because of their lewd behaviour and inappropriate language. There's a lot of talk about the Alpha Male relating to their boorish behaviour when they left telephone messages for actor Andrew Sachs relating to Brand's sexual relationship with his granddaughter, the dancer Georgina Baillie. By any standards what they said to his answering machine was beyond acceptability and they have suffered financially for it, probably not a lot in their estimation, but at least the public outcry has been listened to and action taken. Will the proposed clampdown by the BBC to ban swear words until 10pm? This might help but why not ban swear words totally? The age of extremes is upon us, but as one journalist said in the national press, the further you are from the middle of the road the nearer you are to the gutter.

At the Olympic Games in Beijing China, true sportsmanship was witnessed and a growing intolerance of temperamental footballers and their like 'earning' thousands of pounds a week has resulted. There are signs of strong women standing up to bullying tactics and supporting their less forceful sisters so, are we entering a time of change? Hopefully. The Alpha Male when mature is a natural leader to be trusted but there is an Alpha Male syndrome where less mature men, and some women, want to dominate, think they are superior to their colleagues, they gain power through intimidation and strut their stuff in a most arrogant manner. It's difficult to come to terms with these characteristics.

Is it possible to be honest in politics, in business or in the media, to be a caring colleague, an intelligent entertainer? If not we're done for. Perhaps there's been too much 'ad libbing' and not enough considered speech. The most popular comedy television programmes have a script - *The Vicar of Dibley, Only Fools and Horses*, programmes such as these are repeated ad infinitum but only because they bear repetition.

The new Bond film has just opened and it's labelled brutal by the critics, little room for humour or humanity and certainly the smooth sophistication of Sean Connery has long disappeared. On the other hand the feel good factor *Mamma Mia* has brought a song to the heart of millions, Abba songs, great tongue in cheek acting and happiness. People dancing with each other in the aisles. Are we becoming less inhibited, more open with each other, demanding a better deal not for more money but for value for money? And above all, demanding respect.

*

Although today, 31st October 2008, there is a great anger raging through the world, might that be waning in favour of a new enlightened age? Are there signs that we are planning ahead, taking time to consider the consequences of our actions, using the 'credit crunch' to bring life back to basics? Is there change in the air? We'll see.

This same paper that carries all the distasteful pranks of Ross and Brand includes a report that Gloria Hunniford has furnished her home in the South of France with many of her daughter's personal possessions. She's reported as saying she feels "like Caron is the custodian of the house making us feel even closer to her when we're there."

I spent many afternoons with Gloria in her home in Lisburn, Co. Antrim as she looked through newspapers and selected stories which could be followed up on radio or television. Caron, then Paul and eventually Michael were always nearby. Caron went on to become a much respected presenter on national television, especially on the children's programme *Blue Peter*. When she died in 2004 at the age of 41, Gloria grieved very publicly for her daughter and the public grieved with her. She used this dreadfully sad time, however, to offer practical and emotional support to others, especially by establishing the Caron Keating Foundation to raise money to help all types of cancer charities working with men, women and children who are coming to terms with an intimate knowledge of cancer.

The Blessing of the Boats, Rosbeg Harbour County Donegal.

Stanley Wyllie, organist and transmission controller with Uel Deane.

20
The Pace of Change

In my case restriction came when I married another employee of Ulster Television and like Gloria Hunniford, Claire Kennedy, Kay Dunlop, Joan McCoy, Katie Major, Pat Carlisle and other women whose only crime was to fall in love, I had to leave the company.

And what was going on in the rest of the province? The late 50s and early 60s in Northern Ireland were years of great change. Right in the middle of this time, came the opening of Ulster Television and the launch of the 45,000 tonne P & O liner Canberra with Adrienne McGuill on board to cover the story for the new station. These events marked the formation of a modern Ulster when everything started to change.

There were telephones for householders whereas before they had been for businesses, farmers and the upper class. Cars were a rarity with the 50s being an age of mass transport but in the 60s they became more common on the roads bringing with them traffic jams and hold-ups, something of a problem. It had been chaotic in the late 50s but with the arrival of trolley buses sweeping in and out of bus stops and the build up of motor traffic, it steadily got worse.

Belfast market was in full flow. Country people travelled to town mainly on public transport as the Province's train service was disrupted in the 1950s when the Great Northern Railway Ireland ceased to be profitable. In 1953 the company was jointly nationalised by the governments of the Republic of Ireland and Northern Ireland and in 1958 the Northern Ireland government closed many lines and the GNRI board was dissolved. This meant the bus service in the north was greatly improved.

The cattle came in big farm wagons, open-sided so the calves could see what was happening around them. I was often held up in the No 64 Downview Avenue bus when some of the sprightly young ones would break away from the herd as they were steered towards the market pens. They'd race down May Street and up Cromac Street with the farm hands dashing after them. When the country came to town there was great excitement. In 1965 a bullock was filmed rampaging round the Court House chased by a man with a bucket. Children were hiding behind dustbins and adults took refuge in a nearby bar. A policeman tried to divert the animal and direct him back to the market pen but only when some bright spark lead out another bullock on a rope did the truculent youngster calm down and allowed himself to be reunited with his mates.

In the city people travelled into work on the bus, those who were close enough went home for lunch on the bus and returned home for tea on the bus. Most didn't eat out and a sandwich at the desk wasn't popular. All this travelling at regular times meant we all knew each other and the journeys were more like a family outing than a bus ride. I had imagined stories for everyone on my homeward journey including one for a very beautiful poised woman with blond hair in an elegant chignon. She had a Mona Lisa expression, a sadness that I built on. In my mind she had met an American GI in Belfast, danced at the Plaza, fallen in love, married, had a few weeks of happiness and then he was killed on active service. My heart broke for her every evening between 5.30 and six o'clock. 45 years later I met her in John Stevens butchers in Upper Queen street. It was the first time I'd seen her since those bus journeys which preceded a regular lift home with journalist Paddy Scott. It was surreal. She was just the same, she hadn't aged, beautiful and wistful, laughing and talking. I couldn't help but tell her how glad I was to see her and admit my fantasy. She laughed again at the thought of being a GI bride. "No love, I married a Belfastman, had a family, I'm a granny now," We talked on about her life and it was very unlike my imaginings. I haven't seen her since. Once in 45 years. Was she real? Did I imagine all this? Was it a divine appointment just to put me right?

*

Following the 'Hungry 30s' and the war years which held back everything, life took off in the 50s with almost full employment, but it was a mistaken euphoria. We lost many of our historic buildings when the army took over big houses then left them in bad condition and with no money available, many fell into disrepair and were left empty. There was a complete change of social division as these big houses gave way to three and four bedroom modern dwellings. No one wanted antiques and large furniture. Everyone wanted to scale down and be labour-saving so the Swedish movement became fashionable through magazine articles. Strip pine and duvets, glass tables and hanging lamps, central heating and Formica. In the 'mid-noughties', from around 2006, we were doing much the same thing, with apartments, Ikea and a credit crunch.

Before the war women who married a work colleague had to leave certain professions. This had become the norm not because the employers were against women but because they didn't want them taking men's jobs. But after the war young women expected jobs and by the late 50s they were flooding back into employment. In my case restriction came when I married another employee of Ulster Television and, like Gloria Hunniford, Claire Kennedy, Kay Dunlop, Joan McCoy, Katie Major and Pat Carlisle and other women whose only crime was to fall in love, I had to leave the company. Before equality legislation was passed, the same ethos applied in other institutions including banks and insurance offices. We were told this was because we might be privy to confidential material and be tempted to pass this on to our husbands. Young women today are amazed and horrified when they hear this but it was a male dominated society and the glass ceiling attitude was accepted and really hasn't changed. Even the introduction of the trouser suit didn't do the trick.

I well remember the Sunday morning, probably in 1959, when my friend Muriel Patterson strode up the aisle of Carlisle Memorial Church, between the pews of upright citizens, wearing navy trousers and matching jacket. She looked smart and attractive and I was really impressed. My poor father. He, like the majority of men in the congregation, was outraged! But, because it was Muriel, he decided to accept modern woman and her wardrobe. Hers was a real blow for freedom. Some restaurants refused women in trousers and when one feminist took her trousers off when challenged, even this brave action didn't gain her admittance.

There was prosperity as the 50s progressed. It was a happy and an optimistic time, the austerity of war had gone and the future looked bright. The Nissen huts built to billet soldiers were taken over by people who'd lost their homes in the Blitz and these little white corrugated homes were like palaces. Councils built on a huge scale. Rathcoole to the north of Belfast was the biggest housing estate in Europe at one time. Then skyscrapers came into view and green space was taken up.

The theatre was strong in 1959 and it was the heyday of the cinema. During the war no films were coming into the north so there was a great feeling of elation when the picture houses reopened and house full notices went up.

In poorer areas some cinemas took glass jam jars for admittance, in the Ritz cinema in the centre of Belfast, it cost 1/9p before 3.30 p.m., but it was great value as the main picture houses featured the Big Picture, a 'B' picture, *Pathe News*, a restaurant and an organ. The Ritz was my first experience of a picture house.

I remember the grand staircase, a huge chandelier, the red curtains opening, and sitting in, to what was to me, a huge restaurant for a birthday tea. The film was Walt Disney's *Bambi* and I cried for days. I think I remember the Compton organ being played by the famous organist Joseph Seal. I certainly do remember his successor Stanley Wyllie who became quite a celebrity before he joined Ulster Television as a transmission controller.

More and more dance halls were beginning to spring up and as eating out hadn't yet caught on, a real treat was a Friday night fish and chip supper, wrapped in a newspaper.

As time went on, cafes opened for morning coffee and afternoon tea, milk bars appeared with juke boxes blaring out the latest hit record, *Rock Island Line* with Lonnie Donegan, *Catch a Falling Star* with Perry Como and Elvis. McGlades Bar behind the *Belfast Telegraph* boasted a grillroom. Gradually people began to treat themselves to a little luxury and adventure. Family outings to the Zoo at Bellevue began with the thrill of chugging up the steep path on an open sided 'toast rack' bus and a picnic in the shadow of the Cave Hill.

For children it was in general a quiet existence, making their own amusement with close friendships in the streets and the discipline of school backed by discipline at home. Perhaps the worst thing of all was having to endure the frightening experience of visiting the dentist as the anaesthetic was administered through a gas mask placed over your face and you'd no option but to breath in and pass out.

On the happier side of life, the Wellington Park Hotel opened in 1965. The foundation stone was laid at the new Lyric Theatre with two trees planted by Michael Yeats, son of W.B. Yeats. The old Troxy cinema on the Shore Road re-opened as the Grove Theatre. A nervous George Best was captured on film as this Irish International legend did his driving test and passed, despite saying he found reversing really difficult.

It was the age of family owned shops and department stores: Thornton, Henry, Sinclair, Robinson and Cleaver with its magnificent white marble staircase which apparently now resides in a big house in Ballyedmond, Co. Down. There was the wonderful general store, The Bank Buildings. There was Anderson and McAuley, the Co-op, Brand, The Athletic Stores and Robbs where the payment system fascinated everyone, young and old. The item was bought, a receipt carefully written and torn out of the book, the money and the receipt were then put in a short metal cylinder which fitted into a container and, using vacuum suction, it whizzed from the counter to the cash office high above and back again with the change and the stamped receipt. Many of the big stores in main towns had this system, only cash transactions across the counter, no cheques, no credit or debit cards.

The days were longer and there was time to shop in a stylish way. You could take garments out on 'appro' – approval - often with no deposit and there was always a fitter who would measure and alter to madam's taste. On the glass counters of these posh shops, there would often be a low oval mirror. I wondered what use it was as it wasn't high enough for a woman to look into to admire a hat or a scarf, so I asked. "That, modom, is for the lady to ascertain whether or not the leather gloves are suitable." Silly me. Some months afterwards, in the same shop, with many of the same loyal and mature staff, I undertook an experiment. I went in to buy a present at the perfume counter – without wearing a hat. I was ignored in favour of other more elegantly dressed women before being served with minimal conversation. Next day I went in again this time wearing a hat and gloves, leather of course. I was served immediately and fawned over like a lady. Just shows, if you want to get ahead – get a hat.

*

And so it was, into this calm and prosperous lifestyle, came an impudent new baby and the impact of Ulster Television was great.

People talked about the advertisements, often to the exclusion of the programmes, probably because so many of them were local and live. On one occasion, as the evening programme *Roundabout* came to an end and the final credits were rolling, the set was pushed to one side and in a corner Frank Carson with a packet of Cream Crackers took his place. He began all right but lost the thread after a few seconds and, as is expected of Frank, he began to extemporise. Quick as a flash and in a moment of genius, he ended by taking a biscuit out of the packet, holding it up to camera and with a wink and a big smile, first uttered the immortal words, "It's a cracker!"

Years later, at the beginning of 2009, Frank had breathing problems and apparently was advised to loose two stone so, he says, he went on a diet of porridge and crackers!

Northern Ireland's crime rate was practically non-existent. There was a campaign to get rid of the death penalty although people were still reeling over the dreadful death of 19 year old student

Patricia Curran who was stabbed to death in Whiteabbey in 1952.

The public was beginning to look outside Northern Ireland for holidays with Nutts Corner the only airport serving domestic flights and Silver City airlines the popular carrier. The airport building with its old fashioned waiting area furnished with pale green Lloyd Loom chairs and tables with their glass tops, was a wonderful place to view the aircraft coming and going. It was here that the worst air disaster in Northern Ireland happened in January 1953 when a BEA Vickers Viking struck landing lights and crashed killing 27 people with only eight survivors. In October '57 a Vickers Viscount crashed killing the seven people on board. The move to Belfast 'Aldergrove' International was still six years away and it was a red-letter day when, in October 1963 the Queen Mother opened the new terminal, Belfast International Airport, beside the village of Aldergrove.

*

The year, 1965, was something of a watershed. Although I was coming to the end of my first association with Ulster Television because of my impending marriage in 1966, I was in my element, programmes were exciting and there was a new one every day. If we production assistants weren't scheduled to be in studio, we were out filming somewhere in Northern Ireland and occasionally 'overseas' in London. Slowly but surely the world opened up, and despite being a girl, I began my travels. It began with a visit to Switzerland to stay with another UTV girl, Susan Gibson from Peacefield, Portadown. On one occasion we got a phone call to the office at about ten o'clock. It was from Susie. She was in Dublin. "I was on the wrong platform. I got on the wrong train and fell asleep. I'll be in as fast as I can." She, and we, were in ribbons of laughter at her misadventure. I'll always be grateful to Susie Gibson as she introduced me to Rosbeg, Co. Donegal where her family had a cottage and on a clear night, you could dance on the beach under the Milky Way. 50 years later you still can! When she moved to work in the International School in Geneva I visited and shook the hay seed out of my hair and, in only two weeks, considered myself cosmopolitan. Then came a holiday with my mother to Paris, France and the world opened up.

In the 60s, however, Belfast city was gradually losing its popularity as people began moving out to the suburbs. This migration was the case in many towns in Northern Ireland as the social gap was less evident than ever, the working class had money and major out-of-town factories advertised for workers, no skill required. In 1962, and to a mixed reception, The Matthew Plan was made public featuring a building stop-line around Belfast, a 'green belt'. New towns were to be created and small towns to be developed. A new 'city' was being talked of in the Lurgan-Portadown area, motorways and ring roads were to be built and there were great plans of expansion. The M1 towards Dungannon got underway followed by the M2 towards Coleraine and plans were laid for city ring roads and link roads. It was the beginnings of a network which was to make travelling much easier and faster.

In those days there were many nurses from the Royal Victoria Hospital going home at weekends and for those living towards the south, 'thumbing' at the beginning of the M1, beside the hospital, was a very safe and cheap way of travelling. Two or three would stand together, put out their thumb, and it wouldn't be long before someone would pull in and offer them a lift. The story which went round was of a man who stopped to offer a young girl transport. She told him she was going to Lisburn, got in the back of the car and off they set. Further along the motorway as he was chatting away when he became aware that she was very silent. When he turned round there was no one there, the car was empty. It was said she was a young nurse who had been killed as she stood by the side of the road and so another ghost story was born.

There was also a ghost in Ulster Television and I saw it. Jack Kinney was clerk of works from day one and knew the building intimately. When the extension was being planned and a hole knocked through to the old building beside the studio, he told me to be careful. He just said, "Be warned. There's a ghost." All very mysterious. I'd forgotten about this until I arrived at the production office at 7.15 one morning in 1993. Absolutely no one around. Dull morning. Opened the door into the long wide room, the door gave an eerie squeak. As I walked in, a third of the way down the office, I saw a veil of mist slowly cross the room, hanging half way between floor and ceiling. It looked like a transparent sheet of corrugated mist. When it had crossed in front of me, it dissolved. I walked backwards and forwards through that door a dozen times and it didn't squeak once. There were no reflections, no smoke, no nothing – just a ghostly mist!

*

Annual events drew thousands. The Royal Ulster Agricultural Society Balmoral Show probably attracted the largest crowds and it was top of the list in the newsroom's daily diary for coverage, from

A modern scooter and the traditional mode of transport in Donegall Quay. The horse trough was a common sight, now more often to be found in up market gardens filled with flowers. Kenneth McNally prize bulls to fashion shows, Women's Institute stalls to children's gardens. Established in 1854 following the Famine, the intention was to improve the business of agriculture and the show grounds soon became the centre for farmers and landowners to come and show off animals and produce. The RUAS has charitable status and monies go towards promoting its objectives and supporting areas of agriculture at a time when it is much needed. When the King's Hall was opened one late spring day in 1934 it became the landmark of this annual oasis of all things wholesome. Today it is recognised as a building of special architectural and historic interest and the show is still a major event on the calendar, although in 2009 the venue came under threat.

Each August the Oul Lammas Fair at Ballycastle-O, as the song says, was an example of the town people heading for the country to see the horse traders do their deals and buy the fresh produce, dulse seaweed and honeycomb *Yellow Man*. It was at the fair in the north coast town, on a film outing with Ernie Strathdee, that we supped the devil's brew in a pub with notable hardmen Silver McKee and Capt. Pollock. Silver was famous in and around the Market area of Belfast. I'm not sure about Capt. Pollock but I believe he was the out of town equivalent. As they say, the craic was mighty. Capt. Pollock bought me a tin bear who clapped cymbals together when the batteries were inserted, a treasure for years until it rusted away. Both men offered their service if a 'contract' needed to be taken out on anyone; names were named but all totally rejected just in case it wasn't a joke.

In Belfast, Silver's name was always coupled with Stormy Weather, both street fighters, one Catholic one Protestant and the firmest of friends. The *Rushlight* magazine of 2002 told a lovely story about Stormy who lived in the Shankill. When television came into being and Ulster Television was making its mark, Stormy's wife wanted a set. The next door neighbour had one, so she wanted one! She kept the pressure up until, unable to hack it any more, the night came when Stormy threw down his *Belfast Telegraph*, went out to the yard and got a length of sturdy wood and proceeded to smash a hole through the flimsy dividing wall and into the surprised neighbour's front room. "You want a television? You've got a television." Then he picked up his paper and resumed reading the local news.

And then there was Buck Alec. I'd see him from the bus on my route to work along York Street. He too was a boxer, a squat powerful man. He grew up around the docks area and was a child who 'bucked' the law, hence his famous nickname. At an early age, Alexander Robinson became Buck Alec, a true legend in his own lifetime and beyond his death in 1995. He joined the reserve police force in the 20s at the time of the then Troubles, during which time he continued his boxing career to become middleweight champion of Ireland in 1927.

Buck Alec spent some years in America where it's said he worked for Joseph Kennedy, father of the American president and became a close associate of Al Capone the Chicago gangster. But in the late 50s he was probably most famous for his home zoo, three lions, a pony and, although I never saw this, between appearances in circuses all over Ireland he exercised his lions along York Street much to the vexation of the local shoppers.

This part of Belfast also boasted another fine boxer and a regular visitor to Ulster Television, Rinty Monaghan who in his retirement offered great stories as undefeated world flyweight champion. He was a charismatic character and I always made a point of watching from the viewing room above the studio when he was on a programme.

*

In the early 60s, wealth and poverty sat side by side in Belfast reflecting employment and unemployment. Some traditional areas, for instance the shipyard, where the *Canberra* was the last significant launch of its kind, and the linen industry, were showing signs of decline whilst other companies were thriving and new names were appearing in the newspapers and on television - Courtaulds, Grundig and Michelin amongst them. As linen houses began to close, trades unions organised protests, hemmers and stitchers carried banners and picketed their workplaces but to no avail. By 1958, 25,000 jobs had been lost and in the shipyard the workforce had reduced from 20,000 to 1300. Although the Shorts SCI vertical take-off and landing plane held great promise, orders were slow and it wasn't an immediate success. On the other hand, Shorts Sky Van, launched in January 1963, proved popular for short haul trips and was favoured by freight companies because of its large rear door which made loading and unloading much easier than in other aircraft.

In politics, trouble was brewing when, in September 1964, the Unionist candidate for West Belfast James Kilfedder, sent a telegram to the Minister of Home Affairs demanding the removal of the Irish flag from the Republican Party Headquarters in Divis

Street. It marked a sinister wind of change. On the 28th of the month, the police broke down the doors and took the flag, rioting was intense and the seeds were set for the terrible years of the Troubles.

West Belfast in the 1960's *Gerry Collins*

Belfast's showbiz couple, impresario Alf Scott and his wife Betty.

21
Showbiz Comes to Town

Mounted police controlled the crowds who had turned out to see the guests, Johnny Ray, Bill Haley and his Comets, Gerry and the Pacemakers with hosts David Jacobs and Pete Murray.

In the early 60s, however, Belfast was jumping. Entertainment filled the air, theatres, cinemas, clubs and pubs and now a new television station. Then in 1963 the spectacular Boom Boom Room opened in Arthur Square in the heart of the city. It was new, it was raunchy and it drew the top names in showbiz. That was thanks to Alf Scott who, with his brothers Sidney and Dennis, was at the centre of business in Belfast. Sadly the brothers died only three years apart, all from cancer. So I turned to Alf's wife for the story of those days and I wasn't disappointed.

Betty Scott was born in London of Cockney parents. Her father was manager of Mr. Teesey Weesey's salon and hairdresser to the glitterati. She grew up in Blackpool and would have been a big singing star if she hadn't lost her heart to this handsome budding impresario from Belfast. It was 1962 when, in true showbiz fashion he saw her perform in a Blackpool club. Alf made his way backstage, invited her to dinner and so enthralled was she that she gave up a promising career. She turned her back on a BBC contract for her own television show, travelling the world singing with the combined service entertainment and the possibility of a part on the West End stage.

It was a remarkable love story for a girl who won a talent show at 12, was a Carroll Levis discovery, who at 16 turned down an invitation from Richard Attenborough saying she wanted to sing more than she wanted to act. She shared the bill with Anne Shelton, Tommy Cooper, Arthur English and Vic Oliver but the main man was Alf Scott, her husband for 30 years and without doubt, the love of her life. So Betty Foe became Betty Scott, soon to be instrumental in spicing up Belfast's entertainment circles.

During those years Alf brought the stars to Belfast and on their way to the famous Boom Boom Room they would stop off at Ulster Television. The opening night of the club was memorable. Mounted police controlled the crowds who had turned out to see the guests. They all wanted to be seen at the new club. Johnny Ray, Bill Haley and his Comets, Gerry and the Pacemakers with hosts David Jacobs and Pete Murray.

"Show bands were big at that time, we had the Miami from Dublin and Dickie Rock, we worked alongside the late Jim Aiken and he continued the big showbiz tradition long after Alf died. Lulu did her first gig outside Scotland with us. Then we opened the Tonic Cinema in Bangor for variety shows. That was where I fell in love with Glen Campbell but Alfie understood! Dear Danny La Rue, who died in June 2009 was such a lovely performer, brought the house down." She reels off the names. "Jean Vincent, Gerry Marsden and the Pacemakers, Adam Faith who'd just bought his brother a butcher's shop and the John Barry Seven, I remember John writing arrangements over the dinner table just like we'd write a postcard."

Looking back to the early 60s it seems incredible that Alf Scott was able to put Belfast on the map with such style. Of course, it worked both ways, the artist got exposure on television and a lucrative booking before a massive and enthusiastic audience and we got the excitement; Alf didn't do too badly either.

I remember Frankie Vaughan singing *Give me the Moonlight* and kicking his leg in our small studio before his show in the Boom Boom Room. I mentioned to Betty how we felt he was very brusque with members of the Boys' Clubs who gathered to get his autograph as he left the building.

"That's not Frankie, he must have been in a hurry to get down to us for rehearsal. It was his main charity and he was very good to them, the nicest kindest man you could meet." An example of how lasting a first impression can be.

Alf continued to develop the scene - the New Vic, the Tonic, the Regal in Larne, the Royal Avenue. He brought us the Rolling Stones who appeared at the Ulster Hall on one occasion and had to be smuggled out to safety via the back door and into a meat truck such was the frenzy of the young women. Joe Brown and the Brovvers, Marty Wilde, Englebert Humperdinck - when he answered to Arnold George Dorsey - Cilla Black, Billy Cotton with Kathy Kay and the dreaded Roy Orbison. Dreaded to me. I saw that show in the Ulster Hall and when he sang *Only the Lonely* I took an instant dislike to the man and that dislike remained. Why? Because he had stuffed, reputedly, a Coca Cola bottle down the front of his tight white pants! Someone else was sure it was a badminton shuttlecock but overheard was the comment which summed it up, "whatever that is, it ain't natural!" The gesture backfired because lot of girls found it an absolute turn off.

On the other hand Little Richard rocked the Boom Boom Room to its foundations in one of the best gigs of them all, and Jerry Lee Lewis will never be forgotten for his rendition of *Great Balls of Fire*.

"When Dion Warwick came for dinner after her show, she went off with my collection of tweed hats and Jack Jones sang *Impossible Dream* to me over a glass of wine." That's what it was like, these big stars jetted in and out creating a wonderful rainbow round the town – they had the 'wow' factor.

Alf died on their 30th wedding anniversary in January 1992. It is testament to his memory that shortly after his death Betty held a celebrity gala in his honour to raise £200,000 for an intensive cancer therapy unit for Belvoir Park Hospital. A ten-piece orchestra, 100 artists, many of them from those days in the 1960s, and not one person asked for a penny piece in payment. She doesn't talk a lot about her award-winning work with the RoSPA Tufty Clubs teaching children road safety, her work with the ratepayers association, her time as a toy lady at the Royal Victoria Hospital or chairing the Lady Taverners of Northern Ireland raising money for mentally and physically disabled children. Interviewing Betty Scott is like peeling an elegant vivacious onion. There are layers and layers of interest and memories and just as you think you're getting to the heart of the matter, there's more. Then you do get to the heart and, just for a brief instant, there's a tear.

"I was sitting with Alf at the end. It was our anniversary, that very day, that very afternoon. Thirty Years." She pauses. "In a lucid moment he just smiled at me and took my hand and whispered, "It's been good, hasn't it?"

*

There was no shortage of visiting entertainers especially at the Queen's Festival each autumn. Most of the artists came to the studios during the afternoon before their evening show.

On one occasion we were due to record an American jazz band. It was a matter of putting the grand piano into the studio, a few stools and letting them rip. And they did, a lively traditional number which they would be playing in the *Guinness Spot* at Queen's Festival later that night. Rehearsal over, we took a tea break for the lighting director to make adjustments. I noted the sequence of shots, checked our times for recording, totted up my timings and then relaxed and waited for the crew and the band to return from the canteen. The elderly black pianist, who was their revered leader, had asked one of his band to bring a cup of coffee for him as he thought the stairs might tire him out before performing. Derek Bailey came and sat in his director's chair, just the two of us in the control room and the jazz pianist on the studio floor. The old man began to play soulful blues. As the other musicians returned each took up his instrument and they began to jam – it was mesmerising. Derek whispered, "nip upstairs tell the boys to come back and quietly take shots. Get sound to bring up the mikes, we'll record this, don't tell the musicians."

This happened and we ended up with 20 minutes of real New Orleans magic. When they finished Derek went out on to the floor and asked permission to use the improvisation rather than the rehearsed number.

"I know, I know," said the old black musician with such a sad smile, "that's our music, music from the soul but that's not what we're about tonight. You'll have to show them what they're getting."

One of the frustrations of the medium.

*

That's the way it was. Life was stimulating. Of course, there were down times, tragedy and unhappiness and little telltale signs of things to come later in the 60s despite the ending of the IRA border campaign of guerrilla warfare. The following statement was released to the media on 26th February 1962.

The leadership of the resistance movement has ordered the termination of the campaign of resistance to British occupation launched on December 12th, 1956. Instructions issued to volunteers of the active service units and of local units in the occupied area have now been carried out. All arms and other material have been dumped and all full-time active service volunteers have been withdrawn.

In September 1964 this was thrown into doubt when rioting broke out in West Belfast.

Music was always in the air and jazz was king. Jack Williamson, Florence Irvine, Aubrey Allen, Alan Hailes, Anne Shaw and Paul Irwin at a Chris Barber concert in the Ulster Hall.

The famous McPeakes with Pete Seeger. Frances lll, Tommy McCrudden, Frances ll and Frances l, better known throughout the world of traditional Irish music as Ma Da

22
The McPeake Phenomenon

"Women aren't built for the pipes.
I remember watching a young French girl,
large breasted, trying to play and they
stopped listening they were so busy looking!"

One of my fondest memories was the day Francis McPeake the First, known to all as 'Ma Da', became 80 years old. Or was he?

It must have been around the time Pete Seeger invited the family folk group to make a two month tour of the United States. That was 1965 and as a result of that visit, they were better known abroad than at home. Indeed there's a story told that when Bob Dylan asked Bono of U2 what he thought of the McPeakes, Dublin born Bono admitted he'd never heard of them.

This legendary Belfast family began their musical journey with Ma Da, who was taught to play the pipes by John O'Reilly, the blind piper from Galway. The famous Presbyterian nationalist Francis Joseph Bigger brought O'Reilly north to Belfast for three months to teach the young Francis, who made a willing pupil. In 1908 he won prizes at the Belfast Feis and the Oireachtas of 1912. His talent extended to becoming unique in his ability to play his O'Mealy pipes as he sang, much in the way The Fureys and Planxty did in later years.

As a family they were and are special, each with their own talent, coming together to form first of all the Seamus McPeake Ceili Band, a group which became world famous. More recently under, the player manager Francis III, a school and a studio opened in Belfast city centre and a contemporary group was formed, known simply as McPeake.

It's 2008 and I'm sitting with Ma Da's son, Francie (Francis III) and his grandson, Francis IV in Café Carberry in the shadow of the Albert Clock in Belfast. This is the area of the Law Courts and Portia is all around. Young women in dark suits and white shirts come and go, a sight only seen in recent years since they invaded the male bastions of the courts, but there are also men with wigs in their hands and piles of papers under their arms. There's a tantalising smell of bacon and coffee. I ask Francie if he remembered his father's birthday party in Studio One back in the 60s.

"I certainly do, we thought we were going to do a number on the show but then the birthday cake was produced, 80 candles it seemed like. It was like a furnace and there was the smell of grease everywhere, it went flying all over the place as he tried to blow them out! You know, the joke was it wasn't his 80th birthday at all. That's why he looked so surprised." After all these years of misinformation this is a show-stopper. "Old people gave their age younger because insurance didn't cover them in hospital after I think 70. So we never really knew what age he was; it always caused confusion but we think he was only 78."

Anyway, it was a great event and McPeake senior sat there, unruly white hair and a benign smile hiding the awful truth.

Born around 1885, he was known and loved as Ma Da all over the world. Pete Seeger said he was the best communicator he'd ever come across and the best reader of an audience. Three times he won the Llangollen International Music Eisteddfod and his name was known far and wide.

"He was on UTV's outside broadcast from Dirty Dicks with Dominic Behan, closest thing to a horror film with the low ceiling and the dark and the cigarette smoke but the craic was great. He went everywhere and the drink was always flowing but he was wise to this and had a whiskey with a lemonade on the side to water it down, so he always had his wits about him. He was a political thinker and he said Irish traditional music was our classical music, the tears, the laughter and the woes of Ireland, the music for your ears and the words for your mind."

The memories begin to come. "We'd get requests for the *Floggin' Reel* from the Catholics and the *Queen's Wedding* from the Protestants; little did they know it was the same tune in different tempo."

In the 50s and 60s, the musical group of family members was made up of Ma Da, his sons Francis II and James, grandchildren Kathleen, Francis III and Tom McCrudden playing between them, two uilleann pipes, two harps, banjo, guitar and tin whistle and vocals. Over the years the family have played for President Johnson in the White House, performed in Moscow and John Lennon once asked Francie II to teach him the uilleann pipes.

"He won't talk much about that," young Francis confides as his father leaves the café to put more money in the parking meter. Once he's back I launch into the unknown.

"I believe you met John Lennon, was he interested in your music?"

The story unfolds concerning a man called Taylor, one of the Beatles management team whose brother was the principal of a school in Liverpool where the McPeakes had been invited to play in a local folk club in the city.

"It was coming near Christmas and the teacher phoned the manager. The manager was bragging that the Beatles film *Magical Mystery Tour* was being premiered during that summer of love in 1967. 'That's nothing,' said the principal, 'we've got the McPeakes here in the school.'

'Is that the McPeakes of Belfast? Been trying to get them for 18 months, want them to do a show.'"

And so it was the McPeakes flew to London, were met on the tarmac by a long black limo, travelled to the Dorchester Hotel where they stayed before attending the premiere of *Magical Mystery Tour.*

The original group, James McPeake, Frances II and the original, Francis - Ma Da.

"We went up into the bedroom and we were getting washed when Ma Da shouted, 'Jesus! Look, they know I've false teeth, they've left me a special tooth brush.' What actually happened was one of the others had already unpacked his bag and put his brush in the glass." What a let down. "But then we went downstairs to the function room there was this revolving stage and we played there. The Scaffold, a group from Liverpool were also on the bill. There were tables all round and we recognised Lulu, Jane Asher and Cilla Black. We met the Beatles. Paul McCartney was very affable, Ringo was OK but George was never my favourite. But they were intelligent boys."

From that meeting, the McPeakes signed up for Apple and the label wanted Kathleen to team up with Mary Hopkin. Lennon wanted to buy the contract and set the boys up in London and have Francis II teach him the uilleann pipes, the 'fairy music' he called it. John also wanted to buy an island off the coast of Ireland and on the day he was sailing over with Yoko, apparently a seagull dropped its letter of love on his shoulder! "Getting it quite wrong, apparently Yoko told him that it was a sign of bad luck so he turned his back to the mainland and never lived on his dream island. You know, he wanted to show that the Irish aren't slow thick people, he saw the beauty of Ireland and the Irish. If he'd bought that island he wouldn't have had to go to India to learn the mystical music there." Francis breaks off to order another coffee before imparting a piece of vital information. "Women aren't built for the pipes you know. I remember watching a young French girl, large breasted, trying to play and the audience stopped listening they were so busy looking."

I began to realise just how famous the McPeake name has been over the years.

Despite all the to-ing and fro-ing, Francis and John Lennon did meet at No. 3 Carnaby Street and after a session, Francis bought John a set of pipes from Mr. Kennedy of Cork and took them on a tour to blow them in. Sadly, despite John having a vision of the fairy music and haunting tunes weaving in and out of an orchestral piece, it wasn't to be. He decided it wasn't quite the sound he wanted.

The McPeakes were the first to play in a group, taking their music from the living room to the concert stage but to leave Belfast to live in London and mix with, as Francis puts it, 'yes men full of a load of bullshit' was unreal and not for them. So they came home. The twists and turns of life, the might have beens but always the superb music of Ireland.

Francis Senior wrote the song *Will Ye Go, Lassie Go* sung a million times or more and recorded by many including The Clancy's, The Byrds and Rod Stewart. Ma Da would surely be proud of the dynasty he began and to know that his great great grand son, Francis V born in 2006 already has his set of pipes standing by.

Ma Da died in 1971 and the family didn't play for some time following his death. In 1980, however, they reformed to teach, record and play – and talk about their remarkable family history.

The modern McPeake sound. Francis McPeake, pipes and whistles, Sean O'Kane, piano accordion, Peter Wallace, vocals and guitar, Nicky Scott, upright bass and Mairead Forde, fiddle.

Paddy Scott, the journalist's journalist. A man whose amazing recall brought back stories long after the event.

23
First Hand Reporting of History

In his cabin he opened the drawer of a small desk
and pulled out the child's vanity party bag.
Look at the contents, he said and I counted
coins all dated before 1912. Keep it, Mulholland said,
in memory of your lucky escape from the Titanic.

No memories of those days would be complete without talking of Paddy Scott, the man who taught me the word camaraderie and who worked as a producer in Ulster Television until his retirement. He died in 1999 aged 93 and a light went out.

In the early 60s we lived nearby each other, off the Antrim Road in north Belfast and he often gave me a lift home in his little blue Volkswagen 'beetle', his voice high with enthusiasm as he talked of his journalistic life. He then graduated to a Fiat which his friend and director Andy Crockart christened the 'jet propelled rosary bead'.

In 1923 Paddy became a pupil at St. Malachy's College and he had a baptism of fire when he first arrived in Belfast from his home in Carrickfergus. Walking from York Street train station to the school on the Antrim Road, Paddy first came across sectarian graffiti on gable walls and experienced the shock of seeing blood on the pavement where someone had been shot dead the previous night. On top of this, his best friend's father was murdered in his public house. Paddy attributed these experiences and the impact of sectarianism as the impetus to become a journalist.

"I felt that the only way to overcome this problem was through communication and education."

The veteran journalist James Kelly told me he well remembers Paddy at Queen's University when he was editing the RAG magazine. He remembers the students cat-calling to the MP's going into Parliament which was situated in the Presbyterian Church's Assembly College from 1921 until 1932. "There was the two faces of opposition, Craigavon and Joe Devlin. The MP's arrived in the train with top hats and the boys came running out of the students union with big sticks and began tipping their hats off. There was a police baton charge and Paddy was in the middle of it!"

Throughout his working life he was in the middle of the action. He was involved with a number of papers including the *Irish News*, the *Irish Press* and the *Irish News Agency* heading their Belfast bureau. His life was often under threat but the story was paramount and these are some of them, told to me on the many chats we had throughout the years.

On a bitter, wet night in November 1952 he was first on the

scene at the infamous Patricia Curran murder scene at Whiteabbey, a peaceful little village between Belfast and Carrickfergus. He talked his way into the house only hours after her body had been found in the wooded driveway of her home. The 19 year old Queen's university student had been stabbed thirty seven times. He knocked on the back door which was opened by Sir Lancelot Curran, in his time Lord Justice of Appeal, Northern Ireland and Member of Parliament for Carrickfergus. He'd been Attorney General for Northern Ireland and a member of the Privy Council of Northern Ireland. Now he was a distraught father, reeling in shock. In the aftermath of finding his daughter stabbed to death, standing in his kitchen, Paddy convinced him that he'd be better to talk to one journalist about his daughter's violent death rather than face dozens. As a result, Paddy left with an exclusive report and a picture which were syndicated around the world. It was only the beginnings of a story which he followed up as it unfolded over the months yet remains unsolved to this day.

*

When the British Railways car ferry *Princess Victoria* sank on Saturday 31st January 1953 in the North Channel off Donaghadee, Co. Down, bodies were being washed up, survivors pulled out of the freezing sea, many taken to the town's Imperial Hotel, headquarters of the emergency operation which swung into action. No journalists were allowed near the scene. No one was talking as Police protected the terrified passengers who were in shock and incoherent. Paddy was on the fringe of the town and determined to get his story. Someone whispered that there was a terrified young cabin boy in a traumatic state, jibbering in his fear. "Let me try to talk to him," Paddy suggested to the policeman on duty. "He's probably from the Islands and he'd talking Scottish Gaelic." This was enough to gain entrance. "Leave me with him for a while till I calm him," commanded Paddy. They did, not realising he was a reporter. Paddy was right; the boy would only talk in his native tongue and together with the journalist's Irish Gaelic they got down to business.

Once he'd heard the whole awful story first hand, right from the beginning of the tragedy, the order to abandon ship at 2 p.m. and arriving ashore, Paddy arranged for the young man to get something to eat and to be looked after as he hi-tailed it back to his desk with the story of the death of the Larne-Stranraer ferry in graphic detail. As a professional he was proud to report that his story beat every other journalist to the front page.

Malcolm Brodie, a newspaperman whose true professionalism allowed him to report on everything from sport to hard news and from the arts to current affairs.

Like Paddy Scott, *Belfast Telegraph* journalist Malcolm Brodie remembers the day the Princess Victoria went down. "It was a dreadful day, I'd been due to cover the football match between Linfield and the Scottish team Airdrie but because of the weather that morning, the team called off the trip. The first flush of morning news was over and we were waiting for the sports reports to come in so, like any newspaper office in those days, between noon and three o'clock on a Saturday, the newsroom was dead. Then the phone rang. I picked it up and it was a woman on the Antrim Road. She told me her husband was a sea captain and they'd shortwave radio. She said, 'there's a drama in the Lough'. She gave me what details she had and it sounded like the *Princess Victoria* was battling against big seas. She was right. The ship was fighting hurricane winds of Force 12, over 100 miles an hour, tossing in mountainous seas when the huge waves battered the rear doors, sheering off the bolts and flooding the car deck; tonne upon tonne of seawater swamped the ship and some 135 souls lost their lives.

"I immediately went up to her house and sat in a wee cubby hole with the radio as she made cups of tea."

He may well have heard radio officer David Broadfoot who remained at his transmitter throughout the tragedy, sending messages in Morse code in an attempt to give an exact position for rescue vessels, although he must have know it meant he would not survive. For this selfless action, Broadfoot was posthumously awarded the George Cross, highest UK award for bravery which can be made to a civilian. There were many other awards for gallantry shown that day.

For two and a half hours Malcolm filed his report down the telephone line to the *Belfast Telegraph*; a young John Cole, later to become a respected BBC political editor, took the copy as the story unfolded. At 4.15 that afternoon, a coaster, *The Pass of Dromochter*, attempted to pick up survivors but send back a message, 'nothing can survive in these waters and we're pulling out.'

Portpatrick Coast Radio Station was giving details as they became available and when he heard figures being talked about, Malcolm did a mental tot in his head and realised the extent of the tragedy.

"My problem was trying to get the boys at the *Telegraph* to believe what I was telling them - that there could be over 100 people drowned."

In fact, it was more. On Saturday, January 31st 1953, 179 set sail from Stranraer to Larne on the car ferry *Princess Victoria*. Only 44 men survived the crossing. Four little children, 29 women and 102 men perished.

There were notable names recorded in the list of dead. Major Maynard Sinclair, MP for Cromac, Minister of Finance and Deputy Prime Minister, was also on board. Major Sinclair was relaxing in the smokeroom when the steward on duty warned that the ship would roll a bit as the weather was rough. At that moment a glass fell off a ledge under a porthole and smashed to the floor. There was a lurch to starboard but she righted herself. A second heavier and more violent lurch threw people across the room breaking chairs and tables. Major Sinclair was thrown to the starboard side of the room. The Princess Victoria never regained an upright position. Sir Walter Smiles Ulster Unionist MP for North Down and Captain James Ferguson who went down with his ship, saluting as the sea engulfed him. But the majority were families, businessmen, passengers and crew taking the routine trip of only a few miles, expecting to leave the shelter of Loch Ryan and move into the North Channel and on to the safety of Larne Harbour. It certainly didn't happen that way and there were many stories told by the survivors after the tragedy. A First Class steward was manning one of the lifeboats, sitting in the bow and holding on to each side of the boat when a huge wave crashed it against the side of the *Princess Victoria* cutting off three fingers on each hand. Others swam to life rafts only to be carried away in the raging sea. One lifeboat filled with women and children was swept against the side of the sinking vessel and swamped.

The inquiry into the disaster found the fault lay principally with the ship's owner and manager, the British Transport Commission, basically because the ship's stern doors were insufficiently strong for conditions in the North Channel. There was also a failure to provide adequate 'freeing' arrangements for seas that may enter the car decks from any source.

Some positive actions were taken as a result of the disaster. Because the standard cork lifejackets were thought to have choked some passengers to death. Today lifejackets must be tied tightly and held down if jumping into the sea to prevent them pushing up and causing neck injuries or suffocation. The design of similar ships was examined in the light of the experience and subsequently stern doors were strengthened and the size of scuppers increased.

Like Paddy Scott, later that afternoon, Malcolm Brodie headed to Donaghadee to follow up on his story, but the tragedy he said was when he came back to the *Telegraph* that evening to find thousands of people standing in Royal Avenue waiting for news. "You've got to remember in the early 50s there was no news broadcasting as we have today, no Internet, no mobile phones, so they came to the source of news and that was a newspaper.

"For the first time in its history," he said "the *Ireland Saturday Night* carried a news story on the front page rather than sport and we put out a special edition of the paper on the Sunday. It was tragic." Malcolm was obviously reliving that last day in January as he added sadly, "I lost a mate that day, a fellow Scot." He's silent for a moment. "We were to meet that Saturday night as usual and go dancing. It wasn't to be."

*

Despite the many and varied stories he covered during his lifetime, Paddy Scott liked best to talk of the *Titanic*. So when the

James Cameron film was previewed in 1997, I invited him to come with me to Belfast's Yorkgate Movie House.

He wrote the following handwritten letter to me, probably that same night when he got home. A moving piece of history.

Dear Anne,

The apt expression of the reaction that comes to my mind on seeing and hearing Cameron's Hollywood version of the *Titanic* story is contained in a quotation from Macbeth (Shakespeare) – *it was a tale told full of sound and fury signifying nothing.*

That may seem a harsh appreciation of the three hour version of the *Titanic* story of which I had a fascination since as a boy of five years and the seventh son (of eight boys) of the chief officer of the Coastguards at the station in Cloughey, on the rocky Co. Down coast between Donaghadee and St. John's Point at the entrance of Strangford Lough. I saw the *Titanic* with black smoke belching out of three of her four funnels as she gained speed, on dropping her tugs, on her passage to Southampton to begin her maiden voyage to New York and destiny.

It was an early April day in 1912 when most of the people from the villages of Cloughey and surrounding farms gathered at the Coastguard station in great excitement and expectation to see the great liner – the largest and most luxurious in the world - sail into and past Cloughey Bay on her passage down the Irish Sea to begin her maiden voyage to New York from Southampton, collecting passengers at Cherbourg France and Queenstown Ireland on the way. The aim was to capture the record crossing of the Atlantic from the rival transatlantic passenger company.

Everyone knew of the size, luxury and capabilities of the world's greatest and most luxurious ship.

My home knew all about the ship especially from my brother John, then a third year apprentice in engineering at Harland and Wolff shipyard, who referred to her as "the big boat 401" apparently the number on the shipyard's list of ships.

The Belfast papers reflected all the enthusiasm and pride in this the second of the luxury liners on the slips of the Belfast shipyard – the *Olympic*, the *Titanic* and the *Britannic* – all catering for the emigrant traffic to America from Ireland and Britain and Europe. The three liners were the brain children of three cousins then leading executives of Harland and Wolff's shipyard – Lord Pirrie the chairman, Alexander Montgomery Carlisle, managing director and chief naval architect and Thomas Andrews of Comber, a younger member of the linen mill owning family, all members of the non-subscribing Presbyterian Church (Liberal minded and with close connections with the independent wing of the Protestant church).

The great family name linking the three cousins was Montgomery. The best known of the non-scribing Presbyterian or Unitarian faith, the leading figure in which was the great cleric Dr. Montgomery, scholar and one of the founders of 'Inst.' (the boy's grammar school Royal Belfast Academical Institution) whose tolerant views on religion, especially towards Catholics, brought on him the wrath of the great Presbyterian champion (but not the scholar) Dr. Cooke.

Lord Pirrie, engineer and naval architect of H&W where he served his time, was, after Harland himself, the chief architect of the success of the Belfast shipyard. He negotiated the deals with the White Star Line for their transatlantic passenger trade and planned the initial stages of adding to their fleet the three great liners – the *Olympic*, the *Titanic* and the *Britannic* – all at the opening decade of the 1900s.

Of the three ships, the *Olympic*, the first of the slips was Perrie's favourite. It was the *Olympic* which brought his body back for burial in Belfast City Cemetery when he died from a heart attack during a cruise in American waters.

The plans for the three liners were agreed by Pirrie and the White Star Line chiefs. He looked after the *Olympic* design and left his cousin Alexander Montgomery Carlisle, the chief naval architect to succeed him as general manager to look after the *Titanic* and the preparation of the building of the *Britannic* on adjoining slips. So Carlisle was the man who built the *Titanic* and his cousin the youthful Thomas Andrews saw it completed.

Carlisle was a strong individualist, hard working, a disciplined student and apprentice. He took a cold bath every morning before cycling to the shipyard at 7 a.m. and was late for work during his five years apprenticeship on only one morning.

He had cultured taste in music and was a keen photographer, a practice he retained all his life. He rose in influence in the firm and succeeded his cousin Lord Pirrie as managing director and chief naval architect during the construction of the *Titanic*. He overworked and had few hobbies (music was one) and when he was in virtual working control of the shipyard, retired early and handed over completion of the *Titanic* and Britannic to his young cousin Thomas Andrews of Comber whose brother became the second Prime Minister, Mr. John M Andrews (M for Montgomery) of Northern Ireland in succession in 1941 to Lord Craigavon (Sir James Craig).

Alexander Montgomery Carlisle, through the influence of Lord Pirrie (a liberal peer), was an Irish privy councillor with the right to sit 'near the throne' in the House of Lords but not participate in the discussions or vote. In retirement he persisted on taking a cold bath each day, cycling to where ever he wanted to go in London and dining at Lyon's Corner Cafes. His cold bath exercises while he had a severe cold, led to his death.

In religion he became a humanist and showed his views by making arrangements himself for his funeral at the Golders Green cemetery leaving instructions, as he paid for the costs, that his body was to be burned, that there was to be no religious ceremony or sacred music, that the organist was to play Franz Lehrer music and that only his immediate relatives be present; only a handful of relatives, including his daughter, the wife of the aide-de-camp to the Kaiser (then in exile in Holland). A short report in the *London Evening Standard* revealed that the sobs of his daughter and the few relatives as the coffin disappeared from view were louder than the light sound of the organist who declined to reveal the identity of the music to the only reporter present.

Whilst in London, Carlisle was a close friend and admirer of Wickham Steed, the well-known author, who wrote a special feature in his prominent magazine on the *Titanic* and planned to travel to a humanist convention in America on the maiden voyage of the liner from Southampton.

Carlisle went there to see his friend off and his ship and his cousin Andrews who also planned to make the maiden voyage and complete work to be done on the liner while on the crossing.

It was customary for the managing director and his wife to make the maiden voyage crossing in the ship. But Andrews's wife was still suffering from postnatal depression after the birth of their first child, a daughter and her doctor advised her not to make the maiden voyage on the *Titanic*.

Just before the *Titanic* pulled away from the docks at Southampton, Bruce Ismay, the chairman of the White Star liner noticed Carlisle standing on the quayside near the gangway. He had come to see off his closest friend Stead.

"Are you not coming with us Carlisle?" he shouted. Carlisle replied, "No, I wasn't asked."

Later, when the fate of the *Titanic* was talked about, he was asked. "Would you have gone if he had said 'Well come along with us.'" He replied. "I would have been honoured to die with my brave and loyal friend Stead."

So three Ulster cousins figured prominently in the history, story and fate of the world's most luxurious liner, the *Titanic*.

Andrews courageously lost his life in the disaster and was last seen advising passengers to put on lifebelts. His last thoughts were about his wife sick at home in Windsor Avenue in Belfast and his young baby daughter. He was among the 1500 passengers who died that night."

*

This was an amazing letter to receive only hours after Paddy and I sat and watched Cameron's film.

During our conversations, Paddy, with his unique memories, later updated the story of the RMS *Titanic* which struck an iceberg in the North Atlantic just before midnight on 14th April 1912 and sank the next day with the loss of 1520, men, women and children. This total didn't include stowaways. The *Belfast Evening Telegraph* of April 15th 1912 carried reports which were amazingly informative given the short time between disaster and publication. One report from New York spoke of the clamour for news and of ladies sobbing hysterically, one frantically inquiring for news of her sister who was returning from her honeymoon. Later, high-class women pulled on their fur coats, raided their larders and were chauffeur driven to the docks wishing to give what they could to survivors. From the day of the disaster, surviving crewmembers ceased to receive any pay and even in death there was the discrimination between rich and poor. First class passengers were placed in coffins. Canvas bags for the rest.

Then, from Paddy Scott, my friend and mentor, came the strangest story of all.

*

"When I became a journalist, on leaving Queen's University, I happened to meet and then interview an elderly man who lived alone in a street off the Old Lodge Road near Carlisle Circus and Clifton Street. I think his name was Mulholland. He was a stoker by trade. Sitting in his back room one day in front of the wee fire he told me that he stoked the *Titanic* on her trials and on her way down the Irish Sea to Southampton. This is his story, Anne. It's spine tingling."

There and then Paddy Scott stepped back in time to 1929 recount this interview with Mulholland the stoker, word for word.

'In 1912 work was hard to come by in Belfast. I was waiting for a stoker's job in a tramp steamer that would bring me work continuously for much of the year. I was offered the job on the *Titanic* but I didn't like short crossings although I agreed to go as far as Southampton. I preferred the long voyages in tramp steamers that took you half round the world's ports. At the end of these voyages after visiting ports in two or three continents, you'd have a nice pay packet in your pocket. You didn't save money on a short transatlantic crossing.

'Anyway I made friends with my mate in Belfast, a fellow stoker on the *Titanic*. On her trials down the Irish Sea he urged me to complete the voyage to New York with him as we got on well working together on the same furnace. I explained my preferences to him about long voyages and told him I'd keep an open mind.

'But my decision was made by the behaviour of a cat that came on board the *Titanic* in Belfast and made a home with the stokers. She had a litter of four kittens on board ship and we kept her, looking after the mother cat and her brood broke the monotony of stoking the furnace. But when we docked at Southampton that cat made up my mind for me. Shortly after we tied up, the cat made a survey of the place. I watched her intently. When I saw her catching each kitten by the back of its head and carry each one down the gangway and on to the quayside, I thought, that cat knows something and has decided that the *Titanic* was no place for her or her kittens to spend their lives. So I took the advice that cat was giving me in a practical way - I said goodbye to my mate and left the ship at Southampton. I gave thanks to God for my choice.

'A few years later, Paddy, my tramp steamer berthed in the port of Valparaiso in South America. I dropped into a pub at the docks for a leisurely pint with a crew colleague. I happened to cast a glance across the bar and my eyes focused on a figure drinking there, something about him which I thought I recognised, something familiar. It was dim where he was sitting in the corner. I looked several times at this man and a movement of his head revealed features like those of my stoker mate on the *Titanic*. I thought no more about it, Paddy, as I had long given him up as one of the crew lost in the greatest sea disaster. But I kept looking at him.

'Finally, curiosity got the better of me and I got up and approached him. As I got closer I almost panicked. It was him. He recognised me too. We greeted each other warmly, even emotionally as I thought he was dead and with the other victims of the disaster at the bottom of the Atlantic with the liner.

'When I recovered from the shock of meeting a stoker mate who had come back from the dead, and a few more drinks, I accompanied him back to his ship where he told me how he got off the doomed liner.

'In the panic and confusion on board the *Titanic*, he said he made his way through the milling crowds of passengers by various routes and corridors to the upper deck and edged his way towards the rail where a lifeboat hung precariously on ropes. There were women and children on board. An officer called out:

Is there anyone here who can row and manage a boat?

I shouted back over the noise, I can and sail one too.

Get in and pull away immediately the lifeboat hits the water.

I got into the crowded lifeboat, did as he told me and pulled away when it began to float. The relief to be away from the panic was overpowering. We got clear of the *Titanic,* away from the danger of being sucked down with her. We kept close to the other lifeboats by shouts and whistles. We were, after many hours, picked up by the *Carpathia.*

'I was the last to leave the lifeboat and as I was being lifted off I noticed amongst the debris on the floor of the lifeboat a small-decorated chain purse used by a young girl to hold her money at a party. I picked it up, put it in the pocket of my jacket.

'And Paddy, in his cabin he opened the drawer of a small desk and pulled out the child's vanity party bag. 'Look at the contents,' he said. I counted coins all dated before 1912. 'Keep it, Mulholland,' he said, 'in memory of your lucky escape from the *Titanic*.'

It was obvious that Paddy Scott was moved by the memories that were unfolding as we talked all those years later.

"I was mesmerised Anne by the story of this man who walked off the Titanic, lived to meet his mate and hear the story of his survival".

In 1929 Paddy had been taking the story down in shorthand, and he told me how he paused as Mulholland stood up from the table.

"He walked to a chest in the corner of the room in Old Lodge Road, lifted the lid and drew out the precious little chain mail purse he'd been given in Valparaiso and put it into my hand. He looked at me sadly saying, 'And Paddy, I've kept it in this drawer ever since.'"

Paddy Scott died on 21st December 1999 at the age of 93.
He never lost his zest for life or his sense of humour as his friend Andy Crockart found as he sat by Paddy's bedside and heard his last words.

"I asked him did he like the new water bed the nurse had got for him and he opened one eye and said, complete with typical finger wagging:
'Although I wasn't consulted, I approve.'"

The remarkable Shay Healy

24
Hands and Hearts Across the Border

Coming from the south as the RTE boys did,
Newry was the Gateway to the North,
whilst for us it was escaping forty miles down
the road to the freedom of the Ardmore Hotel
where we could eat, drink and sing and where,
on occasions, love blossomed.
Most of us were just embarking on a career path in
broadcasting and the journey united us.

We had a great rapport with the other television stations in those days. The boys played golf around the UK network stations and at home the BBC, RTE and Ulster Television would hi-tail it to the Ardmore Hotel on the outskirts of Newry town, now a thriving city sitting snugly between the magnificent Mountains of Mourne in South Down and the Ring of Gullion in South Armagh. It was our chance to meet up with the boys from Radio Telefis Eireann, known and loved as RTE, the public service broadcaster of Ireland, a statutory body run by an authority appointed by the Irish Government. On January 1 1926 it went on air initially with radio programmes followed by television on the last day of the year in 1961, so making it one of the oldest continuously operating public service broadcasters in the world. Not that any of this information mattered to us, we were a bunch of 20-somethings on the crest of a wave.

Coming from the south as the RTE boys did, Newry was the Gateway to the North. For us it was escaping forty miles down the road to the freedom of the Ardmore Hotel where we could eat, drink and sing and, where on occasions, love blossomed. Most of us were just embarking on a career path in broadcasting and the journey united us. We were in the big bubble of 'the meja' as it was called - the media, it covered a multitude of excitements but television was surely the biggest bubble of all.

One young man was electric. He wrote, sang and worked in RTE. He turned out to be Shay Healy, a most attractive man and a good friend. In later years I remember him doing a BBC radio programme from Ormeau Avenue during the workers strike when he said, 'sure you've only to stick your nose out of the door these days and someone will picket.' Undoubtedly he was a natural wit.

Perhaps his moment came in 1980 when his song *What's Another Year* sung by Johnny Logan, won the Eurovision Song Contest in The Hague. The song instantly reached No.1 in the UK charts and over three million copies were sold.

"That was an extraordinarily exciting time. We were met by thousands of well-wishers at the airport and myself and Johnny became national heroes. To this day, people still like to tell me where they were on that famous night."

There was an interesting build up to that ultimate moment and an insight into the inner working of the southern broadcasting company.

To start at the beginning. Shay lived on Wilfield Road on the borderline of Ballsbridge and Sandymount, on the fringe of the Dublin suburbs and his story is one of a young man with stars in his eyes. The difference is that Shay Healy became one of those stars.

"Wilfield Road dead-ended into a playing field that hosted Pembroke Cricket Club in summer and Monkstown Rugby Club in winter. So, in a house full of Gaelic speakers, I grew up playing Protestant games. In the early sixties there was almost an equal ratio of Protestants to Catholics on our road. All of us were neither rich nor poor and I grew up to be a true egalitarian after a childhood that happily was free of trauma.

"I lived quite close to RTE and many times in its first two years of operation I gazed longingly over the walls, sensing rather than knowing that something inside those walls was calling to me. My mother used to write and read children's short stories for BBC Radio. She also contributed to RTE Radio magazine programmes. She knew she was trapped in domesticity, having to rear six children, four girls and two boys. I don't know why she chose me, but she invested her knowledge and her time in me so that she could vicariously live out some of her dreams through me. She encouraged me enough that I read my first article on the Petronella O'Flanagan Show on a Friday afternoon when I was only 15. I think I fell instantly in love with that word "show" and deep down I knew that I was a bit of a show-off."

In 1963, RTE chose twenty-two young men to be trainees in cameras, sound and lighting. Shay could scarcely believe his luck that he was one of the chosen ones. After six months of training, he opted to be a cameraman.

"Cameramen were like fighter pilots," he told me. "Swooping and shooting anything that moved. The presence of an audience in studio for shows meant there was an audience for us too. We could show them what a great bunch of technicians we were. During *The Late Late Show,* the cameras frequently panned around the whole studio and if by chance you were caught on camera, working on this exalted show, you were close to being a celebrity as dammit."

The *Late Late* was first broadcast on Friday 6th July 1962 at 11.20 p.m. and claims to be the world's longest running chat show hosted in those days by the famous Gay Byrne. Gay was unique, he presented the programme for 37 years and has been looked up to and emulated by many chat show hosts ever since. But it was just one of an astonishingly varied range of programmes Shay recalls.

"We did four-camera music shows, 'live' dramas, shows with the RTE orchestra. We did apres-dinner chat shows and farming programmes. It was all grist to our mill. We did not differentiate between working on the *Late News* in Studio 3 or working on the fabulously exciting *The Showband Show.* It was all television to us. And for my own history I had the very first shot on the very first Irish soap opera, *Tolka Row.*

"Television had the country in its thrall and we were at the centre of this new universe, creating the excitement that was changing the very fabric of Ireland. The glamour was a powerful scent wafting on our daily breeze. The collective spirit in RTE was part of the joy. We had unanimity of purpose and in those fabulous years between 1963-1967 when I was part of it, we worked together and played together. The weatherman was as much a part of our gang as was an electrician, a vision mixer or a film editor.

"I do remember how eagerly we anticipated our annual trip North to meet our colleagues from UTV. Due to my fascination with Smirnoff, I have a lot of fuzzy memories. There were nights in the Ardmore Hotel in Newry and in The Wellington Park in Belfast, where we sang a repertoire of rebel songs that would all too soon be proscribed on radio, North and South."

Another of our company was Noel D. Greene whose name was to come into homes all over Ireland and the UK when he became a network producer in years to come. How proud we were to see him listed in the credits, popular shows like ITV's *Punchlines* and *The Krankies Klub.* He was a close friend of Shay's and the two were real hits with the guests at our wedding in 1966. Shay recalls their friendship.

"Noel joined RTE the same day as me. We quickly became best friends and when the time to choose arrived, he also opted to become a cameraman. Noel was macho man, parachuting and rallying with gusto. But one night in the RTE Social Club, we locked the door of the snooker-room at his behest and he confessed to me that he was gay. It was a big admission in 1967. I hugged him and told him that our friendship would never be based on his sexual orientation. I was very fond of Noel. He had a wicked sense of humour. He went to London and had a successful career as a producer at ITV until his obscenely early death."

I reminded Shay of his visits to Belfast and his contributions to BBC Radio programmes.

"I used to like to write parodies and funny ditties and I can just about dredge one verse from the blacked out areas of my memory.

Up in Belfast
Fights can break out very aisy

Especially if you meet up with a man called the Reverend Ian Paisley.
Our politics and religion make him laugh
And that's why I'm standin' here waitin' for the milkman so as I can grab some milk bottles to make Molotov Cocktails to throw at the buses in Belfast.

During his time as a cameraman in RTE, the "ballad boom" began in Ireland and Shay became a performer and MC at gigs all over Ireland. He was also the folk correspondent for *Spotlight Magazine*, the bible of Showbiz in Ireland.

"In the middle of all this madness, I married Dymphna Errity on September 5th, 1967 and almost simultaneously switched sides of the camera to become the host of *Ballad Sheet*. I quickly achieved by ambition to be famous and landed myself a radio show on RTE called *Preab Sa Cheoil* and through Tony McAuley I also landed a show on BBC NI Radio. I can still hear the announcer intone gravely, "And now *Folkweave*, a programme of folk music."

There followed years in America where he became a restaurateur although singing was still top of his bill.

He and Dymphna emigrated to Boston, sang in Music City, and spent the summer of 1975 in Hyannis on Cape Cod, a happy sojourn in fine weather, he says, still singing in a glorious, unforgettable time.

After the Eurovision success he had a cult television show *Nighthawks* but in the late 2000s he calls himself a multi-media artist.

"I've written a couple of novels and a gig memoir. I've made lots of documentaries about characters as diverse as Roy Rogers and Phil Lynott from *Thin Lizzy*. I also fancy myself as a photographer and journalist. And, of course, I still write songs. Most recently I have had three tracks recorded by the phenomenally successful Celtic Woman and I also have written for the new sensation of Irish folk, The High Kings."

Who'd have guessed that a life could be crammed with so much variation. We didn't look ahead in those days of heady fun, it all just seemed to happen, and it happened big style for Shay Healy. He has even written his own gravestone inscription which he hopes will read:

He had an adventurous life and a lot of laughs -
do not resuscitate.

The fashion of the day.
Miss Adrienne and friends.

Rowel Friers working on the cover of his autobiography, Drawn from Life.

25
Special men in my life

Years later, Rowel was called to an art house in London to verify a painting attributed to the late William Conor.
He did recognise it but it wasn't signed.
"Take it out of the frame please," he requested.
This was done and Rowel turned it over and there, sure enough, on the back was a greasy stain where the egg had hit the canvas.
A true William Conor.

At school, we used to snitch coloured chalk from the blackboard box to use as rouge, eye shadow, lipstick, and to mix blue and red to fashion black eyes for sympathy. When William Conor was at school he used chalk to satisfy his need to fashion faces and figures of the men and women he saw around him. He was only ten when his music teacher came on these drawings and realised immediately that the pupil of Clifton Park Central National School was special. Subsequently he went to the Government School of Design in Belfast later to be renamed the College of Art, where his journeys to and from the city centre would accord him the characters he craved for, the shawlies, the mill workers and the men from the yard.

When I was travelling home on the 64 Downview Avenue bus from the Ormeau Road to Fortwilliam, I saw the mill girls stretched across the pavements of York Street, arms linked, singing *Our Queen Can Burl Her Leg* at the top of their voices. I also remember how we had to watch our time to avoid the bus being caught in the midst of thousands of men, dark trousers and jackets and flat duncher caps, the empty piece box which once held their lunch under their uxter; they were making their way home from the shipyard as the evening drew in.

It was at that time William Conor arrived in our office in the early 60s. He was coming to the end of his presidency of the Royal Ulster Academy and would have been about 83. I met him in reception and took his large heavy portfolio and led him upstairs. Derek Bailey came down the corridor to greet him. By this time Conor was acknowledged as an extra special man.

*

William Conor was born in Fortingale Street on the Old Lodge Road off the Antrim Road in Belfast. His father was a wrought iron worker so he was born into a family where creating was important. Like his father he was an artist but to earn a living, his first job was with David Allen and Sons as an apprentice lithographer. In 1914 he was appointed a war artist and commissioned by the British Government to produce official sketches of soldiers and munitions workers during the First World War. He was prolific and his work today is much sought after. There are examples of his art in boardrooms and bedrooms and his crayon and watercolour works are in the permanent collections of the Ulster Museum.

When he left Belfast for London in 1920, he was immediately absorbed into the social world of the top artists, Sir John Lavery and Augustus John amongst them. The following year he was accepted to exhibit at the Royal Academy. He was already recognised in Dublin and then became one of the first Academicians when the Belfast Arts Society became the Ulster Academy of Arts in 1930 and a full member of the Royal Hibernian Academy in 1946.

Taken from Rowel's book, this picture shows William Conor (extreme left) with colleagues in David Allen's and Sons. Jeremy Friers

Above all, he loved Belfast and Belfast people, men, women and children. London couldn't hold him and he returned in 1921 to open studios in Chichester Street, then Wellington Place and his final studio on the Stranmillis Road, subsequently becoming the sophisticated Café Conor.

Artist Joe McWilliams remembers him well with his big floppy bow tie and fedora hat, a character at the Art College and a painter whose true genius was yet to be realised.

He excelled with official commissions but he will be best remembered for his portrayal of the man in the street, the working class heroes and the Orange processions. It's been said that he raised the art of crayon drawing to the level of genius.

And here he was opening his portfolio propped up on my desk. It was filled with sketches. Crayon, charcoal, watercolour, oils, all mediums were represented. Derek was selecting drawings to illustrate Conor the artist in a forthcoming series. I watched as they went through the higgledy piggledy papers, small medium and large, some on drawing paper, some on blotting paper. This man obviously couldn't stop and used whatever was to hand. He was a perfectionist to a fault as we soon discovered – to our long term cost.

"Not that one," he said, taking a drawing of a woman and her two children and screwing it up then firing it into the wastepaper basket. "I won't want you to use this." Another work of art lands in the basket. He thought they weren't worthy for a programme about his work. There must have been a dozen discarded drawings and we didn't even think to rescue them when the delightful elderly gentleman left the building.

In and around 2007 even a scrap of a William Conor would be worth tens of thousands. Some paintings would sell for over £80,000, even £100,000 but that's not the point; sometimes a little doodle or a preliminary sketch tells more about the artist than the finished work and our little treasure trove is long gone in some landfill site no doubt built over many times.

*

It was much the same with the work of Rowel Friers, again one of our finest creators. For him it was most often the cartoon style but again he favoured the wee man in the duncher and the bent fag hanging from between his lips.

Rowel was a regular in the studio, especially when it came to the late evening programme *Flashback,* a hard hitting review of the week's news featuring film stories, newspaper headlines and articles with Rowel's brilliant cartoons giving the subject a satirical edge.

Friday morning saw Derek Bailey and Ernie Strathdee on their knees in the Preview Theatre. Surrounded by newspapers, dailies and provincials, they were cutting and pasting. Ivor Mills would pop in and out to give a hand before he presented the show later that evening. The script was written as we went along, me on typewriter, the boys still weilding scissors and Rowel away with snips of stories which he turned into an integral part of the fast moving programme. *Flashback* was conceived as a way of getting value from the newly opened news room and the team, Fred Corbett, Bill McGookin, Derek Murray, Rory Fitzpatrick, Paddy Scott and Ian Sanderson amongst them. Robin Walsh and Colm McWillams followed in the tradition. Film was re-run, photographs of people in the headlines and reporters straight to camera were used.

The jigsaw came together early evening as we rehearsed. It seemed every programme had a highlight. When the opening of the first Chinese Restaurant in Belfast coincided with important Orange (Protestant) and Green (Nationalist) talks, Rowel combined them with a cartoon showing Basil Brook, 1st Viscount Brookborough, Unionist and Eddie McAteer, Leader of the Nationalist Party talking over a Dim Sum Chinese meal, complete with pigtails and chopsticks. The caption? *The 'Olange and Gleen Talks'.*

Rowel Friers (centre) admiring a portrait of R.H McCandless.
With him is Nelson Brown, College of Technology, and the poet John Hewitt. *Jeremy Friers*

In 1965, when Irish premier Seán Lemass came to Stormont, Rev. Ian Paisley was there with his followers armed with snowballs and proceeded to pelt the Taoiseach's car. Ivor had fun with that image, wondering what balls the Reverend gentleman would be making next!

Rowel became a dear friend who never took sides when it came to politics or politicians. They all left a lot to be desired as far as he was concerned.

"The only side I'm on," said Rowel Friers, "is sanity. I just make fun of all the madness." He was describing his work as a caricaturist, the best-known cartoonist of the Troubles. The Oxford Dictionary defines a 'rowel' as a spiked revolving disk at the end of a spur. A name well chosen for Rowel, sharp as a tack in his observations and able to pack a punch with his talents and get a dig in at the same time.

Rowel experienced the madness at first hand. He was born in the year of partition when the Northern Ireland Parliament was created in 1920. He spent his entire life in the Province only to die in 1998 following the Good Friday Agreement, which created the Northern Ireland Assembly. Yet few knew the background which made this man so intensely sensitive and a genius in his chosen profession.

At Park Parade school, he told me, his ambition was to be a monk.

"I had this romantic idea of the Robin Hood character and all I wanted was to sit in a cell all day and draw, wearing a dressing gown and no tie." Although it wasn't quite like that, Rowel had his cross to bear suffering as he did from mental illness. His description of his 'black dog' was told without emotion.

"Sometimes I would get this light-headed feeling at school and my guts would grip. I felt removed from reality, everything would go silent, people were walking about like a dream I couldn't relate to. I was isolated and alone from everybody. My mother used to tell me to run my wrists under the cold tap." If only it had been that easy. There was shock treatment which he hated. Sessions where he sat in the waiting room ashamed and frightened, watching people who all looked like zombies realising he probably looked the same to them. He had four serious breakdowns in his life, times when he didn't want to see friends yet wanting to see them. The mixed up emotions and depression could stay for months. Once the moon was shining through his bedroom window on to the white cover of the bed. "It seemed to fall in the shape of a cross. My hands were resting on my chest and I was convinced I was dead."

The power of this man was his ability to talk about the bad times and the good times knowing he might be able to help someone. "They think it's something to do with over-sensitivity – a lot of painters and artists get it. Churchill had his black dog."

And then it was on with the conversation.

He grew up in East Belfast, in the Lagan Village, a short walk from the City Hall and the shipyards. His first job was at 15 when, like William Connor before him, he was an apprentice lithographer before attending the Belfast College of Art at a time when it was a powerhouse of creativity. He was soon contributing to all the major publications in Ireland, his cartoon comments and political satire gracing many magazines and newspapers, including the *Belfast Telegraph*, the *Irish Times,* the *Belfast Newsletter* and the *Daily Express, Punch* – even *Men Only*.

He was awarded the MBE in 1977 and died two years short of the new Millennium. Always a part of my life, he is still missed, his laconic comments stimulating lively conversation. I recall his theory for peace in Northern Ireland at the time of the frightening confrontations between Catholic residents and Protestant marchers on the Garvaghy Road in Portadown during the 12th of July marching season.

"Build raked seating on either side of the road, sell rock with Garvaghy printed through the centre. I'll design a T-shirt, one for each side and we'll do postcards and set this up as a worldwide tourist attraction." He had a habit of taking the wind out of people's sails and defusing the most tense of situations.

Rowel didn't move far from his birthplace ending up with his wife Yvonne in a rambling old house in Holywood, Co. Down where his paints and paintings were all around, again like Conor, scraps of paper holding delightful drawings and canvases on shelves and tables. His memory and creativity is perpetuated by his two sons, photographer Jeremy and graphic designer Timothy, and his nephew, the painter Julian Friers.

*

Nor did William Conor move far from his birthplace in North Belfast. William Conor OBE died not long after we met over his portfolio in the production department of Ulster Television. He was buried in 1968 from his home on Salisbury Avenue off the Antrim Road. I hope that teacher, Louis Mantell lived long enough to realise how important was his mentoring of that 'special pupil'.

There's a lovely story told about William Conor and it's attributed to Rowel Friers. Apparently Rowel was visiting his old friend in his Salisbury Avenue home where Conor lived surrounded by his paintings, so many that some were lying face down on the floor.

Rowel was invited to take a late breakfast and so an Ulster fry was prepared and served, but the fried egg escaped, slid off the plate and on to the floor, landing on a painting back side! Waste not want not. The egg was scooped up and put back on the plate. Years later, Rowel was called to an art house in London to verify a painting attributed to the late William Conor. He did recognise it but it wasn't signed. "Take it out of the frame please," he requested. This was done and Rowel turned it over and there, sure enough, on the back was a greasy stain where the egg had hit the canvas. A true William Conor.

*

The late Lawson Birch was a popular visitor to the studio, a sought after artist who ended his days in Donegal, painting the beautiful landscapes and introducing a new concept, photographing the bottom of rock pools through the clear Atlantic water and then re-creating them on canvas. I commissioned a series of small studies of Rosbeg where my heart lies, and we planned the handover in our old haunt, the famous Nancy's Bar on Ardara's main street. On quiet mornings we'd sit at the cosy fire, Margaret McHugh would make us an Irish coffee and her son Charles would keep an eye on general consumption as we'd chat about everything in life but most of all about Ulster Television, the people, the programmes, the fun.

Lawson was a practical joker. His fellow artist, Dan Dowling, remembers the time he hatched a plan to cut a superior art critic down to size. He drew a sketch à la William Conor, signed it and put it in an old battered brown envelope. One evening at the Arts Club in Belfast, then the exclusive headquarters of male literati, genuine artists and social members, he got his chance. The main room was being refurbished and the carpet was rolled up for removal; he eased the brown bag underneath allowing one corner of the envelope to stick out. All evening, he and the members waited for the art critic to notice and investigate but he didn't rise to the bait. Eventually Lawson pointed and gasped, "What's that sticking out from under the carpet?" The butt of his joke investigated, thought he'd found a genuine Conor and claimed it for his own. For all anyone knows he still boasts of his windfall.

Lawson Birch was the first artist to gave painting lessons on local television.

When I think of the men who impressed me in those days, I think of Patrick Moore. Big, confident, precise and I admit he scared me. As a production assistant in the early 60s, one of my jobs was to time the over-all programme making sure the individual items would add up and we wouldn't 'over run'. Because our studio shows were sandwiched between commercials breaks and the powerful network programmes, we had to fit the slot perfectly, opening caption on the second, closing caption on the second, no over run was tolerated. I still waken up in a panic having dreamt I've lost 60 seconds somewhere on my timing sheet not knowing whether to say so or see if I can somehow claw it back before the end caption!

With the man who was to become respected as Sir Alfred Patrick Caldwell-Moore, CBE, Hon FRS, FRAS who, in 2001, was elected Hon. Fellow of the Royal Society an extremely rare honour for an amateur scientist of any discipline, I had absolutely no problem!

He'd arrive, monocle in place, tie under one ear, jacket buttoned over his stomach, bark out that he would take 3 minutes and 18 seconds - and he was spot on. He must have been around 42 when he came to Northern Ireland as director of the newly constructed Armagh Planetarium, a post he held until 1968. This amateur astronomer was the most professional presenter. He had the gift of enthusiasm, didn't suffer fools gladly and had the whole studio enthralled. After sorting out his script, the next question would be about his dear mother, a woman he adored and admired.

When I talked to him for this book, he remembered driving to the studios in his old car. "The Ark, almost as ancient as Noah's craft. I still have it!" he barked, "doesn't do more than 38 miles an hour." I asked him what make it was. I should have known. "Ford Prefect!" A true hitchhiker of the galaxy. Terry Moseley, past president of the Irish Astronomical Association and astronomer with the rare distinction of having an asteroid named after him, thanks Moore for giving him an excitement about the subject.

"I often drove him from Armagh to Ulster Television and the talk was always about astronomy. He was incredibly informative. I was 19 at the time, and had only seen him on television so I didn't know him until then but he literally opened up the heavens to me. He'd a photographic memory, I believe a genius in his own way."

Terry had bought a book written by Patrick, became instantly hooked, made a telescope and, when he heard that Moore was coming to Armagh in 1965 to take up the post of director at the Planetarium, the young man got in touch and found a mentor. "I went to see him at St. Mark's Place, a giant of a man 6' 4", talking 300 words a minute! He said he'd brought over three telescopes with him and I was welcome to use one, it was too good to be true." The two men have been close friends and worked together ever since, both benefiting from each others knowledge and passion for the mysteries of the night sky.

Patrick Moore brought the heavens into our lives on 26th April 1957 when the BBC first screened *The Sky at Night* which became the longest running television series with the same original presenter. We were in awe of this slightly dishevelled professorial type when he arrived into Havelock House. I think of him as a bustling man, a barnstormer, tilted forward in enthusiasm, rapid conversation and piercing gaze, one eyebrow raised permanently probably due to looking through a telescope most of his life. As time went by we learned more and more about this unique man. Member of the British Astronomical Association at the age of 11 and later its president, co-founder and former president of the Society for Popular Astronomy, author of over 70 books on astronomy, all typed on a 1908 typewriter. We learned that he was educated at home because of poor health in his childhood, and that his developing interest in astronomy began when he was six years of age. Proud of his RAF career as a navigator in Bomber Command and much saddened when his fiancée, a nurse, was killed by a bomb which fell on her ambulance.

He grew up on live television. Once, like UTV presenter Julian Simmons years later, he swallowed a fly as he spoke but kept up his rapid-fire commentary on some galaxy or other. His demeanor belied his mischievous humour. In 1976, this was used to good effect for an April Fool spoof on BBC Radio 2, when Moore announced that at 9.47 am, a once-in-a-lifetime astronomical event was going to occur: "Pluto will pass behind Jupiter, temporarily causing a gravitational alignment that would reduce the earth's own gravity." Moore informed listeners that if they could jump at the exact moment that this event occurred, they would experience a temporary floating sensation. The BBC received many telephone calls from listeners saying they did – and did!

The best April Fool I achieved in Ulster Television was to leave a message for a po-faced director to ring Mr. C. Lyon at a Belfast number. We stood outside his door as he duly dialed the number and found out it was the zoo! We ran away giggling like schoolgirls. He was not impressed. The worse experience was when my uncle's young race horse got loose and was grazing on the grass a few hundreds yards from the main Belfast to Carrickfergus road. I ran to him and gave him the awful news. "You won't catch me that way," he laughed. I didn't know what he meant and pleaded with him to come outside and catch the horse. "I know you're a great practical joker but do you think I'm going to fall for that." He wouldn't listen. I was in tears. "Good try darling girl," he said, "but I know it's the first of April." I'd forgotten. Eventually we caught the horse and I understood the meaning of biter bit.

Patrick Moore was showered with appreciation by his peers. In 1945 he was elected a Fellow of the Royal Astronomical Society, in 1968 he was awarded an OBE and 20 years later he was promoted to CBE.

He became a 'Sir' in 2001, when he was knighted 'for services to the popularisation of science and to broadcasting' in recognition of his remarkable *Sky at Night* programmes, also a British Academy of Film and Television Arts (BAFTA) award for services to television which perhaps included his musical compositions, two operettas and his accomplished playing of the piano and xylophone.

On May 2007, he was in the headlines again when he stated that the BBC was being "ruined by women". Was he being mischievous? "The trouble is that the BBC now is run by women and it shows: soap operas, cooking, quizzes, kitchen-sink plays. You wouldn't have had that in the golden days."

I hope he was thinking of Ulster Television.

Sir Alfred Patrick Calderwell-Moore, a star in his own right. Irish News

'Anne's role to be reversed,' said the newspaper. 'Petite Anne Shaw has been calling the tune for her fiancé Alan Hailes since they met in Ulster Television.' I bet that was written by a man!

The thrill of meeting Bruce Forsyth, the star of Sunday Night at the London Palladium and asking him to sign the visitors book. A gentleman who turned the studio to bedlam.

26
Some of the Greats

"I was a professional driver paid by the British Motor Corporation and they made it very clear from the start that we were a British team so in all the press reports I was a British driver. But, a few weeks later, when I was caught smuggling a camera through customs in Heathrow, they decided to make a thing of it to put others off trying the same thing and the paper headlines screamed, 'Irish rally driver caught smuggling'."

In those early days of Ulster Television one of the most popular and exciting programmes which came to us from the network was *Sunday Night at the London Palladium.* As it happened, every November my father and mother would travel to London to dad's firm's annual conference and I would tag along, popular because I could book seats for ATV's live televised Palladium show. It was a thrill to walk into the old theatre, secure in the red plush seats, excited at the though of what was going on behind the huge crimson curtains that hid the stage.

This West End theatre has a great history dating back to 1910 when the wooden structure was rebuilt by Fredrick Hengler, the son of a tightrope walker who wanted to use it as a circus venue including an aquatic display in a flooded ring. Then it became a skating rink before it was rescued by Frank Matcham, the famous theatrical architect who designed the Grand Opera House in Belfast. It held 2286 patrons and in those heady days it was a venue for variety.

Tommy Trinder was the first host but then came a whirlwind called Bruce Forsyth. The dancing Tiller Girls high-kicked their way across the stage and he'd tag on at the end kicking higher than any of them, and, when the revolving stage would turn to reveal that night's game of Beat the Clock, he would use it like a scooter, pedalling with one foot in a mock attempt to make it go faster.

When we talked of those days I asked Bruce if he recalled the name Paddy Hopkirk, a Belfast man who appeared on the show. "Hopkirk. Paddy Hopkirk." Thinks. "Mini Cooper S? Monte Carlo Rally?" Spot on - 44 years later.

When Paddy Hopkirk and Henry Liddon won the Monte Carlo Rally in 1964, there was great excitement locally and nationally and indeed, one Sunday night, sitting in his red Mini Cooper S registration 33 EJB, Paddy joined Bruce on the revolving stage of the London Palladium. "Only time we ever had a car on the show. Marvellous," was the compere's memory. Over to Paddy.

"Absolutely marvellous," he had the same memory. "Never forget it, especially because at rehearsals I discovered my hero was on the show, my God, Tommy Cooper, even the musicians were falling off their instruments he was so funny. During transmission, Bruce was in front of the curtains and there's the noise of a car racing past and the squeal of brakes. 'Who's that?' asks Brucie. 'Paddy Hopkirk,' replies his gag man. 'Why didn't you stop him?' 'I tried to,' and the gag man turned round to reveal tyre marks right across his back as if he'd been run over. Laughter and applause." Paddy warms to the subject. "The curtain goes back and I drive onto the stage and do the interview, then at the end I'm on the revolving stage with the rest of the performers, Tommy Cooper and the Tiller girls." He's reliving every moment.

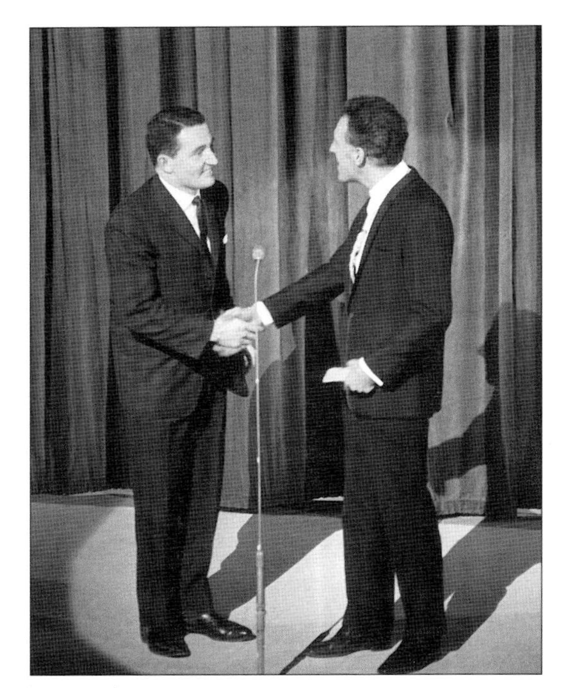

Paddy Hopkirk on the stage of the Palladium being congratulated by Bruce Forsyth on winning the Monte Carlo Rally in 1964. Paddy Hopkirk

"Everyone enjoys fame," he admitted, "I'd be telling porkies if I said I didn't love those few days in the limelight, especially when people really want to see you." It's said that 28 million viewers tuned in at the height of the Palladium days, nearly half the population of the UK.

"It's funny that after the Palladium show I drove the car to a restaurant and parked it outside and while I was having a meal it was stolen. The guy crashed it in Cromwell Street and I had to go to Bow Street court next day because I was the 'keeper' of the vehicle but the 'thief' hadn't actually been a car thief, just a young man who couldn't resist the thrill of driving the winning car in the Monte Carlo Rally!"

Staggering to think that same car is now sitting in the Gaydon Motor Museum in Warwickshire and is valued at around £800,000. "The Monte Carlo was like winning a gold medal, it wasn't for the individual it was for your country, it was a nationalistic thing. I was a professional driver paid by the British Motor Corporation and they made it very clear from the start that we were a British team. So in all the press reports I was a British driver. But, a few weeks later, when I was caught smuggling a camera through customs in Heathrow, they decided to make a thing of it to put others off trying the same thing and the paper headlines screamed, 'Irish rally driver caught smuggling'.

Paddy was our hero. He may have been described as a jovial Irishman but Hopkirk was an aggressive driver hunched over the wheel in his determination, skidding round the sharp bends, a bank of spotlights blazing, now in the air 'yumping' over the humps then racing flat out down the icy mountain pass. Technically, Paddy drove a Mini Cooper S with 1071cc engine. The car was fitted with a lower final drive ratio than standard and after the rally was road tested by several motor magazines. The top speed recorded was approx 93 mph with a 0-60 mph time of 12.0 seconds.

In the deep snow of the French Alps the Mini Coopers were nimble and benefited from front wheel drive but it was on the last stage at the Grand Prix city track in Monaco that Paddy pushed the machine to its limit and made it home just in front of Bo Ljungfeldt (Sweden), Eric Carlsson (Sweden) and Timo Makinen (Finland) and history was made, the first British win since Ronnie Adams in 1956 and it was our man at the wheel.

And in 2009? What is he driving?

"Yes, you've guessed it Anne, I drive a works Mini Cooper S - very sporty. But I must be honest and also tell you that I work for BMW as a Mini brand ambassador. But even if I didn't, I would run one anyhow!"

*

Brian Waddell, who had come to Ulster Television from the *Belfast Telegraph*, was motoring correspondent reporting on anything that moved on four wheels from go-carts to Mini Coopers. He suggested taking a film crew to Monte Carlo to meet up with Paddy, bringing congratulations from home to the celebrations in Monaco. This was accepted by management and the team returned with a half hour documentary. When they were there they flew from Nice to Corsica to interview a doctor who claimed to have a cure for leukemia. This was the first time stories were covered in Europe and as Brian puts it with a smile, "our first time outside of Conlig."

Brian went on to establish his own local production company long before it was the popular thing to do. In 1988 Brian Waddell Productions was born in a small upstairs office in Holywood, Co.

The Mini Cooper S takes pride of place on the revolving stage but the driver only had eyes for the top of the bill, Tommy Cooper.

Brian Waddell came to Ulster Television from the Belfast Telegraph and went on become Controller of Local Programmes and then to open his own production company.
Apparently, when he was a teenager, he bought and dismantled two old cars and built one sports car!

Down and in the years that followed he gained worldwide recognition as a programme maker.

In 2004 he made a documentary for BBC Northern Ireland commemorating the 40th anniversary of Paddy Hopkirk's famous victory. During filming, and under direction of his son Jon-Barrie Waddell, Brian met up with his old friend to reminisce as they sat on the Col de Torino in the French Alps.

Brian has brought new talent to the screen and engaged top names in his programmes. His headquarters moved to a flash new office block, still in Holywood, with a New York office run by Jon-Barrie. His daughter Nikki is involved in development and based in London and Jannine is managing director of the company.

When I was Brian's PA in the mid-60s he had a spelling dilemma on the morning he was to register his baby daughter's name. It was to be Jannine but was it one 'n' or two. Time was running out so I was dispatched to the public library to look up names – no Internet in those days – and returned with two 'n's. How well that little baby and her family have done since that day.

*

Television is now a sophisticated industry with immediate access to anywhere in the world but it started with basic equipment, an enthusiastic workforce and stimulating contributors. It was risky and irreverent and the element of surprise on live shows held the audience.

I asked Bruce Forsyth if he remembered the day he caused mayhem in Studio One at Ulster Television, "I remember a scooter I think, was it a scooter?" I told him it was the roller caption on wheels. "You see the mind is a marvellous thing," he said, "it's an encyclopedia but you need memory jogs don't you? I left out a whole piece in my book, oh dear, I got the childhood and the RAF though."

What a nice man, so generous with his time. I'd written to him asking for an interview and one day my husband came to the back door and shouted to me that I was wanted on the phone. I was sitting with George Loughridge who had taken time for a cup of coffee between helping me top the apple trees. As Alan came closer I asked who it was. "Bruce Forsyth." George choked on his tea and I calmly thanked Alan and took the phone. I have to admit my heart skipped a beat.

"Anne. Bruce Forsyth." He omitted adding OBE awarded in 1998 for his outstanding work in the world of entertainment.

"Darling, I've just found your letter, I've been away, am I in time for your book?" The reply was obvious. "For you Bruce, we'll hold the presses." We got on well after that and had two lovely conversations during the run up to his show *Strictly Come Dancing*, a show he said he was thrilled to be working on. What a performer. Even into his 80s he is still showing the young ones, who'd never even seen him perform at the London Palladium, what a graceful dancer he is.

Although some reports claimed that *Sunday Night at the London Palladium* was watched by as many as 28 million viewers, others say it was under 10 million. Which ever, it was one of the most watched programmes and it attracted top artists. A vicar in Surrey even brought forward the time of his Sunday evening service by half an hour so his congregation could get home in time such was the impact of the programme. And we saw the host's energetic behaviour at first hand on that day when he came to visit Ulster Television.

By now I was a production assistant. This meant working with a director acting as his secretary, tea girl, timing programmes and calling camera shots on fast moving musical shows. Working from a script, it was a matter of shouting out which camera the director had pre-determined he'd select next – 'coming to camera one, on one, standby three, coming to three, on three' and on and on. *Roundabout* was a panic most nights because it was a small studio, probably not much more than 30 yards square with up to ten items coming from this space during the teatime programme. This meant shifting people in and out of the scene dock doors, a musical group, lambs, half a dozen politicians, a model showing the latest creations, you name it and it was on *Roundabout*, a sort of in town tonight. This mixture, a variety show in itself, appealed to the audience and made this one of the most popular live programmes of all time.

It was into this mix that Bruce Forsyth arrived in 1961. I was on the programme that night, stopwatches primed, list of items, how much time for each and all added up to the second. Great. Forsyth was hilarious, Ivor Mills was in stitches and on the cue to windup the interview, Ivor made all efforts to shut the man up and say goodnight. Time was ticking but mayhem suddenly broke out as the funny man from the Palladium jumped on the caption roller used for the end credits and scootered round the studio with cameraman Alan Hailes in hot pursuit.

I don't know how, but we somehow finished the show on time, albeit without the end captions.

*

Although more associated with the BBC, Belfastman David Hammond was often in the building. There was something about the man that was mesmeric; a film maker, a broadcaster, a teacher and perhaps above all, a musician. He was described by Seamus Heaney as a prince among performers who made the whole of Ireland a better place. He died in August 2008, aged 79, and he was buried in love and admiration in St. Finnian's Church of Ireland in the east of the city. He promoted peace wherever he went and as a dear friend of Derek Bailey, I met him on many occasions. A handsome man with a stillness about him which was calming belying a razor sharp mind. His distinctive voice captured his audience, even at his funeral, which he had planned with typical care and attention. When a recording of David singing *The Banks of the Bann* faded in the stillness of the church, there was a heartbeat and then spontaneous applause.

Following his death there were many tributes to David in the media. All the major Irish and British papers carried detailed obituaries and there were special programmes on television. Writing in the *Guardian*, Seamus Heaney described him as a 'natural force' for good in Irish life with a gift for television filming-making and song. He told about the day David received an honorary degree from Dublin City University and was invited to

My favourite picture of all time. 1963. Meeting my heart throb, Adam Faith.

come to the podium and say a few words in response.

"So he rose in his robes, looked down for a moment at the hundreds of graduates and parents in the hall in front of him, then threw his head back and started to sing."

*

My life has always been peppered with influential people: David Hammond, Derek Bailey and Paddy Scott amongst them, and having been asked to leave school at fifteen, these men were my teachers. Television attracted people with a will to learn new technologies, to translate life into pictures and have unbounded enthusiasm for everything and that got us through. We worked hard, 37 hours a week was the laid down union limit and whilst we filled that into our time sheets, the majority of us worked many more hours because we loved being together in the building called Havelock House.

One memorable day, handsome fair-haired Adam Faith was booked for the programme. A new record to be plugged meant a tour of the television stations and, knowing my passion for this little power packed singer, I was allowed to go with the driver to collect him at the airport. It might have been the tight Jaeger elasticated belt or the extra high heels, but I was so overcome I don't remember my first sighting. I do remember sitting in the back seat, himself beside the driver and he was giving off rings round him about some newspaper article in which he was described as 'a virgin'. Now why he was so cross I don't remember either, I was just so mesmerized. Whether he was a virgin or not never became apparent but it was my first taste of how the 'media' can invade a person's privacy and it seemed outrageous that they could print such a word let alone such a claim. I guess as his career flourished, he learned that that was small beer.

He was a delight and I was thrilled to meet him again in 1963 when we were in London to film for a programme called *Heads or Harps*, an investigation into how much the average English men and women knew about Northern Ireland. It was fascinating and the answer was not a lot.

"What is the capital of Northern Ireland?" asked our presenter Charlie Witherspoon. "Northern Ireland? That would be Dublin." "No, *Northern* Ireland." "Where's Northern Ireland?" And so it went on. We didn't have a high profile in those days so people could be excused for genuine ignorance. "What? Our Queen's your Queen?' outraged vendor at a flower stall. "How come?"

Many years later, in 1998, I was part of a theatrical production with entertainer and dancer Lionel Blair, I played his mother, and coming towards the end of rehearsals in Islington, the London cast were asking questions about our opening in the Grand Opera House in Belfast and in the Gaiety Theatre in Dublin. They still didn't know much about the island even after our high profile Troubles. "Do we need passports?" "Is Dublin hundreds of miles away from Belfast," "Do you have square pin plugs?" I was asked. "What about banks, do you have them over there?" Another added, "Are they the same as ours?" This wasn't rudeness it was just that they hadn't thought about Ireland and when they did, their thoughts were very out of date. The assurance that pleased them most was that we received *Coronation Street* and *EastEnders* on our television sets with square pin plugs!

On the other hand, that trip to London in the early 60s opened our eyes too. We could walk off the street into a café or restaurant at any time during the day and get a meal. Derek Bailey was so delighted when he saw a shop window filled with men's shirts for 19 shillings 19 pence, a penny short of one pound, he bought two.

I was walking down Regent Street with two of the boys, Paul Irwin and Gil Henderson, when I was approached by three well dressed and attractive women. I didn't catch what they said but the boys muscled in immediately and told them in no uncertain terms that I was with them and to get lost or words to that effect. Then they had to explain the word lesbian to me and the age of innocence was over! The boys were also on hand that evening when our interviewer, Charlie Witherspoon, in his sexy Y-fronts, knocked on my door with his trousers in one hand and a needle and thread in the other wanting me to fix his zip. Charlie was left standing as I was whisked off to a coffee bar and some London nightlife!

We also visited Rediffusion's Studio 9 Kingsway in the city centre. Going up in the lift was a tiny elfin-like boy, colourfully dressed with a shock of curly brown hair. He was talking ten to the dozen about a singer he'd just seen. "She's amazing," he told his companion, "great voice and she sings in her bare feet." He was Leo Sayer and she was Sandie Shaw, both to become big names in the pop scene. Sayer was being part-managed by Adam Faith, and Sandie Shaw was also spotted by Adam my hero who took her under his wing. He introduced her to the right people and within two weeks she had a record deal with Pye Records, so the incident in the lift must have been during those two weeks. Her song, *Always Something There to Remind Me* shot to number one in the UK singles chart in the autumn of 1964.

Three years later she won the Eurovision Song Contest with Phil Coulter and Bill Martin's *Puppet on a String* and she became known throughout the world. It's strange that she says she always disliked her feet and apparently had corrective surgery 48 years later.

Although Leo Sayer was in floppy casual gear that day, his debut single *The Show Must Go On* was making him a big bit and he had his own gimmick, he wore a white pierrot style outfit, with full makeup. Sayer was still causing comment almost 50 years later when he shared the controversial *Big Brother* show house with the late Jade Goody - but he had the wit to walk out.

My spirits rose with the lift that Thursday. We were going to the *Ready Steady Go* pop show studios and with a little bit of luck Adam Faith would be there and I could gaze from afar. Sure enough, there he was and although I have the photograph to prove it, I can't remember anything about our meeting. Struck dumb again might be appropriate. Certainly all the fuses blew in ecstasy. I was so overwhelmed I must have had a little death.

Sadly, his own death was premature. He'd had a heart complaint, he worked too hard, he chased life and caught it, but it took its toll. That distinctive voice, the acting career, the financial prowess all came to a standstill the Friday night he came off stage in March 2003. He'd been appearing in the stage show *Love and Marriage* in Stoke-on-Trent and just made it to the hotel before a heart attack claimed his life. He was a character and I wish I could remember what we talked about; and I wish I hadn't worn that dreadful pink head scarf.

*

On 17th September 1961 a film story took us to Baltray Golf Club, four miles from Drogheda in the Republic of Ireland and situated at the mouth of the River Boyne. A links course, it was highly rated amongst regulars and visitors, described as a hidden gem which could be gentle or challenging attracting players of all handicaps. On that September day, the player we were interested in had a handicap of 5, but he was beginning to feel the pains of bursitis in his shoulders. This inflammation of the small fluid filled sac that reduces friction between the joints was to hamper his game in months to come. He was Bing Crosby.

It was his first visit to Ireland. He'd been making the film *Road to Hong Kong* in England and came to Ireland to attend Leopardstown races the previous afternoon followed by some fishing then nine holes at Baltray next morning. Later that day, more golf with a fourball at Woodbrook, Co. Wicklow. With the US ambassador Grant Stockdale, professionals Harry Bradshaw and Christy Greene, he played to raise funds for the Irish Society for the Prevention of Cruelty to Children. Rule 3 in the programme stated that 'under no circumstances will any of the players break into a run'. Therefore, there was no necessity for spectators to break into a run either and everyone had a good view of the great man.

We were waiting for him in the bar looking out on to a windswept course where the tail end of a hurricane which had ripped through the United States was now making its presence felt in Ireland. But it was bright outside and deemed the best place for the interview. Then, through a door at the end of the bar, in came this dapper man, smiling, his eyes crinkly and kind - Bing Crosby, crooner, actor, total star.

As the camera was set up and interviewer Anne Gregg selected her spot just outside the big picture window and under a balcony, this great man came over to me and asked me if I could mention to the director that he'd like to keep his golfing cap on during the filming. I assured him that would be no problem. He tapped his head, winked and said he wouldn't want the raging gale to ruffle his hair. I think I must have looked at him rather blankly but I soon worked it out that he was referring to his toupee. As a result of this meeting, Derek Bailey subsequently filmed Crosby's life story thanks largely to the contacts he made that day.

Only a couple of weeks later Bob Hope visited, again for golf, and again Anne was the interviewer on the film story in Banbridge. Not my turn so I missed that story and getting to meet Bing Crosby's great friend. He must have been something else as Anne was walking on air when the crew got back - apparently Bob Hope just fell in love with her on the spot.

*

We also had our home grown stars and many of them appeared in a very special play, *Boatman do not Tarry* by John D. Stewart, a hour long drama which was shown on the eve of the company's 8th anniversary. And it was shown throughout the network of television companies to audiences all over the United Kingdom.

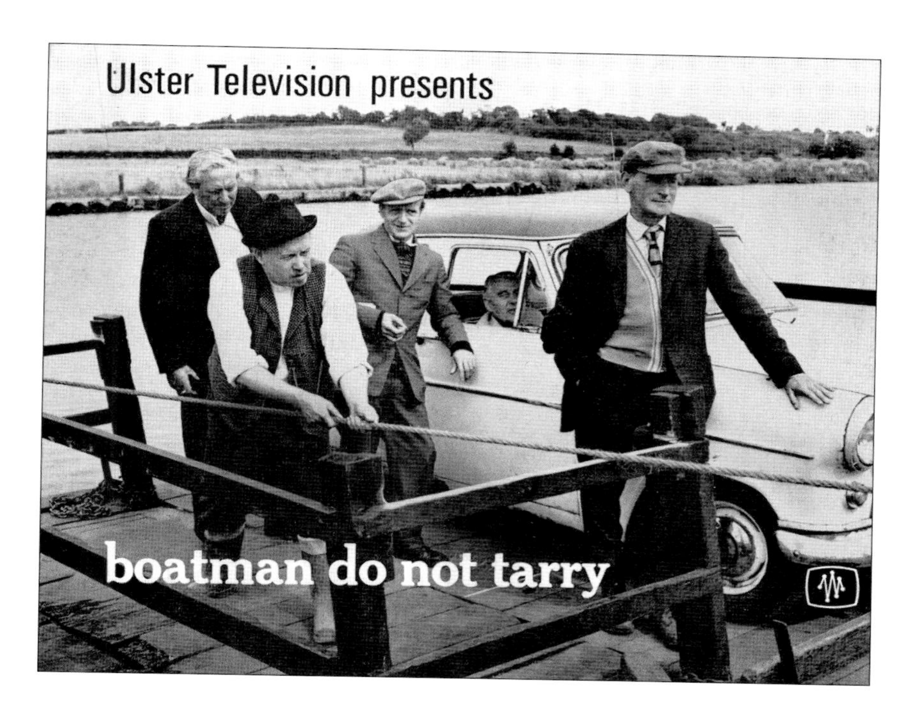

One of the publicity photographs for
Boatman Do Not Tarry
a local play by John D. Stewart, directed by Derek Bailey.
It was transmitted on the network to audiences throughout the United Kingdom.

The cream of Ulster's acting fraternity appeared, Patrick McAlinney, J. G. Devlin and Elizabeth Begley. Margaret D'Arcy remembers being the Minister of Development and Uplift. "I was called in to keep the peace! But you know it was terribly sad. We all thought it was the beginning of good drama on a regular basis, Derek Bailey was the director and he was so full of enthusiasm. We were hoping for great things but it never happened."

Boatman, however, was a great success. "I thoroughly enjoyed the play and so did those who watched it with me." So wrote *Belfast News Letter* critic W. J. M. who admitted that he expected this to be "just another production in the classic tradition of local TV drama that laid the Ulster accent on with a trowel and depended on outlandish 'Irish' situations for effect." But he was pleasantly surprised. "Particularly from the production side, *Boatman* was excellent having a polish that one normally associates with one of the big cross-Channel stations. The story surrounds the Cleghole ferryman in the heart of Ulster attempting to hold the community to ransom until compensation is extracted from a harassed Stormont. I got the feeling that director Derek Bailey, both on location at Bannfoot and in the studio, had determined to avoid camera clichés like the plague. He succeeded admirably."

It is worth recording the actors in this landmark play designed by Roy Gaston. Patrick McAlinney, J. G. Devlin, Elizabeth Begley, Margaret D'Arcy, Ronald Adam, Michael Duffy, Oliver Maguire, John McBride and Maurice O'Callaghan, Sean Reid and Louis Rolston. They all continued to head cast lists both here and on national stages for years to come. But Selwick Damel, the bull who had such an important part, wasn't heard of again!

Two favourite men, Tom McDevitte and his alter ego, Barney McCool from Coolaghey.

27
The split personality of a gentleman

The first half dozen years of Ulster Television were probably the best simply because television was evolving.
It was like a great colourful ball of dough to be manipulated and shaped to fill the small screen. No idea was too outlandish, it was taken and kneaded until an end result was arrived at.
Sometimes it was make do and mend as Barney McCool recalled.

Barney McCool was a rare bird, hard to pin down. A man of all trades who could tie up his trouser legs with straw and turn his hand to taking in the hay, walking behind a plough, sowing the seed potatoes or just hanging over the gate putting the world to rights. I first met him in his the early 60s when he came into UTV to tell the viewers of his life. The ups and downs of married life with Mary Anne. The doings of the vet Mr. Hughie O'Donnell and the wee hen woman. With his stumpy clay pipe clamped between his gums, he'd recount the goings on, the loves and life of the little village where he was born and bred, the romances at local dances or the Coolaghey Operatic and Dramatic Society, CODS for short. One woman, he said, was practically on her deathbed but had to hang on to hear if Mary Anne got the pension or not. "And it took Mary Anne three months to get the pension sorted and by then the woman said, 'ouch, the notion of dyin' was off me!'"

He used to come into the studio and lean over our garden gate to tell his tales.

"One day someone had the bright idea that there should be a shower of rain but no one had time to work out the finer details of how it would be administered so, one of the props boys, his name was Isaac King, just tipped the bucket all over me – it was a downpour!" And it was live and the viewers loved it. They'd come to the front door sometimes by their hundreds just waiting for Barney or some other personality to leave after the programme.

But Barney fooled them because his best friend and mentor, Thomas Page McDevitte was the man behind the old farmer, a kind, beautifully dressed, generous gentleman who could make his way through Northern Ireland without a second glance, but if he was to put on his soft paddy hat and take out his teeth, he'd be mobbed.

Who was this man who was born at 11 p.m. on 22.11.11? "Multiples of eleven have pursued me all my life," he told me. "When I was 22 there was shooting over the Lifford and Strabane border and when there was a lull I ran out of the house down the road to the butcher's. A woman pushed in in front of me for a quarter pound of mince and as she left the shop, a shot rang out and she fell. If she hadn't pushed in and I'd had my turn I wouldn't be here today."

On 22nd April he met his wife and moved into No. 22. His phone number added up to 22. During his many years working on the railways, the majority of his transfers were on 11th or the 22nd of the month. When he was 11, his composition at school drew attention from the teacher.

"She said, Thomas Page McDevitte, you'll be a journalist."

So it came to pass. For many years he provided a column for the *Tyrone Constitution* and since it began just before Christmas 1959, he wrote over two million words. Even the most avid reader of '*the Con*' might not have realised this because Tom didn't write under his own name but as his alter ego the soon to be famous, Barney McCool, that rare bird from Coolaghey which is half way between Drumnabratty and Tullyrap just half roads between Raphoe and Ballindrait.

Tom gained legions of fans through his writing and his broadcasts on Radio Eireann, every month for 20 years. Television interested him and he applied for a job as office manager at the new station. Instead he ended up in front of camera a legend was born.

He talks about the early days. "I was on the first ever *Roundabout* with Ivor Mills and Anne Gregg. They set up a cardboard gate for me to lean over – definite instructions 'over' not 'on'. But it looked a bit bare so they sent out for a bush. A props man Isaac King lay at my feet holding the bush and after a while he began to shake and the bush trembled. I had a letter from a woman who wrote how nice it was to see a wee country man out in his field with the good fresh air blowing in the trees." That same day he happened to see the credits go through during rehearsals and immediately asked that Tom McDevitte be replaced with Barney McCool. After that he lead a double life until he died in December 2005 in his 95th year.

I visited him in his comefy home in Finaghy in the shadow of Black Mountain, and the cards celebrating his 91st birthday were still on the mantelpiece. From sons and daughter, grandchildren, great-grandchildren, friends around the world and the congregation of the Methodist Church in Finaghy. The room was stacked with books, papers, magazines and the walls covered with pictures of trains reflecting his 40 years service with the Great Northern Railway which gave him untold material for radio and television and his weekly column in the *Tyrone Constitution*. In May 2000, when he was awarded the MBE for services to the community and journalism, the Queen asked him about his writing.

"'I write a weekly column for a provincial paper, Mam, from the historical to the hysterical.' Then she asked me which newspaper and when I told her the *Tyrone Constitution* in Omagh immediately she enquired, 'Oh, how are they?' She was referring to the terrible bomb atrocity in the town two years previously and I loved her for that."

That day at Buckingham Palace was a red-letter day for the man born in Strabane but a man who belonged to all Ireland. Indeed in his time he cycled every county from Malin Head to Mizen Head chatting all the way.

"Strabane, a town of great neighbourliness where no one thought in terms of denominations. I grew up there and now I just accept people as they are; it never dawns on me to wonder what's their background. Sure we all come into this world one way and we'll all go out one way."

He made no difference between people and welcomed all. A few days before we talked, a woman had come to his door looking for money. He discovered she was from Bosnia. Where another would have maybe given a few pence and closed the door, Tom gave her hospitality.

"As she left she said, 'I will pray to my God for you.' And I told her I would pray to my God for her." I pass the comment that many a person would have ignored the doorbell in such a situation. "Isn't it Hebrews Chapter 13 where it says, *be not forgetful to entertain strangers for thereby some have entertained angels unawares.*"

This was his philosophy of life, give everyone a fair hearing and listen.

"I've always been interested in accents," he proved the point by launching into a story which required him to be a 'wee man' from Kerry, then another from Cork and, of course, his other self from Coolaghey.

Between trains and Barney McCool, Tom travelled the world, but working on the railways was his real joy, with all the twists and turns.

"In February 1936 I was a relief clerk in Dungannon when I was told to go to Armagh. The message came by Morse code and the girl who took it made a mistake and took down Ardee instead of Armagh and in the confusion I was bundled into a train and sent to Ardee. I stayed there for six months and as far as I know they're still looking for me in Armagh!" Eventually he moved to Dundalk, cycled with the local Methodist minister to services and met his wife, Gladys O'Neill. They had a long and happy marriage until her death in November 1990.

It was hard to keep up with this remarkable gentleman. He'd go into one book to give you a quotation, then reach down photographs, proudly showing off his MBE alongside Elizabeth

Taylor and Julie Andrews who received their awards on the same day. All he would say of these two ladies was that he liked Julie Andrews!

We paused as he went off into the kitchen and returned bearing tea and cakes. We took up our conversation. Then he dropped his news, he had a touch of cancer he said, but he passed it off as a minor irritation. It was to claim him not long after.

Our conversation that day roamed all over the place. Tom McDevitte had a crystal clear mind, names and dates didn't defeat him and his memories are history.

"I got a second hand bike when I was 14 and I certainly appreciated it. My father, Walter E. McDevitte, was a leader of the Methodist Church in Strabane and he was strict. Sunday was a day of rest and there was no cycling." But 14 year old young men can be a bit wayward. "Well, I got the bike out this Sunday and with a push and a wobble I rode the half mile to Lifford. Then the bike turned left and I ended up in Donegal Town 32 miles away, tired, hungry and penniless. I set off home but I was exhausted. Then I saw a wee thatched cottage and a woman looking over the half door, wrinkled and kind face. 'Where have you come from?' she asked. 'Strabane,' I told her, 'do you know it?' 'Sure wasn't I hired in it when I was 14,' and she asked me in. Small room, tiny fire in the grate; she took down a porringer, a wee saucepan to make tea, and asked me would I like an egg and proceeded to boil the egg in the tea. Well, I can tell you, I don't like hard boiled eggs or black tea but it was like nectar." She gave him a kiss, blessed him and sent him off home. It's obvious he can see it all in his mind's eye, especially what happened when he got home and found his father had called out the police. But the story didn't end there. "My father had reason to be on that road the following week and passed the wee house which was all shut up and bolted. In Killybegs he heard that the old woman had been found dead of malnutrition, lying by the side of the road. Yet she had given me her precious food."

Everyone loved Tom. He was a man of his word who quotes his father's advice, 'having put your hand on the plough, don't turn back'.

He did his best to spread the principles of Tom McDevitte through the medium of Barney McCool and by speaking at dinners, introducing events, broadcasting and writing.

When his family bought him a helicopter ride for his 90th birthday in 2001, it was the highlight of his life, although looking down on the chimney pots caused him to think how close we are, yet how far apart. At the time he wrote of speeding over Belfast with the thousands of houses and families below.

'... some of whom don't realise how much they have in common but persist in only seeing the comparatively small items which divide them. Haven't we a common land and a common Lord? With all due reverence, if He was a Belfast man He'd be tempted to cry out, 'Away and catch yourselves on, have a titter of wit.'

We mulled over his life that day and, thinking about that trip in the helicopter, he paused, holding his cup in his hand and quoted:

"What matters that at different times our fathers won this sod,
What matters that at different shrines we worship the same God?
In fortune and in fame we're bound by stronger links than steel
Neither can be safe or sound but in the others weal."

Tom gloried in the music of male voice choirs, he toured churches and chapels throughout Ireland with the Ballyclare Male Choir singing to 'priests and parsons, nuns and nobodies.'

He was proud to be their Vice President and his wish to have Yvette Anderson, daughter of his long time friend Joseph Locke, conduct the Ballyclare Choir and the BB Centenary Choir at his funeral, was agreed without hesitation and with much love.

Tom died at the age of 94, Christmas time 2005 and to this day he's the only man who could publicly announce that he knew me when I was "a lovely slim wee thing" and get away with it. When it comes to Tom McDevitte it's true, he was part of my growing up.

We lost two great characters in one man, Barney McCool and dear Tom McDevitte.

Many children had their first taste of life outside the home when they visited Romper Room and they never forgot the experience. It was a valuable lesson in growing up.

28
Changing values

She's not behind the door when it comes to nude scenes but even she is giving voice to the unease many people are feeling at the pornographic element in so many shows.

In October 2008 newspapers carried the story that broadcasters have come up with a system that shows adverts during the programmes. The new technology developed for ITV is called 'automatically placed overlay advertising'. More science fiction.

Apparently areas such as blue sky or blank walls in programmes can be identified as a place in which commercial logos and messages can be placed. Certainly this technique is used in news programmes where a blank gable wall can be used as a background to information on the decline in house prices for instance, comparisons in house price percentages or a graph of profit drops and gains in the money markets.

The proposed advertising system has been developed because people using advanced technology can skip through commercial breaks and so threaten advertising revenue. Will the viewers accept such intrusion into serious dramas or sensitive documentaries? Until September 2009 product placement was not allowed on television but the downturn in advertising revenue changed that and commercial television will now feature brands and be paid for the privilege.

Back, in March 2009, many people were shocked at the possibility of advertising types of contraception and pregnancy advisory services on television. At the end of that month a commercial was shown on ITV, Channel 4 and Sky for the morning-after pill. Millions of viewers saw the cartoon-style ad depicting a woman waking up in bed next to her partner - and then heading to a chemist to ask for the pill. Although it was screened shortly after the 9 p.m. watershed, hundreds of viewers, mostly parents, phoned in complaining.

The Broadcasting Committee of Advertising Practice responsible for writing and enforcing advertising rules, has said the commercials would give information about contraception and a range of options for pregnant women, including abortion. These would run throughout the day and evening. In general the older generation were against it although younger people said the proposal made sense because information dispels ignorance. Adults felt that such tuition should come from parents and backed up by teachers. Many teenagers on the other hand said no information came from any quarter, they just heard from their friends. When asked, all agreed that there is a difference between making love and having sex but when you've had a few drinks, or many drinks, that is forgotten. Time will tell.

Will such a message from a television campaign have the desired outcome or be so glossy and entertaining that it will excite the imagination and the message will be wasted? Or will public opinion prevent the campaign getting past the planning stage?

I wonder what the future holds? Children and teenagers have to grow up quickly and absorb a lot of information, but they also have their own opinions, they make their voices heard. No shortage of studies on the subject; in mid 2000 another report found that two out of three children said there is too much sex on television, that they believe sexy pop videos are made to cover the lack of talent with so called 'stars'. Even the stars are throwing up their hands in horror. In 2003 Helen Mirren said she was shocked by the sex and nudity on television. She's not behind the door when it comes to nude scenes but even she is giving voice to the unease many people are feeling at the pornographic element in so many shows.

Standards were always of the highest with the hard working celebrities: Jimmy Greene, Diana Bamber, Tommy James, Adrienne McGuill, Brian Durkin, Denise Brady and Ernie Strathdee.

Thank goodness, after years of being ignored, the public's concerns are being addressed by some television companies. I believe there should be a concerted effort to lobby them, not only the public putting their point of view but parent teacher associations, leaders of youth organisations, sports organisations for young people and church groups. After all, we are the consumers of the media so we have a say in the menu. When the balance is skewed towards perversion we should be demanding it be put right. I used to laugh at campaigner Mrs. Mary Whitehouse. I thought her a woman with no sense of humour, with no comprehension of modern outlooks on life. How wrong I was. We couldn't believe it when she said it began with *Tom and Jerry* cartoons, the little person being set upon by the big person, abused and the subject of much violence. Her message was that when the big cat bashes the little mouse, a sense of bullying, revenge, hurt and manipulation is instilled in the young mind. What would she make of the suggestion that condoms and pregnancy advisory clinics should be advertised on television? Maybe I'm being a Mrs. Whitehouse!

Remember being 'at home' with Ozzy and Sharon Osborne? *The Osbornes* was first shown in 2002 and was viewed worldwide, an amazing piece of reality television watching a family who used the 'f' word more often than Billy Connolly and that's saying something. A shaky camera filmed them at Christmas lunch. That's boring for a start. I am inclined to think this was a total set up as surely parents, no matter how dysfunctional, would allow their children and their children's friends to speak in such a manner? I asked a teacher about this and she laughed at me. She assured me that, in her experience, such language is common in the home and the classroom.

The 'f' word was mild as the Osborne lunch progressed. Why would anyone want to watch this? At that time I began to take notes on what I considered unacceptable content on television. One evening, admittedly quite late and well after the 'watershed', was a programme called *F*** Buddies*. Again, there was nothing clever or interesting about it, it seemed to comprise entirely of men and women who wanted a sexual relationship without commitment. So what? Is that a production worth spending money on and is it worth wasting time watching? Then there was a programme about a family who got rich making porno films and sex 'toys'. Now that was revealing. The son of the family had to watch young women perform on a settee before making a decision whether or not to employ them. That done he went home to his young son and played in the garden. Why do we get upset about the Internet when we can watch explicit pictures on the television set in the front room? Slap 'educational' on it and anything goes.

*

Some say there's evil around, some say a satanic revival. It seems these production company decision-makers are sitting round and laughing at their audiences for being so gullible.

We the public must take some responsibility because if we don't these pathetic offerings will slide further down the time scale and the mythical nine o'clock watershed will cease to exist. In fact, it's begun. As I write in 2009, an example is *Coronation Street*, children out of wedlock, murder, adultery and *EastEnders*, children out of wedlock, murder, adultery and that's mild. The point is, this is considered family viewing and today there's a television set in every room, even children's bedrooms so a no holes barred offering like *Big Brother* is available to teenage minds.

Attitudes are shaped by television and God help us if it's programmes like these that are moulding our children's attitudes. An Independent Television Commission report confirmed that gratuitous sexual content in television programmes has more than doubled in a period of only five years. A BBC programme about Charles II boasted bigger and better graphic scenes of a sexual nature, no doubt excused as it was a modern look at this *Merry Monarch* who fathered 13 illegitimate children from several mistresses. This has a brutalising effect on adults and children and lowers behaviour standards.

A taxi driver told me how he had been waiting for an arranged fare in the Shaftesbury Square area of Belfast when a young man tried to hire him. He explained he was already booked. The man then pushed his girlfriend towards the open window, pulled her sweater up and offered her for sex if he'd take them where they were going. Apparently she didn't object. Try driving through this area after midnight any weekend and you'll have the light taken from your eyes when you see girls half-dressed and half cut. Do they watch these programmes about Ibiza and Majorca and the holiday resorts where anything goes and then try living the same life style in a bleak Bradbury Place?

*

More recently I have a feeling that standards have improved slightly when it comes to pornographic type material. Now it's reality television which is distasteful but passes apparently because it's reflecting real life. The problem now is that the majority of television programmes are made on a limited budgets. Peak time viewing is dominated by cheap programmes, game shows, talent shows, reality shows. A survey in the United States I believe, found that the attention span of the average viewer was four minutes. Hence the quick fire magazine programmes where subjects are skated over but rarely developed. It's the pace of life. Everything is instant, food, communications, even fingernails! When did you last get a well thought out and written letter in the post? When did you last get the ingredients together and bake a cake? Is it still possible to get a slow boat to China?

To a great extent creativity has been strangled. Profits, which became the Holy Grail, are threatened to the extent that Russian media firms are apparently poised to buy into British television channels crippled by the credit crunch. At the beginning of 2009, ITV share price had fallen from 80 pence to 28 pence making it vulnerable to a takeover. There's a trend. In the middle of January '09 the *Sunday Express* reported that billionaire and former KGB agent Alexander Lebedev bought the controlling interest in the *Evening Standard* newspaper for £1.

The Internet is also having a great influence on television, radio and newspapers and now all three arms of the media have their Internet departments carrying news directly to people's computers. No matter what you want to find out or catch-up with, just key in the appropriate address and there it is. Internet has its advantages but also its disadvantages, as there seems to be little control over material you would prefer not to come into your home.

What changes inside the last fifty years! From black and white, innocent television to fast, colourful adult programmes.

Perhaps we'll get back to worthwhile content some day – if television as we know and love it lasts that long.

When Jimmy Greene left Ulster Television to work in London, the newspapers bade him a fond farewell on their front pages. The caption read: 'It was a case of 'stiff upper lip' last night for UTV anchor man Jimmy Greene. The occasion was his last appearance in the Round About show. He was seen off by Maggie Gilchrist, Shelagh McKay and Anne Shaw.'

29
Looking Back

I was in a changing room in a store when I heard two men talking outside the curtain.
"Can you lend me your gun, mine's jammed. The boss says I've to work late tonight."
I was terrified. I came out and saw the young men working away stocking shelves and chatting. The boss was nearby. It all looked so normal that, to my shame, I said nothing. Years later I heard the same conversation but this time I saw the people and challenged them. Then it clicked. They were talking about a pricing gun.

For me writing this book has been a joy although transporting myself back into the early 60s has its disadvantages. There comes a time when you have to drag yourself back into 2009! The time between has been a constant source of exciting and interesting episodes, journalism in all its shapes and forms offers a varied path and, from the day I climbed the fire escape at Havelock House, I have very rich memories to look back on.

From the film editors to the logging clerks, the secretaries and their bosses, studio crews, runners and technicians, they all belong to this story. From holding a smoking cigar under the title caption of a war film to give atmosphere to the sophistication of a live link with the State of Maine, U.S.A. via the Early Bird Satellite only five years later is incredible and that progress has continued over 50 years and will continue. I've only covered the first six years, gone off on tangents admittedly as the notion took me but it was indeed a time which was rich and rare and impossible to cover in its entirety. I've left out so much and so many but, on this occasion, space doesn't allow.

There are times when mothers come to me and admit despair at their child's exam results. "What will happen, where will they get work? Perhaps journalism or public relations?"

Journalism or public relations only work if you have the privilege to be given space in a newspaper, a magazine, on radio or television. Otherwise what's the point? A good writer must have a story to tell and the ability to tell it in such a way that the public's attention will be held. Some people say we're lucky to have that space. It's not a matter of luck, it's constant work, always looking for stories, coming on a story which is taking place before your eyes, as in the Troubles, and having the experience and discipline to report it accurately and describe it in word pictures.

Sports journalist Malcolm Brodie is a true professional in the art. Ernie Strathdee and Malcolm were a famous twosome, Malcolm being the new boy in 1959. "Ernie knew my weaknesses and guided me through studio protocol, we'd that team spirit that's so important when you find yourself looking at the wrong bloody camera! I found it fantastic, even down to waiting on the clips of film from the 'bath' in Joy Street where George Craig used to develop it and rush it down to Havelock House. It was such a change for me from the written word, now I was having to memorise up to 10 match reports, no autocue to help, boards with scores being revealed as I spoke. One Boxing Day, Ernie and I had attempt and we'd expected it to take about ten minutes but Buster made it first time and Ernie was able to see it through to the end of the time allowed without any waffle. I asked him once about being in the ministry and why he left it. ' One day in the pulpit I said to myself, I'm not in the right place and here and I got out of it.'"

For Malcolm all sport was his meat but football was his main diet. These were the days of Jackie Milburn, Tommy Dickson, Danny Blanchflower, Alex Russell and Peter Doherty. "Television was open sesame for a journalist like me, taking me to places I wanted to go. I'd the best balance for a journalist, to have the command of writing for a newspaper along with radio and television, with those three together you were going to be recognised, whereas you could write in a newspaper for years and you would never be recognised. People would know your name but if you're on television you're instantly spotted. And as well as that, I got 5 guineas a programme!"

Malcolm was 12 when he came from Glasgow to live in Portadown and never lost his distinctive Scottish accent, another distinguishing aspect when it came to broadcasting. "It was very satisfying when you knew it was a job well done, deadlines met, at one time interviewing every captain of every team in the Irish Cup, travelling round doing 16 interviews a week then watching the programme and being proud when it worked but utterly depressed if we'd made a balls-up!"

Ernie Strathdee with his sparring partner Malcolm Brodie, Malcolm as usual with a notebook peeping out of his jacket pocket.

I must acknowledge Leslie Dawes for an insight into interviewing. When I was a PA I often went with him on film stories and it gave me an opportunity to watch his technique, how he gave his subject confidence before the interview and 'debriefing' them afterwards. I realised at that time how important it is to honour your interviewees, to trust and treat them with respect.

Would I recommend the media as a career? Yes. We now have three grandsons, Jonathan, Daniel and Charlie and I would love to think that in their lives they will have the same stimulation and interest I have had. When you are your own boss you have to be

to give the results from the tiny announcers box, true bill, sitting on the same chair, Mutt and Jeff, cheek to cheek! Ernie had been celebrating all day but we got the report done but it must have been obvious drink was taken. People say I fell off the stool at one stage but that's not true! I was shattered when at the end of the programme Ernie suddenly announced, '1234567, all God's children go to heaven.' I think we were off air, but I was never sure."

Ernie was the supreme broadcaster. I remember one night we were trying to break the world weight-lifting record on *Roundabout*. The late Buster McShane was ready to make the on your toes, making your work, dealing with people in such a way you get the best from them and they get the best from you. With a pen and paper we are indeed mightier than the sword and the influence for good in a station such as Ulster Television is important. On the wider scale there are problems but at a local level there have been many notable contributions to the people within the Ulster Television area.

*

When Ulster Television and BBC were growing up in Northern Ireland, the story was backed up by pictures; one day it changed and now pictures are supported by 'sound-bites'. For me that's a sadness. We don't go 'filming' any more, now it's a 'shoot'. I often wonder if anyone over heard a journalist saying he or she was shooting next morning what they'd make of it.

During the Troubles, I was in a changing room in a Belfast store when I heard two men talking outside the curtain. "Can you lend me your gun, mine's jammed. The boss says I've to work late tonight." I was terrified. I came out and saw the young men working away stocking shelves and chatting. The boss was nearby. It all looked so normal that, to my shame, I said nothing. Years later I heard the same conversation but this time I saw the people and challenged them. Then it clicked. They were talking about a pricing gun.

Leslie Dawes was an interview with class, he always had an unexpected angle with his stories.

When it works, journalism can take you round the world as it has for me. Bangladesh and the dreadful conditions for the people who live in constant fear of flooding, where villagers tie their children and their livestock in the highest branches of the trees when the rains come. Rwanda a year after the 1994 Genocide and the aftermath of almost a million killings of Tutsis in only 100 days. To see the bones of hundreds of men and women and little broken skulls of children massacred by machete and clubs, all piled in a church. They had fled there to take sanctuary but it made no difference to the Hutu Interahamwe paramilitary. Standing by a river where only the year before, women were lined up, their hands tied and their babies strapped to their backs and both pushed into the deep water. So many bodies that they dammed the river which overflowed and flooded the fields. The Sudan where I realised what it is like to have nothing, watching a woman drill a little line in the desert sand and plant a bean. There was no hope of it growing but she put her faith in God that somehow her action would ensure food for her children. China and Hong Kong, all over Europe, so many adventures.

Looking back I would like to have worked at ITN in their news gathering operation. The nearest I got was in the late 70s when I was working with the BBC World Service, I presented a programme about local groups of Catholic and Protestant children visiting America and Scandinavian countries. The hope was such trips would break down barriers and they would realise they had more in common than they thought. To an extent these were successful but intimidation back home put paid to most friendships flourishing.

One interview involved me travelling to Newry during the Maze hunger strike. I had instructions to pull in at a designated lay-by where a car would pick me up and take me into the heartland of a Catholic estate. I would be returned to my car after the interview. I did as planned. A car was waiting. The back door opened and I walked over and got in. There were three men in the car, their faces partially obscured with turned up collars and woolly hats pulled down. Not a word was spoken. I was driven through the estate, black flags hanging from upstairs windows. I was taken into a house and a room which was sparsely furnished, a couple of chairs and a table, a woman with a small child. The men stood aside as I interviewed the woman on the bulky Uher tape machine. I couldn't help noticing tell-tale bulges which implied to me they were armed.

It was a good and fair interview in which she welcomed these trips and hoped they would benefit her children in the future. When it was over, we said goodbye. I was ushered out of the house, into the car and back to the lay-by. Still not a word had been spoken between the men and me. As I prepared to leave and walk to my own car, one of the men got out and opened the door for me. I thanked him and he said, "Ok Anne, goodbye."

I was fine, I had my story, I was on my way home. I got as far as Banbridge, a few miles north of Newry when I began to shake. I had to pull in and I cried, from tension, fear but also for the reality of the lives lived by children in this part of the world.

I think my silver spoon was being born with a low boredom threshold. When the challenge goes I leave. So it was with BBC although I loved my days as a broadcaster and the people I met and interviewed. My first BBC broadcast was for forces overseas and I was three and a half years of age and I well remember the round table, green baize covering and green light. The recording was sent to India where my father was serving and my immortal words were – "Father Christmas brought me a doll's house with real electric lights". In later live radio broadcasting life I had a fixation about coughing! Beside me on the round table with the transmission light in a hole in the middle, was a plethora of medicines, cough sweets, throat sprays, drinks, even Fisherman's Friends. One Thursday morning as I sat with headphones on listening to the tail end of the nine o'clock news and waiting for the signature tune of *At Home with Anne Hailes* to begin, I was aware of a panic behind the glass panel where the producer and sound man were sitting, now standing, now running around, now coming into the small studio. "What's wrong?" The soundman replies, "Terrible *schash* noise, can't find out where it's coming from." He rushes out again. More leads are unplugged and replugged, the mic tested, no answers. Time is ticking. Then I realise what is causing this interference on the mic. I called through, somewhat sheepishly, "I think it's my Rodoxon dissolving in the glass of water."

In 1982 I was invited back to my old hunting ground when Ulster Television asked me to become a producer/presenter. What good years those were.

*

At one time the powers that be thought two secretaries, Brenda Adams and Anne Shaw, might make it to the screen. Here with Ernie Strathdee, Colin Lecky Thompson and Tony Finigan we were screen tested but we were too happy working behind the scenes. In fact, both auditionees did eventually present, direct and produce programmes, Brenda in London for See Hear.

People are the essence of life and I've had a wonderful selection through my career, most of them within the media. Ulster Television was a family for years with Brum Henderson our godfather. He was a kindly man and expected the same from his staff. When Phyllis Allen was receptionist, she remembers a farewell party for one of the technical boys who was emigrating to Canada. He got his carriage clock and said goodbye. "A couple of weeks later there was a hammering on the outer door late one evening. I opened it and there he was standing, clock in hand and tears in his eyes. 'I've come home,' he said, 'take the clock and give me my job back.' He was given back his job and worked on for years. It's interesting that when he said he'd come home, he meant home to Ulster Television." Phyllis experienced the same understanding. She had a small daughter and thought she would have to give up work. After a short time she realised it wasn't going to work out financially so she talked to the Managing Director who asked her what would she like to do, would she like to work in the afternoons? "He even asked me what time I'd like to start! You wouldn't get that consideration today."

Phyllis proved her worth the day another hammering came to the door and a group of hard men piled into the foyer. "They were after one of the reporters. I just had time to get a message up to the newsroom and then I confronted them and told them they couldn't just walk into a television studio like that. I said, 'you'll just have to settle down now or I'll call the police.' In the meantime the reporter was able to get to the roof and hide." The men left but later, as Phyllis was driving from the building on her way home, they threw stones at her new blue car. "The roof was chipped and it was quite damaged but UTV paid for a complete re-spray."

The world, even the universe, is covered by cameras today, everywhere you look. Technology has allowed instant access to stories anywhere any time. Compare that to 50 years ago when 16 millimetre film stories from Derry were handed over by the cameraman, to a motorcyclist who brought it over the Glenshane Pass and down to George Craig in Joy Street, Belfast. He processed them, then brought them to Havelock house for editing. It wasn't long before it changed. Processing was done in-house by Ronnie Dwyre and his colleagues. Then a studio, run by Cyril Troy, was opened in Derry. Until videotape came into use, there was quite a time delay between an event and transmission.

There was always the fascination of contributors. Richard Hayward who died in 1964, a dramatist who was an expert on Ulster dialect, wrote a travel series on Ireland and the story of the Irish harp. He was also an agent for Fox's Glacier Mints!
John Hewitt, poet, an ardent labour activist and a Freeman of the City of Belfast. Michael Longley called him the poet who held out the creative hand rather than the clenched fist. In our house he was Jack, who holidayed in Ramsey Isle of Man and fancied Auntie Muriel Robert's sister Dorothy. "He'd read his poetry to us," my mother reports, "and we'd tell him to put them away and forget about being a poet." He didn't!

☆

Norman Kernahan reported on football matches. We always knew he was in the building, this sweet aroma would drift through the studios. He smoked a pipe filled with a mix of Cavehill dung and heather - at least that's what he told me! Transmission controller Glen Clugston who was trumpeter with the Muskrat Ramblers. It was strange to work with him by day and dance to him at the Drill Hall in Queen's at weekends. The death of poet and playwright Louis MacNeice in 1963 sent shock waves through the production department. He joined the BBC features department in 1941 and was responsible for many classic productions and was one of the 'Thirties Poets' along with Auden, Stephen Spender and C.Day Lewis.

We met the people at the height of their trades and professions. As receptionist, Shirley Andrews was a 'meeter and greeter' of people from prime ministers to the GPO lady with a bun and a little leather bag who came every month to disinfect the switchboard.

Shirley joined the company in 1961 as a secretary in the production office typing scripts for *Roundabout* but soon graduated to the giddy heights of reception sitting under the Lady Antrim mural answering the phone and asking visitors to sign in. "If I'd a penny for every time someone would ask me if they wanted a mime I'd be rich" making reference to the popular BBC programme *What's My Line* chaired by Eamonn Andrews also known as Amen Andreds or Shamus Android. They were happy and carefree days. Russ Conway played the piano outside the scene dock doors and we all stood round. Only when he finished playing his hit *Side Saddle* and we'd given him a round of applause did I get him to sign his contract. Lulu called unannounced one day with her manager, Shirley phoned the production office and the singer was on the programme that night. "Frankie Vaughan came in to perform and I liked him but his manager was difficult and insisted Frankie had a good profile and a not so good profile and the director should shoot him only on his good side!" It wasn't total vanity. These were stars who got to the top by giving their audiences a perfect product.

Brendan Behan will always stand out in my memory, known as 'a drunk with a writing problem' who said if it was raining soup the Irish would go out with forks! Few know that he painted the walls of Donaghadee light house when he was employed by the Commissioners of Irish Lights.

I feel another book coming on! I've left out more than I've put in, the characters, the colleagues and the times.

Kenneth McNally's iconic 1960 photograph of the golden days in Belfast when Smithfield Market was a fascination to young and old, rich and poor. It was destroyed in a dreadful fire in 1974.

30
A Toast to Absent Friends

Television was something of a playground to us, colleagues became friends, friends became partners and many of the originals are now grandparents, looking forward to great grand parenthood. Some call us the *Old Timers,* some *The Wrinklies* but the young ones love to hear the stories we have to tell. So close have those friendships become that, at the time of writing this chapter, in the late spring of 2009, we gather in the Kitchen Bar in the Victoria Centre of Belfast on the first Thursday in every month. There are many other little 'cells' lunching together, often with our younger colleagues.

On the first Thursday in October 2008 a group of us talked over bangers and mash and, as usual, raised our glasses to absent friends. One of our number, Eddie Crook was seriously ill and we updated ourselves on his progress.

Eddie and his wife Sheila came to Northern Ireland in 1959. They lived and grew up on the same street in Chorley, Lancashire. They knew each other all their lives, married in 1956 and were happy together with their three children, Jane, Jonathan and Simon. Theirs was a true love story.

Two weeks after we raised our glasses to Eddie in the Kitchen Bar, to the day, almost the hour, we gathered again in Roselawn Cemetery for his funeral. Sheila, her three children and her grandchildren were surrounded by Eddie's colleagues. His son, Simon followed his dad into television, the image of his father, never take no for an answer, searching out every question, hating unfairness or pressurising tactics. Simon has a wonderful zest for life just like his dad.

Eddie and I danced together at the UTV first anniversary party in Thompson's Restaurant in Arthur Street. We danced well and he said, 'Thank you Ginger'. I replied 'Thank you Fred' and we were Fred and Ginger for 49 years.

At that lovely service I think some of us left the playground and grew up, realising that almost 50 years had slipped by. I certainly did, Eddie was one of our gang and we were missing part of our life story.

We've lost more dear friends since, these boys and girls who became men and women. And with each passing, life is diminished but always we have come together to support and share with those left to grieve.

Television is considered an ephemeral medium to work in but certainly in Ulster Television there have always been strong ties which bind us to each other. Not only the *Old Timers* but the younger people who have also experienced working in this evolving industry.

Tom McDevitte, a man of the country, down to earth, never a bad word to say about anyone. A gentleman who was loved throughout the country, from the wee woman in Outram Street to the families in the big houses.
Tom spoke to people through the voice of Barney McCool.
His wit and wisdom is remembered to this day.
Kenneth McNally

31
The Wee woman from Outram Street

Who was the wee woman from Outram Street? I never found out. She was held up to us as our audience, the essence of Ulster, the hard working mother living in a terrace of houses in the city of Belfast. She ruled the roost, she probably worked out, cleaning perhaps or serving in a shop, with a family of youngsters at school by day and playing in the street until teatime. Simple games. A rope round the lamppost to swing on. Numbers chalked on the pavement for hopscotch, bad luck to break the joins on the flagstones. A playing card fixed with a clothes peg to the spokes of a bicycle transforming it into a motorbike.

Was her man a labourer or did he work in the shipyard? Had he work at all? When he came home, often via the pub, did he expect her to have the tea on the table and his slippers warmed at the stove? Probably, because that's the way it was before the days of the Pill and the microchip. Him and 'her indoors' made a good partnership. Both had their own responsibilities and lifestyles and neither strayed into the other's quarter, except after tea.

In Outram Street and many others like it, once the children had done the dishes and put them away, as a family they would sit round the fire, turn on the television and welcome their friends into their snug little home.

That's how I saw the wee woman from Outram Street off Donegall Pass and she was our audience that memorable Hallowee'n night, Saturday 31st October 1959.

But this wee woman wasn't really typical. There was no typical profile because the public in its entirety took to the new station. Perhaps the message we were given from on high was 'don't be too sophisticated or smart assed for the man in the street'. No fear of that, sophistication wasn't an option. Raw enthusiasm was. More often than not it worked for all our viewers, including that woman and her family, always loyal to their local television station just round the corner.

Today, of course, she would probably have a second home in Spain, a car, all mod cons and a job in a supermarket. Like the audience, the product changes. The television of 1959 is a very different entity approaching the 50th birthday of Ulster Television in 2009. 2009. Science fiction dates, we didn't even know what a millennium was in those days let alone think we'd ever see it.

We were about to embark on an adventure to beat all adventures in a decade that would go down in history. So it's been fascinating to put these first few years down on paper, random thoughts of fun and the frantic pace of life, the fear of making mistakes with live television and the career ladder open to all with swift promotion and a fair dollop of glamour. The development of Belfast and Northern Ireland, the good times and the approach of very bad times.

Looking back can be bitter sweet. Perhaps it's a case of,

'don't be sad for what you have lost,
be glad for what you had'.

I gratefully acknowledge special help from the following:

The Irish News, Kathleen Bell Librarian.
The Belfast Telegraph, Paul Carson Library Assistant.
Belfast News Letter.
Belfast Central Library, Archive Department.
BBC Northern Ireland.
Roger Dixon, Folk and Transport Museum.
Derek Bailey.
Bill Armstrong.
Eric Caves.
Paul and Felicity Clements.
Susie Hailes.
Jeremy Rowel Friers.
Kenneth McNally.
Allen McMurtry.
Brian Garrett.
Pat and Phelim Donlon, Tyrone Guthrie Centre.
Gerry Collins
Alan Hailes.
Sheelagh McCully.
Rev. Robin Roddie.
Paul Kirne, Compton Lodge, Sapcote. Lincs.

And many other friends who contributed to this book. I thank you all.

Adam, Ronald 79
Adams, Brenda (Barrie) 75, 76
Alcorn, Roy 42
Allen, Phyllis 104
Anderson, Gerry 102
Andrews, Shirley 195
Angela, Countess of Antrim 16
Armstrong, Bill 42, 46
Armstrong, Louis 26
Aylward, Gladys 26
Baguley, Michael 17
Bailey, Derek 16, 27, 42, 92, 101, 104, 105, 115, 123, 124, 129, 133, 148, 167, 169
Baird, Brian 55
Bamber, Diana 72
Beagan, Martina 118
Beatles, The 12, 28, 152
Begley, Elizabeth 18, 36, 181
Behan, Brendan 13, 125, 129, 195
Behan, Dominic 129, 152
Bennington, Fiona (McDonough) 63
Bennington, Jenny (Osborough) 63
Bergman, Ingrid 26
Best, George 28
Bilney, Jim 53
Birch, Lawson 171
Blair, Lionel 106, 179
Blaney, Billy 12, 42
Bleakley, Christine 62
Boyce, James 92, 102, 105, 121
Boyd, Brian 103
Boyd, Stephen 37
Brady, Frank 75
Broadhurst, Ronald Brigadier 104
Brodie, Malcolm 127, 156, 191
Brown, Harper 34
Brown, Bill 90
Browne Maire (Mahaffey) 63
Byrne, Gay 164
Carlisle, Pat (Shaw) 140
Carnegie, Colin 71
Catherwood, Andrea 42
Catherwood, Harry 42
Carson, Frank 16, 18, 83, 141
Caves, Eric 42
Clancy Brothers 131
Clancy, Liam 131
Clark, Paul 49
Clarke, Jean 62
Clinton, President Bill 72
Clugston, Glen 53, 195
Cogan, Alma 93
Cole, John 157
Compton, Jimmy 27
Conor, William 167
Cooke, John 66
Corbett, Fred 90,169
Corry, Audrey 12
Corry, Peter 12
Courtney, Olive 23
Cradock, Fanny and Johnnie 111
Craig, George 191, 195
Cranmer, Philip (Professor) 103
Creagh, Jim 34
Crockart, Andrew (Andy) 42, 101, 132, 155
Crook, Eddie 197
Crosby, Bing 13, 28, 180
Curran, Patricia 142, 156
Darbyshire, John 110
D'Arcy, Margaret 181
Dawes, Leslie 192
Dawson, Tom 15
Day, Muriel 45
de Winter, Maureen (Shaw) 95
Deane, Uel 105
Devine, Candy 66
Devlin, J. G. 18, 36, 181
Dick, George (Professor) 104
Dixon, Gus 53
Donlon, Pat 116
Doonican, Val 46
Dougal, Andrew 12
Dowd, Pat 53
Dowling, Dan 124, 171
Drew, Ronnie 43,130
Drinkwater, Madame Gertrude 124
Duffield, S. Gordon 33, 75
Duffy, Teresa 61

Duke of Abercorn 33
Dunlop, Kay (McMurtry) 140
Durkin, Brian 31, 45, 72, 74, 78
Dwyre, Ronnie 195
Eames, Robin (Lord Eames) 52
Elliott, Isobel 15
Ellis, James (Jimmy) 18,43
Faith, Adam 28, 179
Feeney, Brian 77
Finigan, Tony 49
Fitt, Gerry (Lord Fitt) 35, 86
Fitzgerald, Ella 66
Fitzpatrick, Rory 169
Fleming, Craig 53, 54
Flintstone, Fred and Wilma 110
Forsyth, Bruce 175
Foster, Ivan 20
Foster, Rodney 27
Friers, Rowel 17, 40, 169
Garrett, Brian 116
Gallagher, Bridie 84
Gallowglass Ceili Band 61
Galway, James 106
Gaston, Roy 90, 132, 181
Gibson, Marion 65
Gibson, Susan 142
Gilroy, Freddie 18
Goddard, Stella 96
Goldblatt, Harold 105
Gough, Liz 12
Graham, Joe 12
Graham, W.F (Billy) 99
Greene, Jimmy 31, 37, 40. 72
Greene, Noel D 164
Gregg, Anne 19. 31, 36, 62, 180, 184
Guthrie, Tyrone 107, 115
Hailes, Alan28, 42, 59, 91, 178
Hailes, Charlie 192
Hailes, Daniel 192
Hailes, Jonathan 192
Hailes, Michael 59
Hailes, Susie (Harkin) 59, 132
Hamilton, Ken 136
Hammond, David 178
Hampson, Tina 106
Hay, Muriel 105
Hayward, Richard 195
Healy, Shay 163
Heaney, Seamus 106, 178
Heayberd, Roy 66
Henderson, Dr. R. Brumwell 1, 16, 45, 125, 129, 194
Henderson, Gil 179
Henderson, Joan 20
Hewitt, John (poet) 195
Hewitt, John (writer) 59
Hewitt, Sheila (Dundee) 38
Higgins, Alex (Hurricane) 59
Hill, Ian 90
Holmes, Frank 53
Hope, Bob 180
Hopkirk, Paddy 175
Hopwood, Fred 90
Houston, Deane 12
Hughes, Barney 12
Hunniford, Gloria 13, 16, 45, 49, 58, 66. 140
Hunter, Mary (McNeight) 20, 51 73, 135
Ireland, Denis 26, 89, 123
Irwin, Paul 42, 89, 115, 179
James, Tommy 45
Johnston, Barry 75
Johnston, James 107
Johnston, Valerie (Stevenson) 75
Jones, Dave 53
Jones, Tom 13,16, 25, 28
Keating, Caron 62, 137
Keating, Don 59
Keith Lucas, David 103
Kelly, Gerry 62
Kelly, James 155
Kennedy, Claire (Irwin) 140
Kent, Mike 46, 62
Kernahan, Norman 195
King, Isaac 85, 184
Kinney, Jack 33, 142
Korczak, Janusz 81
Kyle, Jack 92
Laking, Norman 53
Lapworth, Basil 18, 83
Larmour, Connie (MacLaughlin) 28, 51, 91
Lecky Thompson, Colin 15, 50, 75
Lennon, John 152
Lillie, Beatrice (Lady Peel) 17
Little, Ivan 49
Longley, Michael 195
Lord Antrim 33
Loughridge, George 177
Love, Walter 79
Lubitsch, Fania 118
Macgaffin, Sean 75, 115
Macgregor, Brigid (McCaw) 62
MacLiammóir, Micheál 92
MacNeice, Louis 195
MacQuitty, William (Bill) 51, 104
Major, Katie (McNally) 140
Makem, Tommy 131
Marshall, David 39
Marshall, Houston 65
Martin, Howard 15
Martin, Maureen 96
Martin, Tony 46
Massey, Brian 97
McAdoo-Toal, Lavina 117
McAlinney, Patrick 181
McCafferty, Nick 53
McCallum, Colin 90
McCandless, R.H. 32
McCord, Jill (Derberville) 29, 90
McCoy, Joan (Williamson) 140

McCoy, Ronnie 15, 47
McDevitte, Tom (Barney McCool) 183
McGookin, Bill 123, 169
McGuill, Adrienne (Catherwood) 13, 17, 18,. 31, 36, 40, 53, 72, 73, 139
McGuinness, Martin 21
McHugh, Margaret 171
McIlroy, Frank 61
McIlwaine, Eddie 36
McKay, Shelagh (Caldwell) 43
McKee, Margaret (Baguley) 67
McKee, Silver 144
McKenna, Denise 45
McKeown, Charlie 42
McKinley, Jill (Gibbons) 75
McKittrick, David 77
McMinn, Irene 77
McMurtry, Allen 38
McNally, Kenneth 74
McPeake Family 151
McQueen, Jimmy 86
McShane, Buster 192
McWilliams, Colm 169
McWilliams, Joe 168
Mills, Ivor 19, 31, 37, 71, 72, 73, 93, 105, 169, 184
Moiseiwitsch, Tanya 115
Monaghan, Rinty 144
Monkhouse, Bob 109
Montgomery, Eric 65
Moore, Patrick (Sir) 171
Moran, Tommy 84
Moseley, Terry 172
Murphy, Father Hugh 51
Murray, Derek 63, 169
Newman, George 46
Nodwell, Eleanor 45
O'Callaghan, Maurice 16, 18, 133
O'Callaghan, Una 133
O'Donnell, Brian (The O'Donnell) 93, 125, 132
Olivier, Sir Laurence 17, 20, 36
O'Mahony, Eoin 119
Paisley, Rev. Dr. Ian 21, 35, 170
Patterson, Muriel 140
Payne, Diana 39
Peters, Silvia 111
Peterson, Oscar 63
Pollock, Captain 144
Pritchard, Jack (Professor) 104
Raymond, Tom 45, 84
Rea, Marjory 84
Reid, Tom 90
Reynolds, S.E. 32
Richard, Cliff 16
Riddell, Patrick 89, 105, 123
Stones, Rolling 28
Robb, William 127
Robbins, Harold 25
Robinson, Alexander (Buck Alex) 144
Robinson, Markey 119
Russell, Audrey 62, 126
Sanderson, Ian 169
Sayer, Leo 179
Sayers, Jack 126
Scholz Conway, John 46, 48
Scott, Alf 147
Scott, Betty 147
Scott, Miles 86
Scott, Paddy 140, 155, 169, 178
Shaw, James (Jim) 105
Shaw, John 15, 96
Shaw, Johnny 28, 96, 135
Shaw, Mike 96, 135
Shaw, Sandie 179
Shields, George 21
Simmons, Julian 101
Simpson, Billy 27
Simpson, Janette 105
Singleton, Basil 18
Smith, Kate 49
Smyth, Zandra 47, 63
Solomon, Mervyn 86
St. Clair, Sheila 40, 74
Stewart, John D 105, 81
Strathdee, Ernie 31, 45, 55, 72, 144, 169, 191
Thompson, Derek 45
Todd, Marilyn Mackie 15
Todd, Richard 34
Tomelty, Joe 18, 71
Tomelty, Peter 61, 84, 102
Tomelty, Roma (Carnegie) 71
Toner, Alex 34
Troy, Cyril 34, 195
Tynan, Kenneth 110
Vaughan, Frankie 93, 148, 195
Vennard, Billy 86
Waddell, Brian J. 176
Wakehurst, Lord 18
Wallace, Albert 20
Walsh, Robin 169
Ward, Bridie 84
Webster, Leila 45
White Eagles 27
White, Billy 66
White, Charlie 55
Whitehouse, Mary 110, 188
Whittaker, Roger 46, 86
Wilde, Marty 16
Willie, Stanley 38, 53, 141
Williamson, Jack 53
Wilmot, Hubert (Hibby) 18, 33
Wilton, Elizabeth (Erskine) 28
Windson, Pat (McBride Hawkins) 62
Wine, Gertie 61, 84
Witherspoon, Charles 89, 179
Young, James 17

.... and many more!